"Brian Wren is that unusual combination of gifted poet-hymnodist, keen theologian, and prophetic voice. He knows well the power of language and the power of God's liberating action to free us from the ravages of flawed maleness and patriarchal oppression. This exciting, important book moves the heart as well as stirring the mind and the will."

—*James B. Nelson*
United Theological Seminary
of the Twin Cities

"I find Brian Wren's book of great interest and potential importance—provided *men* read it and take it to heart! It is the only work I know of that is from a man addressed to men about the problems with patriarchal religious language and the need to redress the situation with the use, among other metaphors, of female ones. I applaud the intent and the product."

—*Sallie McFague*
Vanderbilt Divinity School

"*What Language Shall I Borrow?* asks Brian Wren. I have borrowed his and often. When I have found male God-language a barrier, the words of Brian Wren have met my need for a God beyond words. His new book shows what happens when a poet begins to do theology. It puts the rest of us to shame."

—*Susan Thistlethwaite*
Chicago Theological Seminary

"What language shall I borrow
to thank thee, dearest friend?"
—from "O Sacred Head, Sore Wounded"
Paulus Gerhardt, 1607–76
(trans. James Alexander, 1804–59)

What Language Shall I Borrow?

God-Talk in Worship: A Male Response to Feminist Theology

Brian Wren

Crossroad · New York

1993

The Crossroad Publishing Company
370 Lexington Avenue, New York, N.Y. 10017

Printed in the United States of America

Library of Congress Cataloging-in-Publication Data

Wren, Brian A., 1936–
    What language shall I borrow? : God-talk in worship : a
male response to feminist theology / Brian Wren.
      p.   cm.
  Bibliography: p.
  Includes index.
  ISBN 0-8245-0907-2 ISBN 0-8245-1055-0 (pbk)
  1. Languages—Religious aspects—Christianity. 2. Sexism in liturgical language.
3. Feminist theology. I. Title.
BR115.L25W74 1989
230'.014—dc19

88-39442
CIP

Contents

Contents

To
Francis E. Holmes
J. Merlin Thomas
George B. Caird†
· · ·
best of teachers

Preface

Those who know me as a hymn writer will here meet a male theologian struggling with an issue he can't avoid facing in his life, ministry, and writing. The themes in this book are not the only things that pull and push me: I try to serve the church with hymns expressing the full range of Christian faith-experience. But male dominance and male imaging of God have become for me issues of faith and justice, challenging me at a profound level of personal identity. I want to share my concerns, respond creatively to the creativity of Christian feminists, and explore ways forward.

I write from the experience of being English, white, male, and heterosexual, and as one who values the Reformed tradition and has been shaped and enriched by it. I hope my exploration will be helpful to others but can't predict how. Yet I am convinced that male dominance and the construction of "masculinity" are theological problems for *all of us*, whatever our color, gender, or tradition.

Free-lance workers don't get sabbaticals, so I am especially grateful to friends in many places who have helped in the writing of this book. Bethany Theological Seminary (Oak Brook, Illinois) gave me time, space, and encouragement as its Scholar in Residence in the Fall of 1985. The Hoff Lectures there, and the Rossiter Lectures at Colgate Rochester Divinity School in early 1987, were the genesis of MAWKI and KINGAFAP (see chapters 1, 2, and 5). San Francisco Theological Seminary and the Iliff School of Theology (Denver) have enabled me to share and develop the material with faculty and D.Min. students, as have the Schuyler Institute for Worship and the Arts, the United Theological Seminary (Minneapolis/St. Paul), Chicago Theological Seminary, McCormick Theological Seminary, Garrett-Evangelical Theological Seminary, the Yale Institute of Sacred Music, Whitworth College (Spokane), and McMaster Divinity College (Hamilton, Ontario). The Christendom Trust (U.K.) gave invaluable help with a grant supporting two months' writing time when it was most needed. In Britain I have shared some of the material with Anglican and United Reformed Church ministers on in-service training courses, at Scottish Churches House (Dunblane, Perthshire), and with smaller groupings at St. Andrews University and New College Edinburgh.

It's customary and correct to point out that those who've read the manuscript can't be blamed for its errors. It's also impossible to express adequate thanks for their critique and encouragement. Susan Thistlethwaite invited me to share the nub of the argument with her Constructive Theology class, then commended the manuscript to the publisher. Charles Allen read the final manuscript, pointed me to some valuable references, and gave critique and affirmation. Duncan Forrester and Laurence and Helen Wareing read earlier drafts and gave constructive criticism, as did Susan Heafield, Kay Welch, James Nelson, and Janet Morley.

Other friends have helped more informally, and naming some of them is an act of love not intended to exclude the many who can't be mentioned. So among others, I'm grateful to the Bender family, Walt and Libby Davis, Joan and Jim Fogg, Stuart Frayne, George and Barbara Hamm, Heather and Ray Hobbs, Sue Hosterman and family, Diana Jackson, Bert and Lucille Keller, Vicki Kessler and Donna Kjonaas, Jean Meade, Marilyn and Maurice Miller, Cathy Thoma, Tom Troeger, Jim Rettig, Wilbur Russell, Gerry and Slugger Smith, Margaret Veneman, and Sue Zabel. To Pam and Charles Allen, and George and Nancy Shorney, I give particular thanks and love, for their caring and generous hospitality and for the invaluable professional help and advocacy of George (as music publisher) and Pam (as my North American Agent).

I dedicate this book to Francis Holmes, who taught me French language and literature at grammar school; Merlin Thomas, who tutored me in the same at New College, Oxford; and George Caird, who sharpened my theological wits and supervised my doctoral work at Mansfield College, Oxford, and whose untimely death still evokes great sadness: I would like to have shown him these pages. As educators, they stimulated my abiding fascination with language; as men they would I think be open to the issues raised. I call them "best of teachers"; there can be no higher compliment to their integrity, love of knowledge, and delight in the art of sharing it.

The Main Question

If
every naming of God
is a borrowing from human experience,
  And if
  language slants and angles
  our thinking and behavior,
    And if
    our society
    makes qualities labeled "feminine"
    inferior to qualities labeled "masculine,"
    forming women and men
    with identities steeped in those labelings,
      in structures where men are still dominant
        though shaken
        and women still subordinate
        though seeking emancipation . . .

Then it follows that
  using only male language
  ("he," "king," "father")
  to name and praise God
  powerfully affects our encounter with God
  and our thinking and behavior;

  So that we must then ask
  whether male dominance and female subordination
  and seeing God only in male terms
  are God's intention
  or human distortion and sin;

1

For if
these things are indeed
a deep distortion and sin,
So that
women and men are called to repent together
from domination and subordination,

Then how
can we name and praise God
in ways less idolatrous,
more freeing,
and more true
to the Triune God
and the direction of love
in the Anointed One, Jesus?

Beginnings

I ask the question in the poem on the preceding page as a man, a theologian-poet, and a linguist. I aim to show that every naming of God is a borrowing from human experience, whether contemporary, traditional, or scriptural, and that though language does not determine how we think, it shapes and slants thinking and behavior.

Both points need to be established, since some assert that particular God-names are revealed as normative, while the power of language is often assumed or denied, but rarely investigated.

If these two convictions can be established, it follows that the way we name and depict the divine mystery of Trinity-God is crucially important, since it shapes thinking, behavior, and our knowledge of God. If our naming of God is distorted, our knowledge of God will be also.

When this is accepted, the maleness of almost all our naming and picturing of God stands out and claims our attention. I shall document this and show that God-language in Christian worship is heavily preoccupied with power-as-control.

As a male human being, this worries me, because I have also become convinced that we live, and are formed as human beings, in a civilization in which qualities regarded as "feminine" are disvalued in relation to qualities regarded as "masculine," and in which men have predominance over women. To name and depict God almost exclusively in male terms reinforces those distinctions, since it suggests that women are unfit, or less fit than men, to represent the beauty and greatness of God in language.

3

It took me some years to recognize the reality of male dominance, and even longer to see it as a theological problem: it is difficult to see what lies under our nose, or hear our own voice and accent when speaking. A number of women have long been familiar with the accents of male dominance and its implications for Christian faith. It is time for men to listen to them and look more closely at ourselves.

I shall therefore begin by citing evidence on the meaning of "masculinity" in our culture and the pervasiveness of male dominance over women. To do so I have to converse with historians, social scientists, and others (female and male) and take positions on issues in their disciplines. This is inescapable if progress is to be made, since theology has little value as a closed circle in which theologians listen only to other theologians. I have justified such choices wherever possible; both where I have and where I haven't, further work needs to be done.

Male dominance is a theological problem because God creates us in two coequal genders and does not intend that one should subordinate the other. A civilization built on male dominance and female subordination is a profound distortion and sin, but not immutable. It has arisen in our history and prehistory, so can change and be superseded.

Language is my particular concern. The systematic and almost exclusive use of male God-language, in a faith in which God is revealed as incarnate in a male human being, gives a distorted vision of God and supports male dominance in church and society. The distortion goes deep, in liturgies, creeds, hymns, and the language of the Bible.

Some agree and find Christianity so steeped in male dominance that they bid farewell to Bible and church. Others say either that God intends men to dominate women, or that the distortion stems from the Fall and will only end in heaven.

My hunch is that many are unhappy with those choices and would like to find a way forward that enlarges our knowledge of God, rejects male dominance and the hegemony of male god-language, and names God anew in recognizable continuity with classic Christianity. I shall argue that continuity can be based on the Bible's attitude toward images, the liberating direction of divine love in Hebrew and Christian Scripture (especially in the ministry of Jesus), the self-critical nature of biblical tradition, and the Christian experience of God's threesomeness, which developed into classic trinitarian faith.

In all traditions of Christian worship, similar God-names are repeated again and again, Sunday by Sunday. If I am right about the power of language, God-talk in worship is of the utmost importance, because it slants and shapes our conceptions of God from early childhood. One reason it is so powerful is that worship looks for an encounter with God and therefore aims not to criticize language, but to open us to meet God through it.

As a hymn-poet, I cross and recross bridges between metaphor and abstraction, the rational and the intuitive, and experience the writing of a hymn-poem as a partnership between them. Reason cannot *rule* intuition, nor can clear ideas command the appearance of suitable metaphors. Yet analysis (say, of themes needing hymnic expression) often sets the poetic imagination in motion. Metaphors and phrases sometimes appear unbidden, but still have to be sifted, analyzed, and set in order. The two activities are different, yet reciprocal: each stimulates and needs the other, and naming them as different does not mean they are polar opposites, out of touch with each other. My experience is shared by people working in other areas of creativity. The importance of this will become clear in the next two chapters: I am emboldened to question the "rule models" of our civilization (whereby reason claims superiority over intuition, intellect over emotion, mind over matter, and masculine over feminine) because they are out of tune with experience. Our culture's rigid separations between these categories should also be questioned, but that's outside the scope of this book.

The two styles of working are partly reflected in my division of material into chapters, which carry the main line of thought, and items in the galleries (hymn-poems, and a piece of hymnological research), which intersect with the argument but stand in their own right. The major part of the book (Part III) consists of theological exploration and critique, counterpointed by hymnic examples. Though my aims differ from those of the systematic theologian, the exploration is not disordered, but focuses on God and creation, gender-based naming of God, the significance of Jesus (including his experience of God as Father), the personhood of the Holy Spirit, and the search for more adequate names for God as Trinity.

In what follows, I am not trying to "speak for women," though listening to feminist critiques has made me look at myself and ask what it means to be a man, and what it ought to mean. As racism is a "white problem," so sexism is a male problem: men need to face it and talk about it with men.

Gender issues are issues of justice. Male dominance permeates the fundamental intellectual quests of our civilization. It manifests itself in models of the economy, the recurring cult of toughness in politics, male violence toward women and children, and some aspects of the nuclear arms race.

To recognize male dominance is difficult and painful: our personal stories are involved, our deepest identity called into question. One man, a biblical scholar, accepted the analysis, but said it made him feel as if he were being asked to accept castration.

My initial response was that when our deepest identity is called into question, Christian faith can make sense of the experience in terms of death and resurrection: if we bear the loss, new life will be given. In writing the book, something more positive has been gained. One particular male problem, especially for white heterosexual men, is that we have had a limited male view of things without realizing it. We have assumed that from our experience we could speak for human beings in general. Because we have thought ourselves universal, we have been unable to see what our particular experience is. As I come to understand why I can't be universal and timeless, I also begin to sense, however dimly, the beauty and value of maleness. One day, men will offer it gladly to our female neighbors, in postpatriarchal society.

Gallery: A Song for Boys and Men

Can a Man Be Kind and Caring?

Can a man be kind and caring?
 Jesus was.
Can a man who's kind and caring
be adventuresome and daring,
   bravely doing right
   walking in the light?
      Jesus did, and so I can:
      I will be a Jesus man.

Can a man be sad with crying?
 Jesus was.
Can a man who's sad with crying,
shed his tears, yet keep on trying,
   loving to the end,
   enemy and friend?
      Jesus did, and so I can:
      I will be a Jesus man.

Can a man be hurt and broken?
 Jesus was.
Can a man who's hurt and broken
show his friends how God has spoken,
   giving to us then,
   power to start again?
      Jesus did, and so I can:
      I will be a Jesus man.

*Brian Wren, from *Praising a Mystery: Thirty New Hymns by Brian Wren*, copyright © 1986 by Hope Publishing Co., Carol Stream, Ill. 60188. All rights reserved. Used by permission.

Part I

Masculinity as a Theological Problem

Masculinity is a problem for Christian theology and ought to be felt as such. My theme is "Masculinity as We Know It" (MAWKI for short): what our society considers to be "masculine," contrasted with what it regards as "feminine." MAWKI is problematic for theology if the Holy Trinity, the dynamic, living, and loving God, is seen and depicted almost exclusively through the eyes of a flawed maleness.

My case has six main arguments. Chapter 1 covers the first three, and Chapter 2 the remainder.

A Case to Answer

1. Among many notions of what it means to be a man, MAWKI has two common factors. One is the importance of being in control, whether of emotion, people, events, the body, nature, ideas, or the "feminine." The other is that maleness is partly defined in terms scornful of femaleness, and values and qualities labeled "feminine" are downgraded or despised.

2. We live in a patriarchal society, that is, one characterized by "the manifestation and institutionalization of male dominance over women and children in the family and the extension of male dominance over women in society in general."[1] For the first time in history, many women are in a position to seek emancipation from male dominance. Patriarchal society was formed over a long period of time, which implies it can change.

3. Patriarchal society is reproduced by profound social conditioning, forming us deep within as "masculine" and "feminine."

11

4. Patriarchy sees the world in terms of questionable oppositions based not on equality but subordination, not this-*with*-that but this-*over*-that: reason over emotion, soul over body, spirit over flesh, mind over matter, "man" over nature, and men over women.

5. Many aspects of MAWKI are dangerous and deadly. They include male violence toward women, the recurring cult of toughness in political and economic life, and the irrationalities of the nuclear arms race.

6. All the above raise important theological problems. Patriarchal Christianity is in danger of worshipping an idol, and we are not protected from idolatry by the fact that much of our God-language is biblical.

1

A Flawed Maleness

Masculinity as we know it, or MAWKI, has two common factors. One is the importance of being in control, whether of emotion, people, events, the body, nature, ideas, or the "feminine." The other is that maleness is partly defined in terms scornful of femaleness, and values and qualities labeled "feminine" are downgraded or despised.

"Maggie Thatcher is the only head of government in Western Europe who has balls." The writer was applauding her for supporting the United States' bombing raid on Libya in early 1986. On the same page of the *Economist* another correspondent castigated the "Eurowimps" who objected to the bombing. "They remind me," he said, "of the impotent man who, unable to have sex, offers his abstinence as proof of his high moral character."[1]

Ten months later, Britain's Prince Edward hit the headlines when he decided to leave the Royal Marines. He was said to have cried for three hours after a quarrel with his father, the Duke of Edinburgh, and even a sympathetic newspaper said his status had gone down from Action Man to Royal Wimp. The big question in the tabloids was whether the prince was tough enough for the training course. "It's a tough course, one of the toughest in the world," said the recruiting literature, "and there is no place for the inadequate or the faint-hearted."[2]

In these examples male sexual potency is equated with the use of force, and peaceableness with impotence. The ability to have or sustain an erection is equated with using military force against an enemy. Having testicles is a symbol of courage (though they can also be a load of balls), crying is wimpish and unmanly, and a small group of war fighters is the measure of manhood. Masculinity is associated with *toughness*, having control over others.

My second group of examples suggests another model. "Mum was smashing . . . but my image of my dad is the one who was never there. It was the neighbor across the road who took me to football matches, not my father." The speaker is one of a hundred British men in their mid-thirties, interviewed in a book about men. Another tells how the closest he got to his father was when he was seven or eight. "We used to go into the wood collecting sticks and leaf mould, and sometimes I could get away with holding his hand. I remember the nice feel of this big rough hand. It wasn't that he didn't like me. Of his two sons I was apparently the favorite, but he wasn't able to express it in any way." The interviewer recalls her own parents, a symbiotic union where mother gave all the emotional warmth and father provided financial support. Financially she depended on him, emotionally he depended on her. When she died, he became a forlorn figure, unable to get close to his daughter. "His constant question, whether I was 'all right financially,' seemed to be the only way he knew of showing affection."[3] Masculinity is here associated with *coolness*, having control of oneself, especially one's emotional side. Yet the stories reveal a sense of loss, in the memory of that big, rough hand.

Individual men vary greatly, but we all have to contend with what masculinity is supposed to mean in our culture, whether we exemplify it or struggle against it. Women have to contend with it too. Following recent trends in psychology, I understand MAWKI to be a sex role stereotype. It used to be thought that sex roles—what is involved in being a male or female person in our society—developed from within, because we were individually preprogrammed to learn them. Any problems were problems of adjustment to the role, not of the role itself. Joseph Pleck suggests it is more accurate to think of "masculinity" as a set of expectations, a stereotype, created as it were by society, which individual men may well find problematic. In simplified terms,[4] society has definite ideas about what men and women should be like, but actual men and women cannot do all the things society expects of them.

People who don't fit the stereotypes of masculinity and femininity are usually ostracized. In general, masculinity and femininity would be less stressful if less rigidly stereotyped.

A key word for masculinity as we know it is *control*. A true man is a man in control—of himself, of others, of events, and of the feminine in himself and others. *Control* is an apt word: it suggests a predominance that can often be taken for granted. If you control a situation, you can allow considerable freedom within it, so that your control is hardly noticed, by yourself or others. Perceiving male control requires effort and a self-knowledge painful yet liberating.

One version of control is toughness. Mr. Tough is the ruthless tycoon, the fastest gun in the West, or the deadliest Ninja in the East. He is a real man because he never backs down, always stands and walks tall, and strives for the advantage, to gain power and influence over others. He's less sure of himself nowadays. The calm assurance of the gunfighter who did what a man's gotta do has given way to the frenetic machismo of Rambo, and Dirty Harry has to boast that he has the most powerful handgun in the world.[5]

Yet though Mr. Tough suffers from performance anxiety, he's still part of the masculine stereotype. Attractive or repulsive, he fascinates the male imagination. White, male college students aged eighteen to twenty-five may not act like Rambo, but they are the biggest market for war games. Thousands play games like Cold War, "where the nice guys are very likely to finish a distant last," and players "seize every opportunity to benefit from someone else's loss." In Battletech, they are in a dark age: "Where once the United Star League reigned, five successor states *now battle for control . . . you can control the Battlemechs* in this exciting game of warfare." In Super Power, the players are in today's world, where "in the eternal power struggle of world affairs, *dominance* of the Third World is vital," and "each player, as the leader of a Super Power, *must try to control* the most volatile regions of the world." The players use economic strength, armed force, and wily diplomacy and know that "with the world as the prize, diplomacy can explode into bloodshed at any time."[6]

According to some social scientists, Mr. Tough is an extreme version of the traditional male role, where manliness means physical strength and aggression. Such a man prefers the company of men, and it is other men who assure him of his masculinity. He has strong bonds with work colleagues, fellow sportsmen, or drinking companions, though the relationships rarely get close. Because few men can totally exclude feelings of warmth and affection, Mr. Tough has tender moments when his eyes moisten and there is a catch in his voice, and this is accepted as manly, provided he doesn't let feelings affect his conduct. The control of tenderness is an important MAWKI theme, and the conflict between toughness and tenderness is part of many boys' childhood experience.[7] Mr. Tough expects women to defer to male authority, and marriage is not expected to be romantic or satisfying. He often has a double standard: his own woman must be faithful, but anyone else's is fair game.

The modern male role focuses more on economic or organizational achievement. Such a man values emotional sensitivity, but only in relationships with women. Maintaining emotional control is crucial, so anger and male machismo are looked down on. This man prefers the company of women, and it is from women that he gets assurance of his masculinity. He works with other men, but doesn't like male camaraderie. He expects relationships with women to be intimate and romantic, and proves his masculinity more by satisfying one woman than by trying to "score" with several.[8]

Both descriptions are caricatures, but I suspect they will be familiar to most readers. The "traditional" tough man has working-class associations, whereas the "modern" stereotype works at a distance from the construction site or factory floor. Labeling them "traditional" and "modern" tells us as much about the labelers as the labeled, yet the clash between them comes out in many films and novels. In the film *Saturday Night Fever* (1977), Tony Manero (John Travolta) lives in a working-class district (Bay Ridge), with bickering, beaten down parents and a dead-end job in a paint store. Disco dancing is the bright side of his life. The life of working-class youth is portrayed as gang fighting or gang banging. The men are tough exhibitionists, the women hangers-on. Stephanie Mangano is the exception. She has an apartment in Manhattan, takes ballet lessons, and reads books. Tony comes to accept her judgment of Bay Ridge. He sees his friends' macho toughness as a liability when it leads to the death of one of them in a fall from a high bridge, and he accepts Stephanie's ruling that they'll be just good friends, after he has tried and failed to forcibly "score" with her. The film ends with him moving (though in an undefined way) to the big city, toward a more middle-class view of manhood.[9]

The "modern" version of MAWKI has less emotional reserve than the examples at the beginning of this chapter. Yet he is still, in a way, Mr. Cool. He expresses his feelings of tenderness to the woman he loves, and sometimes to his children, but not to other men. The stereotype says he controls his feelings; in reality he often doesn't know what his feelings are, or has difficulty in expressing them. A group of men was asked by its two women tutors to confront the difficulty they had in expressing warmth by telling others in the group what they liked about them. The request was met with silence, ten minutes of displacement activity, then an attack on the tutors for making such an absurd request—after all, they didn't really know one another. It took twenty-five minutes before one man turned to another and said, "I like you"—and this was in a course called "Sexual Politics for Men"![10] "I find it very difficult to express feelings about things," says another man, "because it's very difficult to understand that your feelings are about something. . . . I can articulate about anything, apart from what I feel, because you have to think so hard about what you've felt."[11]

Being self-confident and in control of one's fate are recurring themes in sport and fiction. Newspaper photos show images of the muscular male body, frozen in a moment of activity, kicking a ball, rushing for the line, or leaping off the starting block. Such images are not meant to arouse desire (though maybe they do) but to suggest invulnerability. "It can't happen to me" is the recurring theme of many adventure stories, where the threatened hero seeks a way out, and usually finds it.

Media stereotypes may not tell us what individual men are like, but they proclaim what men are meant to be. One of the things men are meant to be is in control of situations in which they meet women. Those who are not are objects of humor, and many TV sitcoms hinge on the hero's inability to control the women in his life. Laughter arises out of the clash between masculine stereotype and wimpish reality: if men weren't *supposed* to be in control, there would be nothing to laugh at. Even so, the comic hero stays at the center of things, and women define themselves in relation to him. Most children's stories still have active boys and onlooking girls. When pleasant things happen to the male character, he is usually responsible for bringing them about. When they happen (much less often) to the female character, she usually has someone else to thank for her good fortune.[12]

Similarly, a 1974 study of women in TV commercials found that nearly 90 percent of the authority figures were males, and women were portrayed more often in domestic roles. Updated studies show little change. Men are shown as taller authority figures and women in such postures as "the bashful knee-bend."[13]

Media images of male sexuality are closely bound up with control. Many films center on male characters, with whom the viewer is invited to identify, and on sexuality as pursuit. Men pursue women, whether in love or lust, crude dominance or tender possession. A standard sequence is the heroine in jeopardy. In a horror film, she has left her bedroom at night and is wandering through the corridors of the darkened mansion. In a thriller, she visits a building where one apartment hides a psychopath on the run. In a science fiction film, everyone flees from the monster, but the heroine trips and twists her ankle. Nearly always, it is a woman who is trapped, without resources to help herself. "Heroes in jeopardy do something about it; heroines don't."[14]

We who are watching (tacitly assumed to be "we men") are meant to find pleasure in seeing a woman in peril, and excitement at her vulnerability and terror. The vulnerable part of ourselves can also be touched, without our having to admit it. We are encouraged to take the male role of superiority ("we'd do better than that") and indulge our desire to rape and conquer, or protect and rescue. "We are superior because we either know more than her (we know that the psychopath is there but she hasn't spotted him yet), or because we can see what any sensible person would do but she, foolishly and pathetically, doesn't."[15] When the heroine does take the initiative, she acts incompetently, overemotionally, or indecisively, so that her failure reinforces her need and our superiority.

Sometimes the male viewer is encouraged into the position of rapist in relation to the woman. We can see her, but she can't see us. Though that is true of film and TV as a medium, it is often played on sexually. The heroine is put in a situation in which, if she knew a man was looking, she would be on her guard—she would not go into the shower or wander around in her nightie. Thus she is doubly vulnerable, because she is in a vulnerable situation and because she doesn't know that we—and the monster or the psychopath—are watching. Sometimes we see her explicitly from the viewpoint of the rapist or the monster, as she backs away from the camera in terror.

But she is rescued by the hero, our positive identification figure. "The camera puts us in the position of the rapist, but the plot puts us reassuringly back in the position of the savior."[16] This again establishes male superiority—she needed us and is now in our debt. The plot also feeds male fantasies of being heroic enough to rescue her, which in real life the male viewer might not be able to do.

What is objectionable is not thrills and excitement in themselves, but the way in which, over and over again, the narrative equates a general *human* excitement of suspense and tension with *male sexual* excitement: power over women, the thrill of possession (whether by toughness or tenderness), and the reassurance of female "weakness" and subordination.

Another standard sequence is the moment in a romantic love story when the hero first sees the heroine and looks at her with love and desire. He looks at her: she is seen, but either does not know she is seen or else looks back only briefly or covertly, then looks away. The ways in which the encounter is presented typically show the man as dominant and active, and the woman as deferential and reactive.

Other ways of presenting men and women are as yet marginal: notable because they stand out. In the standard sequences, masculinity is associated with taking the initiative and having control of the situation. There is a suggestive similarity between these story lines and standard views of male sexuality. MAWKI sexuality is goal-oriented: seduction and foreplay are means to the end of climax (orgasm), a quest in which a man moves out of himself and into another. The adventure story is also a quest in pursuit of a goal. The hero moves outward and onward, the goal is attained through possession (whether of gold, secrets, a woman, or power over others), and thus a climax is achieved. Men are the central actors who make things happen, and women function either as the goal of the narrative or the reward for achieving it. Even if the narrative is about war, crime, or business, the drive to its climax is often bound up with the promise of a woman at the end.

To summarize: "the visual representation of male sexuality puts women in their place, as objects of a 'natural' male sexual drive that may at times be ridiculous but is also insistent, inescapable, and inevitable. Such representations help preserve the existing power relations of men over women by translating them into sexual relations rendered both as biologically given and as a source of masculine pleasure."[17]

Perhaps it is because male sexuality is so closely associated with control that many men find it difficult to see themselves as objects of female sexual desire. If I desire her, and her role is to be desired and to respond, then I have the initiative (in theory at least). If she desires me and does not wait, but boldly takes the initiative, then *I* have to respond and lose control of the interaction. To admit that my body is desirable to her is to feel more vulnerable than a "real man" wants to be.

One result of the importance of control in the varied versions of MAWKI is that masculinity is partly defined by negatives. Boys, whatever they positively are, are *not* feminine. They are not sissies, they don't cry, and they don't go running to mother when they are hurt. Whatever our society regards as "feminine," men and boys are definitely not that. In part, this results from our sharp separation of "masculinity" and "femininity" as polar opposites: one is bound to be defined by contrast with the other. But the contrast is not like the contrast between a vine and a honeysuckle, Beethoven and Dostoyevsky, or bacon and eggs. Most people would see these as differences between two equals: I might prefer Beethoven to Dostoyevsky, but would find it difficult to claim that one was superior to the other. The masculine-feminine distinction, however, has a built-in contrast of superiority-inferiority. The MAWKI theme song, "boys are not girls," has an overtone of scorn: "boys are not *girls*."

This is not just a matter of men defining themselves as superior: our culture itself seems to rate what it labels "masculine" more highly than what it labels "feminine," and is not alone in doing so. "Although different societies have very different views about what qualities are masculine," writes John Nicholson, "such qualities are invariably more highly valued than those thought to be feminine."[18] Another researcher summarizes studies showing how women and men are represented in media images and language use. One theme emerging clearly "is the equation of men and masculinity with normalcy . . . and the equation of women and femininity with deviance." Men's attributes and activities are presented not as the partial account of half the human race, but as if they were the norm or standard by which what is "human" is measured: women's qualities and attributes are presented as a deviation from that supposed norm.[19] What is normal is by definition of superior value to what is deviant.

Thus, deep within the meaning of "masculinity " is an assumption of superiority in relation to the feminine: this assumption is as built-in as vowels to consonants, wings to an aircraft, or mortar to stone. Equally deep is a flight from the feminine, in which the drawbridge goes up if feminine qualities come too close to the male self.[20] That is why MAWKI is important for Christian theology: either it is God-given, to be rejoiced in and submitted to, or it is one of the most profound and pervasive sins we know.

Patriarchal Society

We live in a society characterized by "the manifestation and institutionalization of male dominance over women and children in the family and the extension of male dominance over women in society in general."[21] For the first time in history, many women are in a position to seek emancipation from male dominance. Patriarchal society was formed over a long period of time, which implies it can change.

A few pages cannot prove this. All I can do is state a conviction and underline important aspects of it, since there is ample evidence in other sources (as in Marilyn French's charting of patriarchy past and present)[22] and elsewhere in this book.

Gerda Lerner distinguishes helpfully between *oppression* and *subordination*. The former implies forceful subordination with victimization of the oppressed. Though the historical experience of women includes oppression, the term is inadequate, she suggests, because women, more than any other group, have collaborated in their own subordination. Moreover, male dominance can involve mutual obligations between men and women that are often not seen as oppressive. The word *subordination* clearly marks a dominance relation, includes the possibility of a voluntary acceptance of subordination in exchange for protection and/or privilege, and does not imply that there is always evil intent on the part of the dominators.

From this state women increasingly wish to gain *emancipation*, meaning freedom from oppressive restrictions imposed on the basis of sex, and freedom to decide one's own destiny and define one's role in society. Its etymology (derived from the Latin *e-manus + capere*, to come out from under the hand of) makes it a more fitting term than *liberation*, which falls under the same objections as *oppression*. Lerner describes patriarchy as a system of paternalistic dominance, being the relationship of a dominant group, considered superior, to a subordinated group, considered inferior, in which the dominance is mitigated by some mutual obligations and varying degrees of rights held by both parties. Her understanding of patriarchy is of a situation in which women are not totally powerless, passive, or deprived of rights, influence, and resources, but in which men hold power in the important institutions of society and women are deprived of access to that power.[23] From a psychological perspective, John Nicholson advances a similar definition: male dominance means a situation in which "men have higher public status (i.e. they get the best jobs and are responsible for making decisions which affect other people's lives), higher domestic status (they are the formal head of the family), and also that they win the lion's share of whatever commodity happens to be in demand in the society in which they live."[24]

Two things are fundamental: recognizing that patriarchal society was formed by men and women in our common history, and coming to terms with our own gender's part in that history. Gerda Lerner persuasively argues that patriarchy was *created* by men and women in a process that took nearly twenty-five hundred years to reach completion. Her analysis of this process in the ancient Near East—including Israel—indicates that the subordination of women, established well before the first written records of human civilization, developed and was consolidated, at different speeds and with different nuances, in a number of ancient societies.

If patriarchy was incomplete and developing in the earliest societies with written records, it is difficult to argue that it was given in the nature of things. The thoroughness and plausibility of

Lerner's argument put the onus of proof on those who argue that patriarchy is "natural." Debates about possible futures for women and men can no longer appeal to naive assumptions about what "always was." If patriarchy was created by human beings, it can, in principle, be changed and superseded.

In some modern societies, large groups of women have begun to emancipate themselves from male control, discover their past, and interpret the present condition of humanity. A look at inherited notions of "history" shows how significant this development is. Men and women have always been actors and agents in the human story (*history* with a small *h*); in that story women, like men, have been central, not marginal. But *History* with a capital *H* is the written recording of the human story, and until recently Historians have been men. They have recorded what some (usually the powerful) men have done or found significant, called this "history," and presented it as the normative account of the past.[25]

It is not easy to deal with a sinful story when that story has our own identity as one of its products. Wisdom comes by facing the truth about our collective past and learning from it, while trusting that the future is, by God's grace, open to new possibilities. We do not gain wisdom by putting the past out of our mind, or pretending that it has no influence on the present.

So it is important (for men especially and male theologians in particular) to hear and absorb the age-long story of what male domination has meant—and still means—for women. We need to open ourselves to the hurt, the pain, the indescribable sadness of that subordination, the injustice and often brutal oppression in women's experience, and the loss of human potential it represents, in both men and women. Only thus will we be motivated to seek new paths.

I cannot retell that story here,[26] but first acquaintance with it has helped shape this book. In the eleventh century Hildegard of Bingen founded an abbey, corresponded with pope and king, composed hymns and an early form of opera, wrote works of science and theology, and supervised the painting of her "Illuminations"—visions of God, whose images and mandalas reach across the centuries with imaginative power.[27] In thirteenth-century Belgium, some women chose to live together in the semiseclusion of small communities, as Beguines. They supported themselves by weaving, lace making, embroidery, and nursing. They set up industries, bargained with the city for tax relief and the right to practice certain occupations, and won those rights. Their poverty, autonomy, sharing, and service to the community are as inspiring today as they were subversive then. They were persecuted; much of their property was seized; some who defied the church were burned at the stake. In the seventeenth century, during the English Civil War, crowds of women demonstrated and petitioned on several occasions for peace, bread, and the release of the Levelers' leaders. In eighteenth-century France women participated in the insurrection at the Tuileries that overthrew the monarchy, took active part against foreign intervention in the Revolution, demanded and got rights to divorce and equal inheritance with men, and formed political clubs when political rights were denied. In every case, women were suppressed and brought under male control, but their example demonstrates the real presence of women as central in history.[28] It prompts me to begin seeing the past anew, and to want a future where women and men make a humane story together.

From the past we inherit a long history of men blaming women for the world's woes. Early Christianity developed a view of the Adam and Eve story showing woman as the means by which evil came into the world (it lacked that interpretation in Judaism). "Eve" (woman) was scapegoated as the cause of "man's" fall. "*You* are the devil's gateway," said Tertullian. "*You* are the unsealer of the forbidden tree. *You* are the first deserter of the divine law. . . . *You* destroyed so easily God's image, man. On account of *your* desert, that is death, even the Son of God had to die." The church "fathers" mostly take for granted, and frequently reiterate, this denigrating view of women, which ultimately led to witch hunts and burnings, though witch hunts also had more worldly motives. In the Massachusetts witch trials (1647–1700), the primary group accused were women, mostly older (aged forty to sixty), single women or widows, with repute as healers or midwives. They had often inherited land and had a reputation for independent-mindedness toward male neighbors and clergy. Accusations of witchcraft meant either death or penury, since they could not flee without losing property and livelihood. "Thus, the witchcraft accusations, which went on continuously for more than fifty years after the Puritans became established in the colonies, served to crush a particular class of women who were dangerous to the normative definition of women in society."[29]

What can a man learn from this story? I have never shared the "fathers' " misogyny, nor believed in the reality of magic, so feel anger at the misogyny and horror at the witch hunts. Yet this past is part of my present, because similar things can always recur while "masculinity" carries within it a negative valuation of the feminine in a civilization in which men have dominance over women.

Patriarchy Maintained

Patriarchal society is reproduced by profound social conditioning, forming us deep within as "masculine" and "feminine."

Media stereotypes portray women and men as different and unequal, and most adults expect them to behave differently.[30] It is a matter of dispute how far the differences we think we see are inborn or inbred. My view is that there is one race, the human race, and that our gender division into female and male, though important, is secondary to what unites us in our common humanity (a point well argued elsewhere).[31] Average differences can be misinterpreted. Some presumed differences are exaggerated, or socially determined, and in no case do they justify male dominance.

For example, men and women differ in visual spatial ability (the ability involved in reading a map, working from diagrams, or playing chess). The difference becomes statistically significant if enough people are tested. Statistically, then, it can be said that "men are superior to women in visual spatial ability." Some have used such evidence to argue that this is the reason almost all chess grand masters are male and less than 1 percent of British engineers are female. Such a conclusion is invalid, since one-quarter of all women have greater visual spatial ability than the average man. The discrepancy between women and men in, say, international chess, engineering, and architecture cannot result from differences in visual spatial ability alone. To claim that it does is to use statistical averages misleadingly, to excuse an injustice.[32]

As regards physical differences, the average woman's body has 25 percent fat, whereas the average man's has 12 percent. This helps to account for male superiority in most forms of physical endeavor, though in long-distance swimming women are faster than men. But childhood exercise can boost heart-lung capacity more than exercise done in later life, and there is a bias toward males in this area: British and American boys are three times more likely than girls to take part in extracurricular athletics. Where women and men have equal opportunities, differences in attainment diminish. In trained athletes the male-female difference in achievement is only 8 percent, compared with the 30 percent difference between Mr. and Ms. Average. The gap between men's and women's world records has narrowed dramatically. In the 800 meters, the men's record came down from 1:46.6 to 1:41.7 minutes between 1939 and 1981, an improvement of 4.9 seconds. In the same period the women's 800 meter record improved by 18.6 seconds, from 2:12.0 to 1:53.4 minutes.[33]

Conditioning may persuade us that men and women are very different emotionally. Yet emotional differences are difficult to measure. There is no way of being sure that what people say they feel is similar to what other people feel. Answers to questionnaires can be misleading. Boys are reluctant to admit fears and distress, as being unmanly. Questions such as "Are you scared if you walk home alone or are in the house alone?" get markedly different reactions from boys than from girls, not because girls are more "emotional" but because they are more likely to get strong warnings about the dangers in such situations and respond accordingly. There is not much empirical support for the belief that women show more "emotional" behavior than men, and some of the evidence is suspect. Men seem to respond to stress physiologically (for example, by changes in blood pressure), whereas women respond more verbally. Women's greater verbal response to stress ("talking it out") may be what gives women the reputation of being more emotional. One benefit is that it enables women literally to "get it off their chest." Men can disguise their feelings, but only at some cost. Stress takes more toll on the male body, and many men find it difficult to seek help, or even recognize their own stress symptoms in time. "A man's upper lip may be stiff, but so is the price he pays to keep it that way."[34]

The most important evidence concerns child care, since it is widely believed that women are more "naturally" suited to child rearing than men. The evidence for a maternal instinct is "rather flimsy," says psychologist John Nicholson, and the fact that women are responsible for child care in most societies does not prove they are uniquely suited to it. Such an argument would be on a par with the disk jockey who says that a million people have bought a certain record, so it must be good. As Nicholson observes, "You have only to listen to some of the records which sell a million to see how shaky this proposition is."[35]

In the United States, researchers found that boys and girls between the ages of eight and fourteen were equally affected, physiologically, by the sight and sound of a crying baby—alterations in their heart rate followed the same patterns. The difference was that girls looked more interested, whereas boys pretended not to notice, a difference even more marked among older children. This suggests that both sexes have similar feelings about a baby in distress, but are conditioned to respond differently. In Sweden, a study of couples sharing the care of an infant showed that in the first three days of life, when both parents were present, fathers spent more time stimulating the child by holding and rocking, whereas mothers smiled more. Mothers did most of the feeding and cleaning, but fathers were equally good at interpreting distress signals. By the time the child was three months old, these parental roles were often reversed. At fifteen months, the mother was the child's main playmate; at eighteen months, both parents played equally with the child; by three years many children preferred to play with their father.

When both parents are involved in child care, their roles are not interchangeable: fathers tend to be more physical, whereas mothers give more intellectual stimulation. In their first year of life, children tend to laugh and smile more at their fathers, but turn to mothers more for reassurance in distress. A study in the United States found that by age one, about half were more attached to their mother, one-quarter were more attached to their father, and the rest were equally attached to both parents. If this has wider validity, the fact that only one child in two would rather be with its mother than its father "makes it very difficult to maintain the view that mothers must occupy a unique position in the life of their children."[36]

It is fair to say that women and men are more alike than different, and that the measurable differences neither explain nor justify the political, economic, and social disparities between them. There is good evidence that our personal identities as women or men are profoundly shaped by parents, schooling, and other features of patriarchal society.

Conditioning starts early. There is more observable variety of behavior among babies of the same sex than between the "typical" boy and girl. Yet most adults *believe* that boys and girls behave differently, and act on their belief. If men and women are shown a baby and told that its name is "Mark," "he" is seen as bouncing, cheeky, mischievous, and strong. The same child, behaving in the same way but given the name "Mary," is perceived as lovely, sweet, gorgeous, and cute. "Mark" is given a toy hammer, and "Mary" receives a doll. If "Mark" becomes restless, this is taken as a signal that "he" wants to play, and "he" gets what he wants—adult attention and interaction in play activity. The same movements from "Mary" are seen as a need for comfort, so "Mary" gets not play, but cuddles, soothing, and smiles. It is a fair assumption that if boys get this kind of reaction most of the time, they are being encouraged to behave independently and to expect that if they make their wishes known, they will get what they want. "But the only lesson girls will learn from their treatment is that they are expected to lie quietly, passively waiting for things to happen before reacting."[37]

Fortunately, parents treat their own children more variably, and the personality of the child is an important factor in the interaction. But on average, mothers spend more time holding and soothing daughters than sons, despite the fact that boys cry more and need less sleep than girls. Both parents smile and talk to girls more, encouraging such behavior in return, and are more verbally affectionate to girls than boys. Since in early childhood our parents are our "world," their interaction with us is likely to have a powerful effect on our identity and behavior.

Schooling also contributes to social conditioning. In mixed-sex classes boys get more teacher time and are punished more for nonacademic faults, whereas girls get less teacher time, are reprimanded more for academic mistakes, and are praised more for conduct and appearance than for attainment. The hidden lesson is that what a girl is good at is being "feminine," whereas academic work is likely to bring criticism if inadequate and less likely to bring praise if good. Moreover, when a boy gives the wrong answer, the teacher is more likely—especially in math and science lessons—to keep at him, suggesting new approaches. When a girl gives the wrong answer, she is more likely to be told not to worry and less likely to be told to try again. The boy's hidden lesson is that he is expected to improve his performance, and that initial failure is a challenge to be overcome by trying again. But the hidden lesson for a girl is likely to be that academic failure is beyond her control, that little can be done about it, and that it is not her fault. "This attitude is known as learned helplessness. It is not of course confined to girls, but it seems to affect them more than boys."[38]

There is no evidence that girls are less motivated than boys to succeed (men and women are intellectually equal, although girls get slightly better exam results than boys throughout school). But there is overwhelming evidence that women are less confident in their ability to succeed than men are. Although men and women are equal in ability, equally anxious to succeed, and have much the same opinion of their own value as individuals, when there is a job to be done, men are more confident than women that they will be able to do it and more satisfied with their own performance. "The difference in self-confidence is the most striking difference between the sexes in motivation, and applies even when the task is one in which women do better than men."[39]

The change between childhood and adulthood has to do with a person's "locus of control." People with an "internal locus of control" take credit for their own success and generally believe they can control by their own actions what happens to them in life. By contrast, people with an "external locus of control" attribute success to something outside themselves. "I'm not boasting," the former might say, "but I did work hard for that." The latter say, "I'm glad I got there. It must have been my lucky day." In childhood, boys can be divided equally between those with an internal locus and those with an external locus of control, and so can girls. But by early adulthood, more women than men have an external locus of control. In other words, between childhood and early adulthood, girls lose confidence in their ability to succeed, relative to boys.[40]

What can explain this? I have already given evidence that being self-confident and in control of one's fate are an important part of the masculine stereotype. Boys aspire to that, and almost everything they hear, see, and read encourages that aspiration. For girls, on the other hand, the insistent lesson of films, stories, advertisements, and many of their peers and role models is that it's still "a man's world," where men are expected to succeed and women to be subordinate, and where men hold the overwhelming majority of positions of power and influence. It is no wonder that many lose confidence and adjust their expectations downward.

I have summarized some of the evidence that "masculinity" and "femininity," as defined by our culture, are more likely to be learned than preprogrammed in our genes. Some of the evidence rings true in my own experience. When I read of the man who finds it difficult to understand what his feelings are, I recognize something of myself, yet can remember being young enough to express feelings freely and easily. Male difficulties in expressing feelings are learned, not innate. The young child feels and expresses fear, hunger, and distress, with or without verbalizing them: to do so is essential for survival. Male difficulties in expressing feelings are also selective: many men find no difficulty in expressing feelings of anger, especially toward people with lower social status. It is "weak" feelings (sadness, fear, worry, loss, loneliness) that MAWKI would have us control.

Dealing with the "tough guy" was another important part of my growing up. Most boys are not physically aggressive. Though they have more rough-and-tumble play than girls, most of it is in fun, and three out of four boys do not show aggressively violent behavior: it is the behavior of the quarter who do that lifts the average above that of girls.[41] But we all have to deal with the rogue quarter of our sex: "As boys, we have to be constantly on the alert to either confront or avoid physical violence. We have to be ready to defend ourselves. We are constantly on our guard. This builds tension and anxiety into the very organization of our bodies. You get so used to living with it that it comes to feel normal."[42]

Watching from the other side of the schoolyard, Mary Ingham recalls how glad she was to be a girl and not have to pick fights or stand her ground. Later, she saw it differently: "I began to envy what that trial by fire gave you: to be able to stand your ground in a world where you were bound to meet the confrontation and conflict you'd avoided at school."[43] I'm not sure how to take that compliment to male conditioning. There's a grain of truth in it, since all children need to learn fortitude and perseverance. Some gain useful skills from the ordeal:

I used to have fights, really nasty fights in terrible tempers, where boys would say, "I'm going to fight you, Tony Taylor— but no hitting in the face." If they said hitting in the face, that was heavy stuff. More likely they'd be in a really bad temper, just going umph! on your arm. You didn't lose total face because you hadn't run away sniveling and you'd actually planted a couple of punches on his arm, not to hit him hard, just to draw away his anger. If I let him give me three really good 'uns, it might be enough, and it often was.[44]

Here is a real fight, but with unwritten rules. Tony Taylor's account shows a boy learning to stand his ground, bear pain, and deal constructively with male violence (placing and accepting punches to release the opponent's anger). Each boy invents his own strategies and does the best he can. But a boy's playground ruled by bullies is not the best training for adult life. The fortitude and endurance of many women in the peace movement do not come from Amazonian schooling.[45] My own schoolyard taught me to fear and avoid the bullies and how to control and hide my fear. I did not learn there how to peaceably and courageously confront them.

Conclusion

I have argued that a key theme of masculinity as we know it is *control* and that built into MAWKI is an assumption of superiority over the feminine coupled with a flight from the feminine. Men and women live in a patriarchal society, which some of us are gradually becoming aware of, but is as yet almost unchanged. The over-under perception of the "masculine-feminine" relationship touches the depths of personal identity. In Chapter 2 I shall argue that it permeates the way human beings think, think about thinking, and make scientific discoveries, and that masculinity as we know it is dangerous and deadly for human society and planet earth.

2

The Cost of Control

Patriarchy is characterized by divisions and oppositions based not on equality but subordination, not this-*with*-that but this-*over*-that: reason over emotion, soul over body, spirit over flesh, mind over matter, "man" over nature, and men over women.

I worked for seven years in a campaign highlighting Third World issues. There were less than a dozen paid workers, and we worked as a cooperative. A frequent question from people in other organizations was, "Who's your director?" followed by bafflement or disbelief when we explained we didn't have one (or the assumption that I must be, because I was the oldest). Frequently the question came from organizations enthusiastic about Third World cooperatives.

Though our political institutions claim to be democratic, in most of life we are accustomed to look for bosses. We think in pyramids, and with good reason, because most of our institutions are organized that way. There are different kinds of "over-under" relationships, ranging from tyranny to near equality: that someone else is our superior can be oppressive, touching every aspect of life, or almost unnoticeable, because the personal relationships are good and there's a shared commitment to the job being done. Yet, oppressive or not, over-under relationships are pervasive. At the heart of Western patriarchal society is a way of thinking and behaving that sees things in terms of opposites: soul and body, reason and emotion, spirit and flesh, mind and matter, "man" and nature, "masculine" and "feminine," and man and woman. Yet the opposites are not equal. Reason must rule emotion, the soul govern the body, spirit be superior to flesh, mind triumph over matter, "man" conquer nature, and men subordinate women. The starkness of these opposites leads to many distortions, as does the "rule model" of their relationships.

Male-dominated Reason

One of the most distinctively human activities is thinking, reasoning, made possible by our ability to know ourselves, know that we exist in nature, and know that we know.[1] Few would deny that this is a *human* attribute, shared equally by males and females, though varying with age and ability. Yet from the beginning of our civilization, reasoning has been identified with men and masculinity. To reason has had built into it an over-under relationship between reason (identified as a masculine quality) and the nonrational, subrational, and irrational in human beings (identified as feminine), in which reason either rules over the others, soars above them, shuts them out, or leaves them behind.

Genevieve Lloyd has charted the complexities of Western philosophy's thinking about thinking.[2] Though the over-under relationship has been expressed in a variety of ways, two themes recur. One is to exalt reason and despise the nonrational. In an early Greek myth, the infant Apollo slays the python that guards the old earth oracle. This releases the powers of the earth goddess, who sends dream oracles to cloud the minds of "men" with "dark dream truth." Zeus stills these night voices and leaves the forces of reason installed at Delphi. Clear, rational thought is here associated with maleness, and femaleness with whatever clouds the mind and hinders thinking.

Later, Philo of Alexandria interwove Plato's thinking about reason with the story of the Fall in Genesis 3. "Mind corresponds to man," he said, "the senses to woman; and pleasure encounters and holds parley with the senses first, and through them cheats with her quackeries the sovereign mind itself." Though his allegories don't imply that women are irrational, they are shaped by his pejorative attitude toward women. "Man" corresponds to "mind," and "woman" corresponds to sense perception. Human beings are urged to leave behind the "weak feminine passion of sense-perception" and give forth, as incense, the "manly reasoning schooled in fortitude." Moral progress does not exclude women, but they will progress only by leaving behind their female character traits, while men progress by strengthening male characteristics. "Mind" does not dialogue with intuition, feeling, and sense perception, but rules over them.[3]

A more modern theme has been to idealize the nonrational, supposedly feminine qualities, while keeping them in a subordinate place. In Rousseau's thought, a feminized nature is seen as benevolent. In The New Heloise, Julie has a garden, where she is guided by the way nature does things, but tames and controls nature. Women symbolize a desired closeness to nature. They are both objects of adulation and sources of disorder. So men occupy public life, and women are excluded from citizenship. Immanuel Kant venerates women's "beautiful understanding," their presumed aesthetic taste and practical sense. But deep meditation and long-sustained reflection don't befit a woman's beautiful nature. "A woman who has a head full of Greek, like Mme. Dacier, or carries on fundamental controversies about mechanics," said Kant, "might as well have a beard." Kant's adulation of "feminine" qualities hides the fact that what makes them qualities is their exclusion from male intellectual attainment.[4]

Thinking has sometimes been trapped within the masculine/feminine rule model, despite the thinker's best intentions. In the early seventeenth century Francis Bacon used a variety of metaphors to explain his new understanding of knowledge and had strong motives of compassion and concern to improve the human condition. Following his predecessors, he spoke of nature in female terms, and of science as the male suitor seeking to unveil her and penetrate her mysteries. Earlier philosophies had ignored experiment and claimed to know nature without, as it were, looking at her and listening to her. Baconian science was a return to intellectual humility. We have no right to expect nature to come to us, said Bacon. "Enough if, on our approaching her, she condescends to show herself." Lloyd quotes a beautiful passage, reminiscent in style of the Pauline epistles, where Bacon says that if there is any humility toward the Creator, zeal to lessen human sufferings, and love of truth in natural things, "men" must put aside "those inconstant and preposterous philosophies which prefer theses to hypotheses, have led experience captive, and triumphed over the works of God," so that they may "humbly and with a certain reverence draw near to the book of Creation," meditate on it, be washed clean and turn away from speculative opinion.[5]

Yet by speaking of our exploration of nature in terms of the male unveiling the female, Bacon built a new version of that over-under relationship into the meaning of the scientific endeavor. In Greek theories of knowledge, "mind" dominated "matter" in order to reach true knowledge, and this enterprise had a patriarchal flavor because mind was associated with maleness and matter with femaleness. Yet moving beyond, or above, the "feminine" was not an essential part of what it meant to know something.

Bacon, however, saw mind dominating matter because matter itself was what the mind was seeking to know. In his sexual metaphors, control of the feminine became associated with the very act of knowing. Though much of Bacon's thought can be expressed without his male-female metaphors, the intellectual virtues of being a good scientist are expressed in terms of having a right male attitude toward the female, which is seen as subordinate to the male. The right attitude is chastity, respect, and restraint, and the scientist's aim is seen in terms of male-sexuality-as-pursuit. He aims to unveil nature and penetrate her secrets. Female nature is mysterious and awesome, yet also knowable—and knowing "her" is closely associated with control. The metaphors do not give us value-free concepts about the relation between knower and known. "They give a *male content* to what it is to be a good knower."[6]

Thus, one of the most distinctively *human* capabilities, rational thought, has been distorted by rule models drawn from the patriarchal hierarchy of male-over-female and "masculine"-over-"feminine." If to be rational means being free of the feminine, then the downgrading of feminine traits is bound up with our understanding of what reasoning is, and how it is done. Philosophers have seen rationality as overcoming the feminine, as ruling and guiding it, ruling yet being nurtured by it, or surpassing but incorporating it; but in every case the over-under relationship has been retained. We cannot move beyond this, says Genevieve Lloyd, merely by affirming the value of the "feminine" in human life, since this is likely to be co-opted by ideas of the male as normal humanness and the female as secondary, deviant, or complementary. "There has been no lack of male affirmation of the importance and attractiveness of 'feminine traits' *in women*," she writes, "or of gallant acknowledgement of the impoverishment of male Reason."[7]

The Male-as-Norm Syndrome

Philosophy has also been permeated by the assumption that maleness is the norm or standard of what is human. "To renounce one's liberty is to renounce one's quality as a man, the rights and the duties of citizenship," says Jean-Jacques Rousseau in *The Social Contract*. The word *man* seems generic, meaning that liberty is the birthright of all human beings. Yet when writing on the education of women, Rousseau says that "they [women] must be trained to bear the yoke from the first, so that they may not feel it, to master their own caprices and submit themselves to the will of others." So the human quality of liberty only applies in practice to men.

Similarly, Kant says that "man" is a rational being, then describes reason in terms that exclude women; and Schopenhauer says that in every respect women are backward, "lacking in reason and reflection . . . a kind of middle step between the child and the man, *who is the true human being*. In the last resort, women exist solely for the propagation of the race." Carol Gould gives these and other examples to support her claim that, in practice, philosophers have labeled as universal human properties those they have explicitly identified as male or associated with roles and functions where males have predominated. Western philosophers have done their work in societies in which reason has been highly valued, males have been dominant in social and political life, and women subordinate or absent. In those circumstances it is not surprising that rationality has been seen as a male or masculine quality. Yet to change that perception would mean allowing women to claim their rights and be respected not only intellectually, but economically, professionally, and politically. The philosophical ranking order has performed an ideological function: it has both mirrored patriarchal society and helped maintain it.[8]

One odd result of the masculinization of rationality, and the related downgrading of the female and feminine, is Schopenhauer's belief that "women exist solely for the propagation of the race," as if this was of secondary importance. This is hardly a rational proposition, since it implies that the attainment of abstraction is more important than propagating philosophers who can attain it. Yet it has had far-reaching *political* consequences. In classical theories of the social contract, the systematic setting aside of the fundamental facts of birth, childhood, parenthood, old age, and death "results in an image of the public or political world as a timeless or static community of adults, met together to transact their collective business."[9] Despite its acknowledgment of our finite, mortal condition, observes Robert Paul, "traditional liberal political theory simply does not take seriously the dominant facts of human life, namely birth, childhood, ageing and death."[10] One of those "dominant facts" is the work involved in bearing and nurturing children and organizing a household. Because domestic work and child care are excluded from political and economic theories, they are ignored in favor of other sectors of the economy and disvalued in comparison with the masculine virtues of toughness, aggression, and competitiveness.

"Man" and Nature

Francis Bacon was not alone in thinking of scientific discovery as male reason penetrating female nature. A careful study of the biomedical sciences in eighteenth- and nineteenth-century France shows that "increasingly, this capacity for scientific prowess was conceptualized as a male gift, just as nature was the fertile woman and sometimes the archetypal mother."[11]

Women were associated with nature, both positively (for their simple, pure morality) and negatively (because of their ignorance and presumed lack of intellectual powers). They were part of nature-the-unknown, having less reason than men, and with uncontrolled passions not amenable to the guiding light of reason. But women were also being understood by masculine science, as in the growing knowledge of anatomy. In both senses, masculine related to feminine by means of control: women either needed to be controlled, because they could not control themselves, or their nature was being uncovered and thus brought under the control of (male) reason.

Anatomical models of the time reflect this understanding. Male models stand tall, even when organs, muscles, and nerves have been lifted away and only the skeleton remains. Female models are recumbent, as if waiting to be inspected, and were, significantly, known as "venuses." One on view in the London Science Museum has blue eyes, flowing blond hair, and a posture of one who awaits a lover. The image of female nature was made explicit in a statue, in the medical faculty of the University of Paris, of a young woman, bare-breasted, her head slightly bowed beneath the veil she is taking off. The statue bore the inscription: "Nature unveils herself before Science."[12]

Penetrating Discoveries

The sexual metaphors coined by Francis Bacon had consequences he did not foresee. For in a male-dominated society, metaphors of unveiling and penetration easily suggest force and subjugation. Gallantry resisted becomes insistence; seduction turns to rape; inquiry becomes attack.

Some of these possibilities are implicit in Bacon's own writing. He called on his fellow men to inaugurate with him "the truly masculine birth of time" and thus achieve "the dominion of man over the universe." The aim was to discover "still laid up in the womb of nature many secrets of excellent use." It was an enterprise for real men: "The Natural Philosophy we have received from the Greeks must rank only as the childhood of science," Bacon wrote. "It has what is proper to boys. It is a great chatter box and is too immature to breed." The aim, then, is not simply unveiling and penetration, but birth. Intercourse between the masculine knower and feminine nature will bring to birth new discoveries, which will benefit humankind. But nature is cast in a passive role: it is the male knower, the scientist, who will court, unveil, and conquer, and the credit for the new birth will be his.

The language is not overtly forceful, though its reflection of MAWKI sexuality is clear to see. But elsewhere Bacon spoke differently. "Nor is mine a trumpet which summons and excites men to . . . quarrel and fight with one another," he avowed, "but rather to make peace between themselves, *and turning with united forces against the nature of things, to storm and occupy her castles and strong-holds, and extend the bounds of human empire,* as far as God Almighty in his goodness may permit." Here is a peaceful intention—scientific discovery replacing interhuman aggression—couched in the language of conquest and colonial expansion, which European nations had already embarked on as Bacon wrote.[13]

The patriarchal relationship, whereby the male knower has control over female nature, mingled shortly after with the conceptualization of Descartes, in which nature, previously seen as organic, became inert matter, fit only to be mastered by "mind." Robert Boyle (1664) intertwined the two metaphors, seeing the world as a "great . . . pregnant automaton, that, like a woman with twins in her womb, or a ship with pump, ordnance etc, is such an engine, as comprises or consists of several lesser engines." Physicist Brian Easlea gives many examples of the scientist, imaged as the penetrating male, acting on nature, imaged as female. A tribute to Boyle said that whenever "stubborn matter" had come under his inquisition, he had never failed to extract "a confession of all that lay in her most intimate recesses." Sir Isaac Newton's teacher, Isaac Barrow, said that the aim of science was to "search Nature out of her Concealments, and unfold her dark Mysteries." Edmond Halley wrote to Newton of the pride that the world would feel in recognizing a man "capable of penetrating so far into the abstrusest secrets of Nature." In the early nineteenth century Sir Humphrey Davy said, of the "penetrating genius of Volta," that his discovery of the means of creating a continuous electric current was a key "which promises to lay open some of the most mysterious recesses of nature."

In giving these and many other examples from the seventeenth century to the present, Easlea points out that he is writing only of an overall direction or tendency. "Within the domain of science most familiar to me, physics, there is, I know, much that is incredibly beautiful," and many "men of science" do not seek power over nature in an aggressive way. Nevertheless, compulsive masculinity predominates over humane concern in important areas of modern science.[14]

As I shall show in Chapter 3, frequent and systematic metaphors reveal their users' thinking and correlate with behavior. When metaphors of male science penetrating female nature are spread among many users, recurring over a long period of time in the excitement of successive discoveries, they reveal habits of thought and behavior characteristic of patriarchal society. Yet penetration metaphors are neither inevitable nor the only possible way of seeing things. Einstein saw physics as a quest for harmony and spoke of the "joy in looking and comprehending." Female metaphors of knowing nature are equally powerful, for the otherness of nature can be seen as the great mystery to which we open ourselves, and which we embrace and hold within. To speak systematically of the scientific enterprise in those terms would give it a different flavor and might have tangible effects on research priorities.

Reason, Emotion, "Man," and Nature

I conclude that two of the fundamental intellectual quests of our civilization, rational understanding and the exploration and understanding of nature, have been modeled from the patriarchal mold. Women have been largely absent or excluded from the endeavor to understand what it means to reason, a tradition that began in a society in which philosophical ease depended on slavery and men ruled over women. Philosophers have defined reason as the freeing of the mind or self from conditioning and circumstances, blind to the fact that their own thinking has lacked such freedom because it has depended on male dominance. In a male-dominated society, the male-female dominance relation became the basic model for understanding what it means to think, and how reason relates to the nonrational, intuitive, emotional, and physical in ourselves and the world around us. It has continued to structure our understanding of rationality, despite philosophers' best attempts to free themselves from it. What constitutes "the feminine" in human beings has not been agreed between men and women, but defined, decided, and imposed by men. The feminine has been defined, here as elsewhere, as having less value than the masculine. The problem has been seen, from a male perspective, as "how can women have powers of reasoning like ours?" (the assumption being that in a female body this must be difficult), not "how can our reasoning be worth anything when it is so detached from valid emotions and takes no account of birth, childhood, aging, and death?"

The relationships between rationality and intuition, and between human beings and nature, have long been seen according to the rule model, as dominance relationships. It is not this or that version of the model that is faulty, but the rule model itself. What is ruled may be respected or despised, listened to or ignored, shut out or allowed into your presence. But as long as it is ruled, it is heard only on the ruler's terms and regarded as of inferior worth. What the rule model lacks is respect for the integrity and validity of the "other." "Care" and "stewardship" would provide better models for the relationship between human beings and nature, whereas "partnership" and "indwelling" give better clues to the way intuition and feeling interact with reasoned analysis. For the present, these relationships (and others like them) are correctly described as "patriarchal" because they are most commonly seen in terms of dominance and subordination, and because their root model is men's subordination of women.

Dangerous and Deadly

The fifth point in my argument is that many aspects of MAWKI are problematic, and some are deadly and dangerous. Several issues could be discussed, but the problem lies in showing how this or that problem is connected with masculinity. I shall focus on themes where connections are clearly seen.

Male Sexual Violence

One issue is male violence toward women. As child abuse comes more into the open, it is clear that the majority of abusers, and almost all the sexual abusers, are men, and that most of the sexually abused are their (our) daughters and stepdaughters. It will not do to attribute this to a generalized "human nature" since it is, specifically, *male* human nature that is most heavily involved. Violence is, to say the least, not discouraged by the MAWKI theme of male sexuality as pursuit, and rape is still often seen as an extension of normal masculine sexual behavior, rather than the opposite of what a "true man" would do. Not long ago a British soldier convicted of rape heard the judge say, in spite of evidence that the accused had broken the woman's ribs and caused bruises and internal injuries, that "clearly this was a man who on the night in question, allowed his enthusiasm for sex to overcome his normal good behavior."[15] Here is a classic example of violence being seen as a built-in and acceptable part of male sexuality.

Few men commit rape, but all benefit from the violence of those who do, since it instills in women the need for male protection, thus helping to keep them in a subordinate place. Few of us men commit rape, but many go in for sexual harassment of women, meaning by this a range of male behavior including suggestive looks, frequent sexual remarks or jokes, unwanted cheek kissing, pestering for dates despite refusals, unwanted touching, pinching, and grabbing, direct proposition, and even forcible aggression. I suspect that, if men spoke openly to one another, few of us could say we had never behaved in this way. Sexual harassment in the workplace seems widespread. In recent United Kingdom surveys, the percentage of women workers experiencing it ranged from 51 percent to 79 percent. It was most frequent in industries that traditionally employed women and was experienced both from male authority figures and from co-workers: one survey found that sexual harassment was twice as frequent, persistent, and likely from male co-workers than from their managers. Sexual harassment is not sexy, being almost invariably a turnoff for women.[16]

The fact that harassment is experienced from male co-workers as well as managers suggests it does not arise exclusively from male-dominated hierarchical work structures, but from the overall relationships of women and men in society. If "violence" is defined as *violation of human personhood by coercive power exercised in a relationship of domination*, male sexual harassment merits that title. It is not rape, but may leave the recipient wondering what will happen if she protests. In this sense, as long as some men are physically violent toward women, the rest of us do benefit, since we can bluff our way through the old paths of predominance. For can she really be sure that jokes will not turn to abuse, abuse to physical harassment, and harassment, eventually, to physical violence if she maintains her objection?

This aspect of masculinity is problematic in two ways. The first is its degrading effects on women. In the simplest of theological terms, it represents a failure of love between neighbors, in this case between neighbors of different gender. The second, related problem is that this failure of love is deeply rooted in the fundamental definitions of male sexuality in patriarchal culture. As long as the masculine is defined as superior to the feminine, combined with a flight from the feminine, the alternative behaviors will be reverse sides of the same coin: the coin is male dominance, with rape on one side and protection on the other. We need a new, humane paradigm of manhood in which the "true man" neither conquers nor protects, but simply behaves as a good neighbor to women, children, and other men.

The Masculine Marketplace

Since we live in a patriarchal society, it comes as no surprise to find its values influencing economic and political thought and behavior. The vocabulary of the current phase of industrial capitalism has a MAWKI tinge, as in the emphasis on hardness and toughness, and on the "realism" whereby nurture and caring are secondary to the quickest possible profit. Today's achievers are "aggressive, restless, greedy, urban technocrats . . . interested in money to the point of obsession," writes the head of a head-hunting agency specializing in business talent. "Let them make a million and they'll strive for ten. That's the way they are and that's the way we want them."[17]

Raymond Williams looks at the economic model where toughness is unquestioningly accepted as a virtue. He argues that since the 1930s the conventional model for the market economy has divided it into three sectors. The "primary sector" comprises agriculture and the mining of raw materials, the "secondary sector" covers the manufacture of goods, and the "tertiary sector" covers everything else, including "services." Since the Industrial Revolution, the "primary sector" has declined dramatically as a source of paid employment. Now manufacturing (the "secondary sector") is going through a similar decline in Western market economies.

The so-called "tertiary sector" is a ragbag—more a lumber room than a clearly defined category. It includes paid work as diverse as construction, transport, white-collar professions, and entertainment. Some of these so-called "services" are the indispensable infrastructure of manufacturing (hence hardly "tertiary" to it). Others include the agencies of public order and the more obvious meaning of "services" as the servicing of individuals.

The three-sector model is an inadequate way of describing the most important features of our economy. It is a model not for the whole economy, but for the three stages of production for the market—namely, the gaining of raw materials, their manufacture into goods, and the distribution of those goods by sale for consumption.

This model excludes work devoted to the care and nurture of human beings (on which the system itself depends for its continuation) unless that work is paid employment. Moreover, the paid caring that is included is relegated to the "tertiary" sector, which is supposed to depend on what is produced by the first two sectors. This is by no means a play on words, since this relegation prompts governments following the model to cut public expenditure on health care and education. Yet the care, nurture, and education of human beings is mutually interdependent with the process that extracts raw materials and turns them into goods, since neither can continue without the other.[18]

The three-sector model originates in the philosophical exclusion of caring, nurturing, and domestic labor noted earlier in this chapter. These essential activities were left out of consideration when our political and economic theories were first developed, because they were associated (by the men who first formulated the theories) with the "femininity" and femaleness that their lordly reasoning downgraded and despised.

The global effects of patriarchal economics are deadly and dangerous.[19] Only by an inconceivable expansion in world trade, stemming from an increase in production surpassing both the probable limits of natural resources and the environment's capacity to absorb the resultant waste products, could the present type of market economy give the middle class in Third World countries the living standards now enjoyed by the middle classes in Western Europe and the United States. Such an expansion would not benefit the majority of the world's people, who live in dire poverty, since the best evidence shows that expansion along these lines does not "trickle down" to them. In the prophetic words of E. F. Schumacher nearly two decades ago, "This industrial way of life cannot spread to all humankind, and cannot last."

If the world economy is to become sane, humane, and ecologically sustainable, the fundamental issue it needs to address is the care-and-nurture question: "What should a society produce and trade in order to meet the basic needs of all its people?" In Western economies, this is overridden by a different question, namely, "What can be produced and sold for the highest financial return in the global market?"—a question stemming in part from male-centered economic models excluding the essential activities of reproduction, caring, and nurturing. When Alan Sugar, the head of a successful electronics company, says that "if there was a market in mass-produced portable nuclear weapons, we'd market them,"[20] he shows both the dominance of that question and its absurdity.

Dangerous Toughness

Mr. Tough walks tall in the world economy, but goes in and out of favor politically. Before World War I, manliness became closely associated with being tough and bearing pain without flinching. When war came, what we now recognize as breakdown under stress was seen through patriarchal spectacles. Since "real men" didn't break down, it followed that their behavior was a moral vice, cowardice. The definition was deadly, since many "cowards" were killed by firing squad. Yet the war also generated a revulsion against macho toughness, with profound aftereffects. The phrase "going over the top" (derived from mass assaults by infantry leaping out of trenches) changed its meaning from "going heroically into action" to "going bonkers, acting in an exaggerated and unrestrained manner."[21]

More recently, the Vietnam War led many Americans to question the equation of masculinity with toughness. Nearly 3 million Americans, mostly men, served in Vietnam, and tens of millions watched the war on TV. "Here was the enemy against whom American men had measured their masculinity for twenty years of cold war," observes Barbara Ehrenreich, "and the enemy turned

out to be women, the thinnest of youths, old men and children."
One Vietnam veteran wanted her to understand how tough the war
was. It was so tough, he said, that his best buddy had to kill an
eight-year-old boy, otherwise the boy, who had a grenade, would
have killed them. His best buddy now had a good job, two kids of
his own—and screaming nightmares.[22] Another veteran tells of
equally painful experiences and recalls how he came home from
the war to a radical university campus where his fellow students
called veterans "baby killers."[23]

Yet the cult of toughness is not dead. When Marc Feigen Fasteau says that "for our Presidents and policymakers, being tough,
or at least looking tough, has been a primary goal in and of
itself,"[24] he is speaking of the 1960s rather than the 1980s. Yet his
study of presidential policy on Vietnam is a reminder of what
MAWKI values can do, and may do again.

Fasteau's premise is that toughness may sometimes be a virtue in U.S. foreign policy, if it serves the national interest and
derives from careful analysis. Whatever we may think of this, it
absolves him from the charge of being "weak" or unpatriotic. He
shows that successive administrations took it for granted that the
United States had to act tough, go on acting tough, and stay in
Vietnam once it had got in. There was scant discussion of what
the national interest was and how it might be harmed by withdrawal. The best-known justification was that if South Vietnam
went Communist, the other Southeast Asian states would also top-
ple, like a row of dominoes. Yet the domino theory amounted to
no more than a paragraph in a document and was contradicted by
the careful assessments of Secretary of State George Ball and of
the CIA.

Fasteau thus concludes that the domino theory was a rational-
ization supporting a policy chosen for other reasons, in particular a
male preoccupation with toughness, and documents this exten-
sively from the presidencies of Kennedy, Johnson, and Nixon. A
friendly biographer commented on J. F. Kennedy's "keyed-up, almost compulsive competitiveness." As attorney-general, his
brother Robert eventually developed the capacity to see events in
human terms, ask what was happening to the Vietnamese people,
and suggest it was time to consider withdrawal. Earlier, however,
toughness was an unquestioned virtue. Of any new appointee or

adviser, his first question was, "Is he tough? Is he tough?" If the answer was yes, he moved to the next question. If the answer was no, the person concerned lost all credibility.

Lyndon Johnson had an even more explicit concern for toughness. According to David Halberstam, "He had always been haunted by the idea that he would be judged as being insufficiently manly for the job, that he would lack courage at the crucial moment. More than a little insecure himself, he wanted very much to be seen as a man; it was a conscious thing." Bill Moyers, one of his closest aides, recalled Johnson saying to him, after a National Security Council meeting, that he feared being thought of as "less than a man" if he withdrew American forces from Vietnam. Johnson's often coarse language reveals a "traditional" view of masculinity. Of his wife, Lady Bird Johnson, he once said (when she had expressed doubts about another matter) that it was like a woman to be uncertain. Doubt was a feminine quality, and so by definition inferior. On hearing that one of his advisers was becoming more of a dove than a hawk over Vietnam, Johnson dismissed his views with the words "Hell, he has to squat to piss." Peaceableness was a feminine posture, despised or even feared. The morning after the first American bombing raid on North Vietnam, Johnson exulted to a reporter: "I didn't just screw Ho Chi Minh, I cut his pecker off." Here is imagery of rape and castration: the opponent is seen either as female or as a weak man defeated by a truly masculine man.

There is a tragic element in Johnson's story. He cared about civil rights in America and about the Great Society, for which he wanted to be remembered. He fought the war, in part, to protect his political credibility and get his domestic programs accepted. Yet in the end "it was the war that destroyed his credibility and brought the Great Society to a dead halt."[25]

President Nixon showed similar preoccupations. In a book titled *Six Crises*, he said that the most difficult part of any crisis "is the period of indecision—whether to fight or to run away." A moment's thought shows other choices: one could *walk away* or *talk away*. But Nixon sees the choice in terms that leave him no choice, because no president of the United States would want to be seen as "running away." "The *substance* of the issue, what is actually at stake . . . has dropped from sight. The emphasis is not on the problem at hand, not on trying to determine what objective is worth pursuing at what cost, but on *himself*—on his courage or lack thereof."[26]

Toughness and coolness, the twin themes of masculine control, coincided in another important figure from the Vietnam years, Robert McNamara, then secretary of defense. His friends knew him as a warm man of deep and humane feeling. But to his colleagues he was cold and machinelike, ruling out all emotion as antithetical to the task at hand.

McNamara was not alone in his attitudes—Secretary of State Dean Rusk cabled his ambassadors to stop using the word *feel* in their dispatches. But whereas Rusk was a cold war warrior, McNamara's role was more tragic. He had, says Fasteau, "a great drive, an incredibly organized intelligence, and a strong commitment to public service." He had humane impulses and a strong ethical framework. "But this side of his personality was compartmentalized, walled off from his professional life. In this tension he exemplified the *best* in American public men and, in the end, the war tore him apart. He could not bring the humane side of himself to bear in thinking about the war. Instead, the cult of toughness went unchallenged."[27] I find this portrait sad, moving, and parabolic. It illustrates the personal cost, and social dangers, of MAWKI, where reason tries to rule a man's "finer feelings" and, in ruling them, ignores them.

Babytalk and the Bomb

I have already noted the frequency with which scientific discovery has been seen as the male unveiling and penetration of female nature, and pointed to the ease with which male-dominated society turns gallantry into conquest and inquiry into attack. Another implication of these metaphors is that knowledge is brought to birth from the relationship between the male knower and female nature, where nature is cast in a passive role in relation to the knower, and the credit for the birth is his.

These themes run like a thread through the development of the atomic and hydrogen bombs. Brian Easlea shows that the pioneer physicists were well aware that their work could have awesome consequences.[28] He quotes imagery of attack, and penetration of nature, from several sources in the years of research between 1898 and 1938. In 1898 Sir William Crookes told the British Association that modern scientists "steadily, unflinchingly . . . strive to pierce the inmost heart of Nature. . . . Veil after veil we have lifted, and her face grows more beautiful, august, and wonderful, with every barrier that is withdrawn."[29]

Such gallantry was easily transmuted into more forceful language. Ernest Rutherford was a great experimental physicist, honored after his death with the title "father of atomic physics." His lifelong attitude toward nature is epitomized by the word *attack* which was frequently on his lips. Though nature as female is only a fleeting image in his writings, colleagues and admirers use such imagery. The discovery of radioactivity meant that scientists "had penetrated one of Nature's innermost secrets," said Frederick Soddy. In 1950, writing of Rutherford's achievement, A. S. Russell said that if he had abandoned physics, the loss would have been irremediable. "The more fundamental the science," said Russell, "the greater is the need of the big advances which only great men can make." Where the great man does not do his work, "the darkness remains permanently unpierced."

Rutherford had the gift of generating enthusiasm among his (male) colleagues, such that "their uninhibited praise of him is very moving."[30] Niels Bohr is also said to have generated among visitors and colleagues "a spirit of attack, a spirit of freedom from conventional bonds and a spirit of joy that can hardly be described." The same speaker, Nobel laureate Victor Weisskopf, said that "the international community of men around Bohr was held together at that time by his personality and by a common urge to penetrate into the secrets of nature."[31] Crucial discoveries could be spoken of as a "birth," as when Rutherford's student C. G. Darwin counted it one of the great occurrences of his life that he was "actually present half-an-hour after the nucleus was born."

The oddity of speaking of something discovered as if it was new life emerging from the womb is explained when we realize that such metaphors belong to the Baconian system, whereby the masculine mind (usually in a male body) penetrates female nature, which then, as it were, incubates the scientist's seed and gives birth to new knowledge, over which the knower has paternity rights. In this metaphor system, Rutherford's discovery meant that he was the "father of atomic theory." When this was widened (by Sir Oliver Lodge) to include "fatherhood" of atomic chemistry and physics, his colleague Frederick Soddy felt slighted and complained bitterly to his biographer—the implication being that Soddy should have shared the paternal credit.[32]

The longing to understand the nature of things and improve the human condition is a universal human attribute. What distorts it is its connection with the MAWKI drive for control, where it is supremely important to win, gain mastery, and prove one's manhood. It would be unwise for me to scoff at this, since it is part of my own formation as a male—as, for example, in the drive to finish this book and see it in print. Nonetheless, it is problematic. Discovery modeled as exploration is a joyful adventure. Discovery as a quest for control has a compulsive element: the urge can never be satisfied, since control is never complete. This combination has made scientific exploration a quest that knows no limits and that can therefore, in principle, be pursued regardless of consequences. Just as Alan Sugar would mass-produce portable nukes if there was a market for them, so it has been axiomatic for Western science that what can be done should be done, come what may.

So it was that Robert Oppenheimer, who led the Manhattan Project which developed the Hiroshima and Nagasaki atomic bombs, resolved his doubts about working on the hydrogen bomb when it became clear that the bomb could indeed be made. In 1949 the program was "a tortured thing that . . . did not make a great deal of technical sense." By 1951 it was "technically so sweet that you could not argue about that. It was purely the military, the political and the humane problem of what you were going to do about it once you had it." (Note the word *purely*—the consequences, including the "humane" consequences, take second place.) "It is my judgement in these things," he said, "that when you see something that is technically sweet you go ahead and do it and you argue about what to do about it only after you have had your technical success."[33] Yet previously, in the aftermath of Hiroshima, he had told President Truman that he, Oppenheimer, had blood on his hands and had later written that "the physicists had known sin and that this is a knowledge which they cannot lose."[34]

The compulsive element in the atomic quest emerges clearly in the Los Alamos story. Many scientists joined the Manhattan

Project and went to Los Alamos out of a well-founded, rational fear that Hitler might get the bomb first and use it. When the war in Europe was over, the rational response would have been to halt the project, or at least slow it down. Yet, if anything, the scientists' efforts intensified after Germany surrendered. This had nothing to do with what politicians were calculating about the Soviet Union and Japan. The compulsion came from within. "What I did immorally," physicist Richard Feynmann later remarked, "was not to remember the reason why I was doing it. So when the reason changed, which was that Germany was defeated, not a single thought came into my mind that it meant I should reconsider why I was continuing to do this. I simply didn't think." Fellow physicist Bernard Feld said, "There was a mesmeric quality about the bomb." He rejoiced to see the end of the war in Europe, as did others. But "nobody stopped and said, 'We are not at war with the Germans any longer—do we have to stop and think?' We were caught up in this activity, which was all-consuming. Nobody worked less than 15, 16, 17 hours a day. There was nothing else in your life but this passion to get it done. We went through to the desert and exploded it—and [were] ecstatic that it had worked."[35]

Such compulsiveness was not confined to American scientists. Soviet physicist Andrei Sakharov writes how he had no doubts about the importance of creating a Soviet H-bomb, for his country and for the balance of power throughout the world, and that, "carried away by the immensity of the task," he worked strenuously at it.[36] At Los Alamos, the urge to succeed was not unmixed with anxiety. One commentator noted a welling up of individual anxieties about the project, which might have added up to a significant protest if someone had organized them. But nobody did.[37]

On the lips of many atomic scientists were "babytalk" metaphors, whereby the bomb's explosion represents a marvelous new birth, discoverers are fathers, and the baby is a male child. They fit into the patriarchal metaphor system going back to Bacon's time. In 1942, for example, the Chicago physicists were congratulated on a new discovery by a colleague whose telegram read: "Congratulations to the parents. Can hardly wait to see the new arrival." In 1949 N. P. Davis wrote of work on the H-bomb: "The thing that waited to be born still had long to wait. It demanded a new idea." The idea came from Stanislaw Ulam and Edward Teller, but controversy raged over who deserved the credit. A critic said scornfully that Ulam had the idea and inseminated Teller with it, so that Teller should not be called the father of the hydrogen bomb but its mother. Another critic, Hans Bethe, recalls having said that "Ulam was the father of the hydrogen bomb and Edward was the mother, because he carried the baby for quite a while." The implication is that, like female nature, the "mother" of an idea has a subordinate, inferior role.

Teller himself was motivated by more than a concern for U.S. national security. He was, he said, fascinated by "the adventure of attempting to do what at one time seemed impossible." He spoke frequently of the work as a magnificent undertaking, and of the intense fascination of this terrible and unprecedented project. He understood himself to be part of the scientific tradition, going back to Bacon's clarion call three hundred years earlier. His ultimate justification for pushing against the limits of life on earth and unleashing such destructive power was that *"we would be unfaithful to the tradition of Western civilization if we were to shy away from exploring the limits of human achievement."*[38]

Issues for Christian Theology

The assumption of superiority over the feminine is central to the meaning of masculinity, as is the flight from the feminine. We men can barely begin to guess what this does to women. Once it is brought to light, the ideology and social structure of our civilization, built over thousands of years, is called into question. This is frightening to women, as well as to men, says Rosemary Ruether, since it rocks every boat.[39]

I suggested earlier that patriarchy is either a gift of God, so that male dominance is to be accepted and rejoiced in, or one of the oldest, deepest, and most pervasive sins we know. Our understanding and experience of God decide which interpretation we adopt, and I unhesitatingly choose the latter. My reasons for doing so are part of the fabric of this whole book, so I shall briefly sketch what seems most important, to provide a vantage point for this discussion. The living God, known to Moses as "I am what I will be—I will be what I am,"[40] is beyond gender and creates humankind as male-and-female, collectively in the divine image and likeness (Gen. 1:27). There is only one God, and God is One, but God is not a single, isolated "being," but Trinity (see Chapter 8, below)—an unbreakable Oneness by the communion of three centers of personhood, so beautifully distinct that their distinctiveness is revealed in Christian history, and so beautifully one that if we encounter one center of personhood, the others are immediately present.

Trinity is distinct from the whole created universe yet effortlessly encloses it, utterly transcending it yet permeating every part of it, the godhead wherein we live, move, and have our being. Trinity is exuberant, dynamic, gentle, insistent, suffering, rejoicing love, exchanging and giving out what we know as truth, justice, and freedom. Each of the three centers of personhood, and their unity, can be spoken of, truthfully yet always inadequately, in concepts and images. The traditional names we all know: Father, Son, Holy Spirit—though it is more correct to speak of the second of these as the eternal Word who becomes Flesh (a fully human being) in Jesus of Nazareth, not merge Jesus into God. There is rationality in the dynamic Trinity, but also what we know as passion, unpredictability, the untameable wildness of Holy Spirit. And through the incarnation there is experience, from the inside, of human life, the joys of the body, growth, love in relationships, mortality, loneliness, separation, and pain.

Trinity creates humankind as female and male. We are created in that otherness and togetherness so that this fundamental relationship can mirror the divine life. There are many ways in which we know human beings as "Other": each person is "Other," however like us they may be. There are also many webs of relationship where, through teamwork, cooperation, and organizing things together, human beings can glimpse, for a moment, the elusive marvel of the Trinity dance of love-in-relationship and, perhaps, weave new patterns on the divine loom or paint new pictures on the canvas of history. Yet the otherness of gender has a particular quality about it. It is the means by which new human life comes into the world and is nurtured. It gives us a certain irreducible difference and otherness, so that "manhood" and "womanhood" can never be independent of each other, or the norm of what it is to be human. In the mirror of gender-otherness, we can know our own limitations, be assured of our own loveliness, and enjoy and appreciate everything that makes another human being different from our own self. The otherness of gender also gives us the opportunity to name and perceive certain qualities as appropriate to each other, and to give, receive, and exchange them between us, just as in Trinity the qualities we meet in each center of personhood are eternally exchanged, given, and received in the great dance of the divine life.[41]

Human beings, and human social, political, and economic structures, do not live in harmony with the godhead, but in disharmony, distrust, separation, sin. Sin distorts, permeates, is woven into who we are and what we do. There is no castle of immunity from sin, in Bible, church, charismatic renewal, feminist strivings, or male identity. Yet the living God who is Trinity always gives birth to new possibilities and new hope. In Jesus, one of us yet one with God, the dynamic Trinity opens up these possibilities in the most complete and creative way, by announcing and embodying God's "kingdom," and by going through crucifixion and resurrection. These two poles of faith—radical hope for newness and radical awareness of sin—have equal weight, though we almost inevitably swing to and fro between them.

Measured against this summary, itself inadequate and incomplete, masculinity as we know it is deeply flawed. As a sex, men stand convicted of a longstanding systemic and personal failure of love toward our female neighbors, which arises not only from individual acts but from our very identity as men, formed in us from birth. Though many of us want to relate to women as equal human beings, most of us fail, so deep-rooted is the drive to be in control of the interaction. We walk well-worn paths of predominance, maintained by the way our most aggressive fellow males behave, and by the ways in which our thinkers have thought, our discoverers have discovered, and our political and economic structures have been built.[42]

The preceding sentence points to something more deepseated than our personal failure as men. If the divine project involves creating us in coequal genders, as the basis for our mirroring of the divine life, it follows that for one gender to dominate the other is one of the most fundamental distortions imaginable. As it developed in our history and prehistory, it served as a model for many other kinds of domination and over-under relationships. It permeates our civilization, from its deepest foundations to its highest spires. It has defined reasoning as associated with one gender, over against the other. It has helped to shape an unstable, deeply unjust world economic order in which labor associated with female gender is excluded from consideration or relegated to the lowest-priority sectors. It perverts the human longing to discover and turns it into the masculine drive for control, which presses against the limits of our planetary home, and in which control itself is an overruling value, an end in itself. And finally, it distorts our vision of God by seeing the divine life exclusively through male eyes and depicting God in the image of male dominance. This implies that the other half of humanity, created co-equally in God's image and likeness, is not fit to depict that divine life.

Issues for Further Exploration

The end of the last paragraph introduces an assumption that needs explanation and defense. If our language about God is harmless, and has no effect on our thinking and behavior, then the fact that all our names and images of God are male is unimportant, however convincing the arguments about patriarchy. On the other hand, if language powerfully shapes our thinking and behavior, then the maleness of God-language, where God is traditionally "He," "King," "Shepherd," "Lord," and "Father," becomes a crucial issue. In Part II I shall look at the relationship between language, thought, and behavior and show how systematic ways of speaking affect what we think and do. I shall then explore how God-language works, and some important aspects of God-language in the Bible, before asking how we might name and praise God in counterpatriarchal ways more faithful to the Christian gospel.

Gallery: Portrait of a Patriarchal God

How would a patriarchal society see God? If we were outside observers looking at the patriarchal society described above, what sort of god would we expect it to worship, and how would a patriarchal god-image compare with the living God revealed in Christian faith?

Going on the evidence of the preceding chapters, my hypothesis would be as follows. The god of patriarchy would be seen as the one who is in control of everything. Though this god might allow a lot of freedom, he would be very much in command—of the universe, daily events, and human destiny. Chance and randomness might be part of new physics and daily experience, but they would not figure in patriarchal worship, whose god would continue to have the whole world in his hands.

A patriarchal god would be the overseer of all over-under relationships and would sit on the top of the topmost pyramid. He would be imaged as the boss, or director, or as a king with complete authority and power. He would be the ultimate *mon-arch*, meaning one who rules alone. If patriarchy had been infected by Christianity, it would have a well worked out doctrine of God as Trinity, but would keep it safely under control. In worship, God would almost always be imaged and adored as the mon-arch, and the Trinity would be more abstract theory than lived experience. As the ultimate mon-arch, a patriarchal god would relate to his creatures by command and decree, expecting a response of submission and obedience, giving protection in exchange for obedience, and either punishment or mercy when obedience was denied. It would be difficult for patriarchal society to envisage any other kind of relationship.

A patriarchal god would have strong overtones of *toughness*. He would be the ultimate Mr. Tough and probably would be regarded as Almighty, the omnipotent one. He would be pictured as strong, active, and triumphant. His relationship to obstacles would be one of conquest. He would see and know everything, but from the outside, with his eyes rather than in his bones. The one who has total control can't allow himself to be affected by that which he controls, or get too close to it. So the god of patriarchy would be very transcendent, very other. His otherness would be, not the otherness of a mysterious closeness, ungraspable by us though embracing all things, but the otherness of distance, authority, and untouchability.

So the god of patriarchy would be one who has total emotional control of himself, the ultimate *Mr. Cool*. He would be invulnerable, unaffected by his creation and its life forms, impassive as well as impassible.* Yet because he would be a god made in the image of patriarchal maleness, tenderness would struggle with toughness in his being, and this would find expression in patriarchal theology. He would either be alternately tough and tender, or else show tenderness and be vulnerable to pain only with part of himself, or as a temporary measure. Because he was in complete control of everything, a patriarchal god would be most comfortably pictured as pure thought, in control of emotion and intuition rather than in harmony with them. If he had a "wild side" of unpredictability, it would sit uneasily with the controlling notion of god as one who reasons, thinks, plans, and purposes. A Christian understanding of the Trinity, in which the three centers of divine personhood continually exchange their energies and characteristics in dynamic oneness, would be accepted only in theory: in practice it would be difficult to accept the "wild" element (Holy Spirit) as fully divine, or shared by the other two centers of personhood. Patriarchal divides between spirit and matter would also make the idea of God becoming fully present in a human being (incarnation) difficult to accommodate: flesh would be suspect, even if the Word becomes it.

Above all, a patriarchal god would be *male and masculine*. Even if patriarchal thinkers realized that "he" must be the originator of gender, their god would always be depicted, imaged, and spoken to in male terms. Whatever theologians might say, religious

---

*Impassible: incapable of suffering injury, not subject to suffering; an attribute of God in traditional theology.

practice would see the male and masculine as the norm of human-ness, and the female and feminine as a deviation from it. Femi-nine qualities would be seen as inferior, and their intrusion into the realm of the sacred would be resisted tooth and nail, whether the intrusion was embodied (that is, women exercising religious leadership) or symbolic (speaking of God in female metaphors). To speak of the divine in female terms, or admit women to reli-gious power on equal terms with men, would entail a revolutionary revaluation of the "feminine" and "masculine," undermine every patriarchal over-under relationship, and expose what claimed to be normative and unquestionable as, in fact, an ideology justifying male dominance. It would turn the patriarchal world upside down. I shall take another look at the above portrait later (Chapter 5). Meanwhile, I invite readers to compare it with the way God is depicted in worship and with the themes and presuppositions of dogmatic and systematic theologies.

Part II
Language Matters

Naming God truthfully is important, since to name God untruthfully is to delude ourselves and worship an idol. Naming God truthfully is especially important if language shapes and angles thinking and behavior, since untruthful God-language will then hinder our encounter with God and our knowledge of God.

People make assumptions about the importance of language, one way or the other. Critics of sexist language (words like *men* and *man* purporting to mean "people" and "the human species") say it shapes our thinking by making women linguistically invisible.[1] Their opponents say such usage is unimportant, assuming that its male form has little or no effect on thought and behavior. Similarly, the fact that almost all our naming and depicting of God is in male terms (*he, king, father*) is either irrelevant or crucially significant, depending on our assumptions about language. Part II of this book is about language, because I have seen few attempts to examine the assumptions above, and none in sufficient detail and depth.

In Chapter 3 I ask how far language affects the way we think and behave, explore the part language plays in communication, and consider the power of language. In Chapter 4 I ask what we are doing with language when we name or depict God. I have suggested that we do so by borrowing from human experience, and it is important to establish this and show how it works. Some argue that God-language works differently from other kinds of language, so it will be important to listen and respond.

3

Language, Thought, and Action[1]

"The problem was to give birth to a boy and not to a girl." The speaker was physicist Robert Jungk, and the problem was how to bring subcritical masses of Uranium 235 into contact so as to generate an atomic explosion instead of a radioactive fizzle.

As already noted, similar metaphors were on the lips of physicists, military men, and journalists during the development of the atomic bomb (1942–45) and hydrogen bomb (1948–52). The Hiroshima bomb was code-named "Little Boy," the Nagasaki bomb "Fat Boy" (later "Fat Man"). At the Potsdam conference in July 1945, U.S. Secretary of State for War Henry Stimson told Winston Churchill of the success of the first A-bomb test by passing him a note with the words "Babies satisfactorily born." Reporter William Laurence described that explosion as "the first cry of a new-born world . . . the birth of a new force." Edward Teller was hailed as the "father" of the H-bomb and announced the success of its first test with the words "It's a boy!"[2]

A critic might see it as offensive to greet the accomplishment of ultimate destructiveness with the joy that attends a child's first intake of breath, to equate success with the birth of a boy and failure with the birth of a girl, and to label as a "birth" the weapons that could end all birthing.

The scientists could reply to such criticism by saying, "I didn't mean that." This implies that the language chosen was not an expression of the speaker's real thoughts; it usually leads into, "What I meant was . . ." Another possible reply is, "I didn't know what I was saying—I now see that this kind of language was

63

wrong or inappropriate." This implies that the speaker did not originally feel that such language was problematic, but has since had second thoughts. Though Edward Teller used such language at the time, he seems to have become less happy about being labeled "the father of the H-bomb," saying that you don't talk that way about making bombs.[3] A third possible response is, "I meant it and still do." In other words, the language chosen did and does express the speaker's thoughts. Finally, the scientists could reply that their babytalk metaphors were "just a figure of speech" or "only a matter of words," meaning that the language bears no relation to their thinking or reveals nothing important about it.

These four replies are often made to criticisms of language use. If I am criticized for using sexist or racist talk, or for speaking of God in mainly male language and imagery, I can reply, as different Christians do, that "I mean what I say," "I didn't mean that," "I didn't realize what I was saying," or "It's only a metaphor."

Language and Thought

To ask whether these responses are plausible means looking at the relationship between what goes on "inside our heads" (thought), its verbal and written expression (language), and our behavior (action). I shall begin with the relation between language and thought. By language I mean the systems of signs and structures through which human beings communicate in speech or writing.

By thought I mean feelings, reasoning, and imagining that we may or may not choose to share with others. Though we can't directly observe how people think, I shall assume that most readers are aware of doing some of their thinking in a fairly articulate way, by, for example, doing mental arithmetic or using "words inside their heads." Some of our "thinking" is, I suspect, inarticulate, inner events that people sometimes describe as "thought-shapes," scraps of words, fleeting pictures, or feelings and intuitions whose relationship to language is not obvious.[4]

Besides relying on such subjective accounts, we can sometimes tell from a person's behavior what they are thinking. "Freudian slips" are usually taken as an accurate indication of what we are really thinking, precisely because we hastily substitute something else. Silence or apparently irrelevant comment can reveal an unspoken opinion. If you are having breakfast with someone who says, "B. should be shot," you may give your opinion on the matter or remain silent. If it's clear that you heard what was said, your silence will be taken as communicating—at the very least—that you have thoughts you don't want to express, whereas your face and gestures may reveal that you don't agree, but don't want to go on record. If you have heard what was said but reply, "Pass the sugar," your words and tone of voice will be taken as conveying that you want to change the subject and don't want your inner thoughts on the matter to be openly known. The other person will find it difficult to take issue with you, since your request makes sense in the context of breakfast, but will know that something more than "Pass the sugar" has been communicated.[5]

Such evidence from behavior, coupled with subjective accounts, suggests that we can to some extent stand back from the language we use and decide whether or not to communicate to others "what we really think." Sometimes language seems deliberately designed to hide what its sender is thinking and hinder clear thinking in the receiver. George Orwell's 1945 essay "Politics and the English Language" has lost none of its relevance. When defenseless villages are bombed from the air, their inhabitants driven out into the countryside, cattle machine-gunned and huts set on fire, he writes, "this is called *pacification*." Robbing peasants of their land and making them refugees is called "transfer of populations." Imprisoning people endlessly without trial, shooting them, or sending them to die in Arctic lumber camps is called the "elimination of undesirable elements."

Today's nukespeak is similarly befogged. Even an unemotive sentence such as "The United States could survive a nuclear attack" (from a Pentagon document) hinders clear thinking. It is unclear what "the United States" *is* and how it might "survive." Is the writer thinking of the people, plants, and animals in the continental United States; the economic infrastructure and the framework of law and government; or an elite with lead-shielded flags and computers?

Unclear language can signify unclear thought without intent to deceive. A scrupulous writer, says George Orwell, will ask: what am I trying to say? What words will express it? What image or idiom makes it clearer? A less scrupulous writer will shirk such effort by throwing the mind open "and letting the ready-made phrases come crowding in. They will construct your meaning for you, to a certain extent—and at need they will perform the important service of partially concealing your meaning even from yourself." Among such ready-made phrases he includes "a not unjustifiable assumption," "leaves much to be desired," and "a consideration which we could do well to bear in mind," each one of which "anaesthetizes a portion of the brain."[6]

It seems that though we can stand back from language, we don't stand six feet above it, with clear thoughts waiting to be dropped into the right words. The process of choosing between different words, metaphors, and turns of phrase is what enables us to clarify what we "really think." Clear thinking (whether in description, theorizing, worship, or theology) needs ordered symbolic forms if it is to be held in memory and communicated.[7]

Orwell's picture of ready-made phrases crowding into the mind and constructing our meaning for us raises another issue: do particular language systems limit what it is possible for their speakers to think? From their study of native American languages and cultures, Edward Sapir and Benjamin Lee Whorf note that some cultural differences seem paralleled by differences in language structure. For example, the Hopi have a different sense of time from European-Americans, and their language does not have tenses to mark past, present, and future. Sapir and Whorf argue that the absence of tenses *causes* the different sense of time. "Human beings are very much at the mercy of the particular language which has become the medium of expression for their society," says Sapir. "The 'real world' is to a large extent built up on the language habits of the group." We see, hear, and experience in certain ways "because the language habits of our community predispose certain choices of interpretation."[8]

Sapir thinks that change in unconscious language habits is possible. By contrast, some of his followers argue that language systems make it impossible to think in certain ways. In *Feminism and Linguistic Theory* Deborah Cameron convincingly refutes such determinism. I shall follow her argument and add to it. She looks at evidence brought forward by Sapir and Whorf. As regards the Hopi, lack of a tense system does not by itself prove a different concept of time, since other ways of marking past, present, and future may be available, as they are in biblical Hebrew.[9] Yet even if other linguistic evidence from Hopi is available, the question remains: is there a causal relation between the Hopi language and their understanding of time, and if so, what is it? Do the Hopi have no European time sense because their language prevents it or because their society does not need it? If their language makes it impossible for them to understand European time concepts, how can their understanding ever change? Complete determinism entails a catch-22 about translation. On the Sapir-Whorf hypothesis, a Hopi speaker is not able to use Danish, German, French, and English tenses correctly until she understands our concepts of time. Yet she cannot understand our time concepts until she has grasped our tense systems.[10]

It makes more sense to assume that Hopi and other indigenous cultures have a different time sense because it suits their needs, not because of some blockage in their language system. Not needing a "European" time sense, their languages may have developed in ways that made it difficult to express the alien idea of moving through time in exactly measured units, from "past" to "future." But languages are flexible, and their speakers adapt them to new situations, by changing syntax, altering word meanings, borrowing words from other languages, and so on. The Inuit, for example, are said to have thirty different words for *snow*. Such fine gradations of vocabulary are needed in the Arctic, and the most convincing explanation is that they were, over a period of time, invented. "It would surely be very remarkable," Cameron observes, "if instead of having a lot of words for snow, they had a selection of terms for horsehide."[11] If their climate changed or their way of life was altered by white settlement, their language would be adapted accordingly.

To take Cameron's example further, we can ask what would happen if a community of English-speaking city dwellers suddenly had to live in Arctic conditions. Many would die, but the survivors would not for long be hampered by the existence of only one noun, *snow*. Experience would teach them about the different types of snow they needed to recognize, and with recognition would come developments of verbs, adjectives, and adjective-noun combinations (*sharded, blizzard dust, going layered, fools bridge*) to name what was being recognized.

It is unlikely, then, that the structure of a language *predetermines* what its speakers are able to perceive, think about, or communicate, or that it *prevents* them from perceiving, thinking about, and communicating important ideas and beliefs. Yet it is difficult to fault Orwell's argument that uncritical acceptance of existing phrases can shape thinking and hinder new thought.

Metaphors We Live By

Many such ready-made phrases are metaphors. George Lakoff and Mark Johnson discuss some of the metaphors in ordinary English speech. When two English speakers argue,[12] they usually describe what is happening in metaphors drawn from war and battle. They *attack* their opponent's *weak points* and *indefensible claims* and condemn them if they *retreat* or *shift their ground*. "My criticisms were right on target," says one. "I shot that argument down in flames," replies the other. At the end of the exchange, the parties will claim that they *won* or *lost* the argument—or agreed on a draw.[13]

Lakoff and Johnson call this metaphor system "Argument is war." They point out that we don't just talk about arguments in terms of war. We actually win or lose them. Though we also use such metaphors as "building a case" and "floating an argument," much of what happens in arguments, from domestic disputes to academic dissertations, is structured by the war concept. Our experience of arguing is not a "mere metaphor," divorced from the way we think and behave, but is indissolubly linked with both.

"Argument is war" does not *control* our thinking about reasoning. It is possible to imagine a culture where reasoning is described in terms not of battle, but of a cooperative dance. When people in that culture reasoned together, they might speak of Gill making the first step, John linking arms with her thought, Jack bringing things to a turning point, and Alice calling the next sequence. Criticism and praise could be voiced by saying that John stumbled over Lucy's point while Alice's verbal leap was well executed. But if we were to watch and listen, we would not recognize what was happening as an *argument*, because the participants would not be antagonists, and no one would win or lose. There *are* alternatives to "arguing" as a method of reasoning in our culture, but they have not yet challenged the dominance of "Argument is war." At present, "winning," "losing," "attacking," and "defending" are our ordinary way of reasoning together. The metaphors structure our thinking and action. "We talk about arguments that way because we conceive of them that way, and we act according to the way we conceive of them."[14]

Another important metaphor in our culture has to do with time. Though there are other ways of seeing time (for example, qualitatively: "good times," "bad times"), our dominant metaphor is "Time is money." I have *invested* a lot of time in writing this book, but lack of a typewriter ribbon *cost* me three hours. I would have stopped writing over Christmas, but I couldn't *afford* the time. So I had to *spend* a lot of time on it and *budget* my time carefully.

On closer inspection, "Time is money" is a metaphor system with three components. Time is seen as a *currency*, to be spent, saved, or invested. Time is also seen as a *limited resource*, like oil or coffee: it can be used up, we can have enough of it or run out of it. Some market researchers speak of *time poverty* to describe a situation in which affluent two-income couples would rather save time than money, because there never seems to be enough time to do all they want to do. "Time is the new scarce resource," they say.[15] Finally, time is a *valuable commodity*. It is precious. We frequently expect to pay for it. People give us their time, and we thank them for it. The three metaphors are systematically interrelated, because in our culture *money* is a *limited resource* and *limited resources* are *valuable commodities*. "Time is money" (which we save, invest) *entails* "Time is a limited resource" (which we have in limited quantities and can run out of), which *entails* "Time is a valuable commodity" (which we value highly and pay for).[16]

These interlocking metaphors do not *determine* thought, since we can think of time in other ways and enter into other cultural concepts of time with sufficient understanding to express them in English. But try living Polynesian or African time in Chicago, Tokyo, or London, and you will find that "Time is money" is not "mere metaphor," but expresses how our culture thinks and behaves. We pay for time, and are paid, in exact time units, by the hour, week, or month. Phone calls are metered by the minute. To live a different concept of time would mean dropping out of the mainstream, so closely are language, thought, and action intertwined.

Lakoff and Johnson's work suggests that although such metaphors do not prevent us from thinking and acting differently, they strongly slant and shape our thinking and behavior. In an educational game called Star Power, the players get locked into an increasingly unequal set of relationships based on competitive trading. The successful players are then told to run the game and are given freedom to change the rules. Caught up in the game mechanism, most attempts at rule changing leave the total system only slightly more biased or less vicious than before. Few participants can envisage playing a totally different game—unless they stop playing, stand back, and think hard. The stock phrases, systematic metaphors, and other persistent language habits of our culture are like a compulsive game. They tie together language, thought, and behavior, so that it is difficult to see through them or beyond them.

Returning to the point where I began, three of the responses to criticism are plausible. "I didn't mean that" is plausible because the language we use may not, on reflection, express our thoughts and convictions. The speaker may be going along with ready-made accepted phrases and metaphors, unaware of what they signify and communicate. "I didn't know what I was saying" is also plausible, for similar reasons, and because our understanding of what language communicates, or what we ourselves think, can change over a period of time. "I meant it and I still do" is plausible, because we can know that we have chosen this set of words, rather than another, to express our thought. The speaker will have to justify the choice, however, if challenged.

To say that language choice is "mere metaphor" or "only a matter of words" is, however, unconvincing if the usage in question is persistent and widespread. It is a fair assumption that persistent and systematic uses of language express what the speakers really think and match how they behave. Equally, it is a fair assumption that the way we speak of God shapes and slants our understanding of God.

Language in Communication

An important feature of God-language (especially in worship) is its relative imprecision. Patriarchal rationality sees itself as superior to intuition and regards the precision of concepts as superior to the imprecision of metaphor. Patriarchal theology tends to regard the language of prayer and praise as beneath its notice, precisely because it is imprecise. Yet imprecision has positive features, as we shall see.

In the grocer's shop of my childhood, my greatest pleasure was watching the method of payment. The assistant took your money and put it with the bill in a metal canister, which was then sent whizzing on an overhead wire to the cashier, who unpacked the canister, spiked the bill, and sent the change whizzing back to the counter.

Popular understanding of linguistic communication works on similar lines. I have a meaning that I put into linguistic canisters (words). I send the canisters across to you, and you unpack them, getting out the precise meaning I put in. There is no doubt as to who is sending, who is receiving, and what is sent.

Ordinary speech shows how ingrained is this idea of communication. We speak of "putting ideas into words," "getting ideas across," "having an idea and capturing it in words," and even of "packing more thoughts into fewer words." One person's words are "full of meaning" and another's are empty. Someone else's ideas "get through to us," though we can't "get our ideas into their heads." One researcher documents more than a hundred such expressions in English, which he estimates form 70 percent of the expressions we use about language.[17] Another linguist calls this the "telementational" theory: sender and receiver share a common code in which certain *forms* (words, phrases) correspond to certain *meanings* (ideas). If I select the exact form, you receive it and match it to the identical concept in your mind.[18]

The grocer's shop image seems appropriate when we have the feeling of choosing one word rather than another to express what is in our mind. Yet with some exceptions (for example, mathematical symbols, formal logic, and internationally agreed upon scientific and technical vocabularies) communication is far from being as exact as telementational metaphors suggest.

Suppose I tell you that "Banbury is twenty-three miles north of Oxford." If you know or guess that "Banbury" and "Oxford" are human settlements of uncertain size, and roughly what "twenty-three miles north" means in terms of distance and direction, you will "get the message" I am trying to send—or rather, you will get a reasonable though rough impression of what's in my mind.

For most purposes we don't need to be more accurate than that, and it doesn't matter if I have a more accurate concept of a mile than you and know both towns and the road between them, whereas you're from Milan, have never seen Oxfordshire, and think in kilometers. But it's already clear that "what's in my mind" when I say or write those words will not be fully conveyed into your mind.

Our presuppositions also make a difference to what we think the sentence means. So does the context—what's been said already and the reasons for our communication. Unless there is further clarification, you might assume that I also mean it's not very far by car, whereas I'm actually thinking it's too far to cycle every day.

We can, of course, converse and clarify the statement further, as I have just done. Yet with our best efforts a degree of uncertainty, imprecision, and misunderstanding are inevitable in much linguistic communication—and often do not matter. "Without some ambiguity, communication is simply impossible," observes Stephen Tyler,[19] pointing out that too many attempts at clarification bring communication to a halt. If I keep on saying, "What do you mean? What do you mean? What do you mean?" I will eventually stop our discussion and probably cause great irritation. It seems that we have to assume more clarity than there ever can be in order to communicate something, however imperfectly.

How, then, do sender and receiver achieve mutual understanding? Consider the following conversation between two people, about a third, whom both know well:

A: Jean seems unhappy at the moment.

B: What sort of unhappy?

A: It's difficult to pin down. She's edgy, a little bit depressed, though not seriously. She's . . . restless.

B: In love?

A: I don't think so. She's friendly with several boys, but there's no one who's close. It's not something she'd hide, if there was.

B (in agreement): Yes. Is she finding schoolwork too hard?

A: It's partly that, perhaps. She can do it, but she seems to find the effort tedious. Maybe because she doesn't know what she wants to do when she leaves school. She had a marvelous time traveling abroad last summer, so staying on at school for another two years is a bit of a letdown. She doesn't enjoy studying for its own sake.

B: If she did know what she wanted to do, would she feel happier? Do you think she'd work harder?

A: Maybe. It might have been better if she'd left school and gone to the College of Further Education. But all her friends are at school, and her friends are important to her.

Words like *edgy, a little bit depressed, restless* don't have exact meanings. And what does it mean, exactly, to say that Jean is "friendly" with several boys and finds schoolwork "tedious"? Though both speakers explore and elaborate, there are many imprecisions in their conversation. Yet by the end of it, *B* has enough grasp of the situation to know how to listen to Jean when they next meet, to form a clearer opinion. There is no point in striving for perfect clarity, because *A* isn't clear herself what she thinks is bothering Jean, and Jean probably isn't either. Not everything the speakers say needs clarification at that moment. Their context, tone of voice, and relationship are also part of the act of communication and cannot be pinpointed in language.

Yet sifting different words and phrases is an important part of the clarification that does take place, because *unhappy* doesn't have a single, precise meaning in our speakers' minds, and neither expects it to. If it had one, and only one, meaning, it would probably have to be one of two hundred nouns denoting different types of unhappiness, and both speakers would communicate instantly at the cost of having an impossibly large vocabulary. The imprecision of nouns, verbs, adjectives, and syntactical combinations is essential to most communication. Because of it, and aided by the nonlinguistic factors already mentioned, the two speakers can explore together what kind of unhappiness *A* thinks Jean is experiencing far more flexibly, creatively, and quickly than would be possible if each noun, adjective, and verb was a container with one, and only one, meaning packed inside it. Their imprecise, flexible language can take account of the myriad changes of human experience, which makes Jean's "unhappiness" different from anyone else's. This is why, "without the indeterminacy that stops us communicating telepathically we would not be able to adapt our language to the novel situations we need it for."[20]

Similar considerations apply when people from different cultures try to communicate, using a common language but coming from different experiences, values, and assumptions. They can never understand one another if language works on the container theory, because they may each be putting different meanings into their word canisters. To communicate in such a situation each must become aware of, and respect, the differences in their backgrounds and world views. They have to highlight shared experiences in order to find points of contact. As the area of shared experience grows, it becomes the basis for more reliable interpretations of what is said: "When the chips are down, meaning is negotiated; you slowly figure out what you have in common, what it is safe to talk about, how you can communicate unshared experience or create a shared vision."[21]

The *necessary imprecision* of most communication has important implications for religious language. It suggests that there are limits to the precision that can be achieved, and that some forms of communication need less precision than others. In preaching and teaching we of course strive to think and speak clearly, recognizing that "communication is an everyday triumph."[22] Yet there remains a large area of uncertainty and indeterminacy. This indeterminate, uncontrolled space between sender and receiver is much broader when metaphors and other imagery are being used and, as Chapter 4 will show, the meanings of metaphors and images in worship cannot be restricted to those perceived or approved by their senders.

The frequent inability of sender and receiver to tie down meanings of their language has a positive value, hinted at by Stephen Tyler. Every act of saying, he concludes, is a momentary intersection of what is said with what is unsaid. It refers back to what has been said, points forward to what will be said, and is surrounded by the glow of what the speakers do not say but is nonetheless part of their communication. Thus, it "transcends the speaker's conscious thought, passes beyond his manipulative control, and creates in the mind of the hearer worlds unanticipated."[23]

In other words, the impossibility of telepathy, and of exact meanings being placed in our minds through the sending of precisely shaped language canisters, is a precondition of human freedom. I cannot control the associations my words will arouse in your mind, since your experience and preconceptions shape and filter what you hear me say, nor should I try to. As we speak to each other, I shall be aware that all communication is difficult, and that sufficient communication, giving the sense of a meeting of minds, is a precious gift and fleeting achievement. Yet I shall also be grateful for the space between my mind and yours, which allows both of us freedom—including my freedom to have thoughts, feelings, associations, and moves toward action sparked by what you have said, out of the interaction between my experience and your utterance, which you can neither predetermine nor predict.

Power in Language and the Language of Power

The indeterminacy of language safeguards human freedom, yet language is widely felt to have power, whether power over people or power to set people free. Having shown that language can slant and angle thinking and behavior, I will scrutinize the widespread feeling that the power to do this resides in language itself, and that the mere utterance of words can change people. "Words that convey no information may nevertheless move carloads of shaving soap or cake-mix," says one student of language. "Words can start people marching in the streets—and can stir others to stoning the marchers."[24] Is that literally true? What is this power of language? Some examples may clarify the matter.

Adolf Hitler gained political power in Germany during a time of economic depression and national humiliation. Nazi propaganda drew on a host of symbols, including flags, parades, rallies, eagles, monuments, music—and language. The language of propaganda helped persuade people to support the Nazi movement, thus giving it political power, and was then used to consolidate that power. Language was used insistently and emotively. One Nazi propagandist said that *Schlagworte* (literally, "hitting words") such as *freedom, race, soil, blood, brotherhood, capitalism, communism, Deutschland*, and *Third Reich* had to replace "the refined old language of diplomacy."[25] By repetition, strong metaphor, and emotive appeals, in contexts in which oratory could override clear thought and enthuse the audience, Nazi propaganda fomented anti-Semitism. Jews were first dehumanized by language, then stripped of their rights.

Repetition and elaboration of powerful metaphors was an important part of this process. The Nazis calculated that only 0.3 percent of the world's population was Jewish, so they had to explain how so small a proportion of the population could be a dangerous enemy. If Jews had been portrayed as human beings, with human strengths and weaknesses, it would have been difficult to foment anti-Semitism to fever pitch. So Jews were defined as demonic and spoken of in subhuman terms: as "bacilli," as a "plague" capable of destroying the non-Jewish population. Lies, repetition, and incessant propaganda showed the power of language—but that power had to be reinforced by other forms of control, and by the exclusion of opposing viewpoints, to reach its full effectiveness. Given such political control, anti-Semitic language did change people's perceptions. The choice of such metaphors as "plague" and "bacillus" suggested an enemy that was "ubiquitous, close, deadly, insidious." It invited the idea of extermination, whether or not the "final solution" was spelled out. Invisible to the naked eye, it required the "expert," the Nazi agitator, to detect its presence.[26]

Once the Nazis gained political power, language was used to dehumanize still further the children, women, and men sent to extermination camps. "The incessant official demonization of the Jew gradually modified the consciousness even of naturally humane people," so that the German public became indifferent to Jewish sufferings, not because of secrecy or wartime conditions, but because Jews seemed "astronomically remote and not real people."[27] Nazi propaganda is a striking example of the power of language. Yet this power did not reside in the words and metaphors alone. The long history of anti-Semitism in Christian Europe prepared the way. Economic depression and national humiliation brought an intense crisis, maximizing the appeal of simple solutions and scapegoats. Control of audiences, and the suppression of opposition, were indispensable supports to linguistic propaganda.

Language of Darkness and Light

The Atlantic slave trade offers another example of the interplay of language with political and economic power. One writer argues that "having defined the blacks as uncivilized, heathens, barbarians, apes and animals, it was an easy step to oppress them into slavery,"[28] which suggests that it was racist language that made oppression possible. By contrast, Basil Davidson argues that "in the early discovery, men of Europe believed they had found partners and allies and equals in Africa," and that the trade then *"produced* among Europeans the mentality of superiority."[29]

The truth may be more subtle. Peter Fryer argues that sudden or limited contact with other nations or ethnic groups often gives rise to odd and prejudiced beliefs, especially in communities that are "ethnically homogeneous, geographically isolated, technologically backward, or socially conservative, with knowledge and political power concentrated in the hands of an elite."[30] Sixteenth-century England was like this, though about to embark on a long period of social change and expansion. So it is not surprising that weird beliefs about African peoples, derived partly from folklore going back to the ancient Greeks, were reinforced by the sudden contact between a northern light-skinned people and dark-skinned visitors or captives from sub-Saharan Africa. Fryer calls this *race prejudice*. It was scrappy, self-contradictory, spread largely by word of mouth, and it performed a psychological and cultural function (interpreting the new and unexpected).

When the drive for profit led more and more English merchant capitalists to traffic in Africans, and the triangular trade generated undreamt of returns, "the economic basis had been laid for all those ancient scraps of myth and prejudice to be woven into a more or less coherent racist ideology." Race prejudice then became *racism*: a relatively systematic body of beliefs, internally self-consistent, spread largely through the printed word, and performing the economic and political function of justifying the enslavement of human beings.[31]

Among the lineaments of race prejudice was a set of linguistic contrasts between "whiteness" and "blackness" going back many centuries. In England, blackness traditionally stood for death, mourning, baseness, evil, and danger. It was the color of bad magic, melancholy, and the nethermost pit of hell. People spoke of the black arts, blackmail, and the black death. When bad people were ostracized they were blacklisted, when punished their names went in a black book, when executed a black flag was hoisted over them. The black sheep of the family was probably also a blackguard. White signified purity, virginity, innocence, good magic, and flags of truce.[32]

Fryer slightly overplays his hand here, since there are positive connotations of blackness (the dark cloud of mystery where God dwells) and negative connotations of whiteness (whited sepulchres) that he overlooks. In general, though, he makes his case, pointing out that it is much easier to fit a new phenomenon into an existing mental slot than do the hard work of rethinking one's categories. One may add that rethinking categories is more than a mental exercise, because it involves *perceiving* in a new way. Conditioned by longstanding categorizations, the eye has to *see afresh* to realize that the words *white* and *black* do not describe the varied textures of skin color. When sixteenth-century English people first met people with dark skins, it was almost inevitable that they would be seen and labeled as "black" and slotted into the categories "black, badness, devils, monsters," given the longstanding black-white, negative-positive contrast and the myths of travelers' tales.[33]

It appears, then, that race prejudice developed, drawing on longstanding positive-negative contrasts between whiteness and blackness, allied with a potpourri of myth and legend. By itself, this would have been unpleasant, but not markedly at variance with prejudices in other societies. It was as Englishmen gained power over Africans that race prejudice developed into racism, to justify dehumanization and enslavement. English racism went through many stages, from the ideology of West Indian planters in the seventeenth century, to pseudoscientific theories in the early nineteenth and "white man's burden" paternalism in the late nineteenth and early twentieth centuries. The effects are still with us. "Long after the material conditions that originally gave rise to racist ideology had disappeared, these dead ideas went on gripping the minds of the living. They led to various kinds of racist behavior on the part of many white people in Britain, including white people in authority."[34]

"Indian Derision"—Offense or Oppression?

Such events cannot be recorded and read without emotion. Nor should they be. When we think through the interplay of language and power, we confront our own histories and have to deal with the sadness, anger, shame, or grief they leave us. One example sticks in my mind and speaks either parabolically or directly, depending on the reader's own history. In *The Language of Oppres-*

sion Haig Bosmajian has a chapter on "the language of Indian derision," showing how native Americans were linguistically dehumanized as they were displaced, conquered, and decimated. By 1901 native American children were being taught "to salute . . . the flag of the United States, at a time when Indian citizenship was not guaranteed, when Indian suffrage was denied in various states, when 'liberty and justice for all' simply did not apply to Indians. The children were in effect forced to salute the flag under which their conquerors and oppressors had marched." A ritual of (American) citizenship asked the male native American to state his "Indian name." He was then required to shoot an arrow, after which he was told: "(Indian name), you have shot your last arrow. That means you are no longer to live the life of an Indian. You are from this day forward to live the life of a white man." The new citizen then placed his hands on a plow to show his choice to "live the life of a white man—and the white man lives by work." He was given a purse and then answered to a new "white name": "(White name), I give you a purse. This purse will always say to you that the money you gain from your labor must be wisely kept." The American flag was placed in his hands and he was told: "This is the only flag you have ever had or ever will have." The ritual was similar for a woman, save that she was given a work bag and purse and told that she had chosen "the life of a white woman, and the white woman loves her home."[35]

If such language was proposed for use in a situation in which native Americans met white Americans on equal terms, and the outcome had no effect on political or economic status, the former would probably see it as *offensive* and tell the latter to get lost. What makes the language *oppressive* is the power politics of the situation: the new citizens are under economic, political, and cultural *coercion* to surrender their culture, way of life, even their names, and accept the values of their conquerors, including their definitions of "work" and male-female roles.

Learning "Time is money"

The above examples suggest that it is misleading to talk about "the power of language" in isolation from its political, economic, and cultural contexts. Lakoff and Johnson recognize that "words alone don't change reality," yet in the same breath argue that "much of cultural change arises from the introduction of new metaphorical concepts and the loss of old ones. For example, the Westernization of cultures throughout the world is partly a matter of introducing the "Time is money" metaphor into those cultures."[36] This sounds as if introducing "Time is money" into a different culture is a benign linguistic process whereby Westerners say, "Let's think of time like this," and enthusiastic natives reply, "Say, that's a great idea!"

The reality is otherwise. In South Africa, the Voortrekker Afrikaaners and the British conquered black African clans and nations and took their land. Before the conquest, there had generally been a balance between land and population. After the conquest, black Africans were crowded into areas too small and infertile to maintain them and their cattle. Traditional agricultural methods then led to soil erosion and an increasingly difficult struggle to survive. Traditional African culture knows nothing of time as units marked off in hours and paid for in cash per unit, by the clock. After the conquest, black South Africans increasingly "accepted" the "Time is money" metaphor, but this was because acceptance was *imposed*—by economic pressures (the need to earn cash to buy food that could no longer be grown, for example) and by deliberate political acts. One such was the imposition of hut and poll taxes, which forced black Africans to take waged labor, since the taxes had to be paid in cash. In 1894 Cape premier Cecil Rhodes was responsible for one such measure, the Glen Grey Act, which replaced communal land tenure in the Transkei with individual landholding. The act limited the size of plots and imposed a labor tax, with the aim of obliging Xhosa men to work in the mines. Rhodes hoped "by the gentle stimulant of the labor tax to remove them from a life of sloth and laziness; you will thus teach them the dignity of labor." Thus did many colonized peoples make their first acquaintance with the metaphor "Time is money."[37]

Asians and Bureaucrats

Language is offensive if it expresses prejudice. It is oppressive if those with the prejudice have power to impose their will on others. In Britain, linguists have examined the problems faced by Asian[38] English speakers in their dealings with social workers, welfare clerks, and other officials. Both parties are speaking English, but there is often misunderstanding between them. The misunderstanding, however, has more serious consequences for the Asians than for the officials, if the former are trying to make claims that the latter have power to accept or deny. Misunderstanding often leads the officials to label Asians as poor communicators and mark them down accordingly. "Undoubtedly the Asians have their own less complimentary ideas about the *gore* (white people)," says Deborah Cameron, "but these are the ideas of people without power. They do not serve as a base for administrative procedures and decisions, nor do they get expressed routinely in the mass media."[39] "When [dehumanizing] language becomes institutionalized," writes Haig Bosmajian, "when it is spoken by judges, religious leaders or presidents, it receives the imprimatur of authorities who have the power and influence to impose their metaphors."[40]

Language and Control

Language has limited power "by itself," but it gains considerable power—to enable, oppress, or liberate—in the hands of powerful users. Since power over others is usually clung to rather than surrendered, it is reasonable to assume that when individuals and groups have power over others, they will use language that justifies their dominance, or makes it seem normal and legitimate, and which ignores, devalues, or dehumanizes those they dominate.[41]

In looking at any systematic use of language, then, it is reasonable to be suspicious. Where particular forms of speech or metaphor are systematically used by people occupying privileged positions in social classes or institutions, it is a fair assumption that their use of language is expressing, supporting, and trying to legitimize nonlinguistic power relationships. When we look at how God is depicted and addressed in worship and theology, we ask such questions as "Is this way of naming God faithful to the core of Christian faith?" and "How far does it do justice to the greatness and mystery of the living God?" But it is also important to ask: Who benefits from speaking of God in this way, from this or that pattern of language and metaphor? What power and privilege (in church and society) does God-talk help to justify, legitimize, and perpetuate—or bring to light, question, and free us from?

Thus, questions about the truth and faithfulness of God-language go hand in hand with questions about who controls or dominates church life and church structures. Since our churches are, overtly or covertly, dominated by men, we should be highly suspicious when we realize that God, theologized as beyond male and female, is overwhelmingly depicted and praised in male terms, as the highest hierarch (king) at the top of every power pyramid (*Almighty* God). When the maleness of God-language is questioned, there are three plausible responses. We can argue that male God-language describes and depicts who God really is ("We meant it, and we still do") and try and justify our conviction. We can decide that, on reflection, it falls far short of our understanding and experience of divine love ("We don't mean *that*—what we mean is . . ."). Or we can say that we once thought it was unproblematic, but now think otherwise ("We didn't realize what we were saying"). What we cannot do is shrug off the question by saying that it is only a figure of speech or "mere metaphor."

Conclusion

Language change is not *all-important*: if it were, then changing language would be all that was needed to change the world. Nor is it *unimportant*: if it were, we could concentrate on doing love and justice, and quit worrying about how we speak of God. To separate language from action is false. Language change is an *essential part of action*. If I cease using racist language I will not thereby end racism. Yet trying out new forms of speech is a necessary part of finding out what I really think. By using nonracist language I also commit myself more deeply than before, even if I can't completely live out my commitment. Language is a public medium. If I use, or abandon, racist or sexist language, or begin to name God anew, I shall open myself to comment and criticism and shall have to explain and defend my usage. It may then be easier than before to act on what I have said.

Language, like tobacco, is habit forming. Some patterns of writing and speaking are addictive and may damage both the user and others who breathe the same linguistic atmosphere. If we see the damage being done and decide to kick the habit, we may get withdrawal symptoms and hostility or derision from other smokers. But in the end, we shall enjoy breathing fresh air.

4

The Nature of God-Talk

Listen to this, you cows of Bashan
*   who live on the hill of Samaria.   (Amos 4:1)*

She has fallen, never to rise,
*   the virgin Israel,*
forsaken on her own soil
*   with none to lift her up.   (Amos 5:2)*

I will meet them like a she-bear robbed of her cubs
*   and tear their ribs apart.   (Hos. 13:8)*

It was I who had taught Ephraim to walk,
I who had taken them in my arms.   (Hos. 11:3)

In Amos 5:2 the nation Israel is not literally a forsaken corpse, nor does Hosea believe that God is a female bear or a mother teaching her toddler to walk. Like the prophets, we use nonliteral language every day and usually understand it intuitively, without a second thought. This chapter invites some second thoughts about language, in order to understand what we are doing with it when we name and depict the mystery of God. I hope to show that every naming of God is a borrowing from human experience and that God-talk is not linguistically different from non-God-talk. I shall begin with the latter and move on to the former, with special reference to biblical language and imagery.

The first quotation seems to be speaking about a group of cows—until you read the following lines:

you who oppress the poor and crush the destitute,
who say to your lords [that is, husbands], "Bring us drink."

It then becomes clear that Amos's subject—what he is speaking about—is a group of wealthy women in Israel's capital city. We do not need to share Amos's view of these women, or of marriage, to see that two thoughts or images are acting together in his utterance, namely, "Bashan cows" and "upper-class Samarian women" (with the associations each suggests to different hearers or readers).

The second quotation also has one subject, but two images acting together. Amos uses the rhythms of the dirge (reproduced roughly in translation) and a word, *fallen*, which in other contexts suggests death in battle, to present the image of a young woman whose tragic death he laments. Forsaken (without the dignity of burial) and a virgin (unmarried, childless, and so in patriarchal culture unfulfilled), her corpse lies on the ground, never to rise again. The other thought, the subject of his utterance, is the nation Israel. Putting the two thoughts together creates a tension or shock, since at the time of Amos's utterance, Israel the nation is alive and well, with conspicuous wealth held by its upper classes. Since the oracle goes on to speak of Israel's cities losing nine-tenths of their warriors in battle, it is clear that Amos is inviting his hearers to see the nation (apparently alive and well) as already struck down, a forsaken corpse whose destiny is unfulfilled, and to mourn her tragic end at the hands of great world powers (Assyria or possibly Egypt). He aims to engage his hearers' feelings and change their perceptions. To accept the oracle as true his hearers would have to recognize the threat of invasion and see it as God's judgment.

In both passages there is *one subject* ("Samarian high-class women" / "Israel the nation"), which is active with *a second idea or image* ("Bashan cows" / "murdered virgin"). Exactly how the two ideas or images act together is more difficult to express. I shall argue that *comparison* and *substitution* are inadequate terms, and that it is more accurate to say that the two ideas or situations intersect, or interanimate each other.[1] Making new connections between different areas of experience is a hallmark of human creativity. The two situations that intersect can be images, concepts, models, activities, and experiences, and the word *matrix* will sometimes be useful shorthand for all of them. Thus in Amos 4:1 one matrix (Bashan cows and their associations for the hearer) intersects with another (Samaria's aristocratic women) to produce the metaphor.[2]

A few other terms will aid clarity and precision. A *simile* compares something with something else ("I will fall upon them *like* a she-bear robbed of her cubs"), whereas a *metaphor* intersects the two instead of comparing them ("and I [God/the she-bear] will tear their ribs apart" instead of "it will be as if a bear was tearing their ribs apart"). In Amos 5:2 the subject is Israel the nation, but we need words to describe the dead virgin image that interacts with it. I shall use the term *intersecting image* to make the distinction clear. Thus in Amos 4:1 the subject is the women of Samaria and the intersecting image is Bashan cows.

The word *analogy* is also useful, not in Thomas Aquinas's sense, which does not clearly describe how language works,[3] but in its meaning of language stretched to meet new situations without the intersecting mechanism of metaphor. If we met extraterrestrials who communicated soundlessly by visible movements of their stomach muscles, we could say they had "said" this or "spoken about" that, without any sense of strain, because our language about communication had merely been extended: by analogy with the human voice's communication through sound waves, we would be describing communication by another means as "saying" something. Analogical speech can also work by negation: to say that God is infinite and invisible is to extend our understanding of *finite* and *visible* in a negative direction, meaning that God is neither. On the other hand, *omniscience* and *omnipotence* extend our concepts of knowledge and power in a positive direction.

Finally, I use the words *image* and *imagery* to mean language appealing to the senses, whether of hearing, sight, taste, touch, or smell. Thus,

> *Leave the gloomy haunts of sadness,*
> *come into the daylight's splendor*

contains visual imagery (of light and dark), whereas

> *Wind was swishing in the trees,*
> *leaves were rattling on the ground*

has imagery of sound (aural).[4] Since (as we shall see) metaphor is the most significant form of God-talk, discussion will center on metaphor, with some reference to simile and analogy.[5]

How Metaphors Work

Metaphor is not just an expression of feelings, nor the substitution of an image for its literal equivalent, nor simply a condensed comparison.[6] On the substitution view, for example, the metaphor "Richard is a lion" is only a substitute for saying that "Richard is brave." Nothing is gained by it, except an emotional effect or, sometimes, brevity: to say that "the chairperson took us on a powerboat ride through the agenda" takes less time than to say she suppressed objections or irrelevancies, kept tight control, and got the meeting finished far more quickly than expected.

The examples illustrate the weakness of the substitution view. "Richard is a lion" is a weak metaphor. Even so, it must mean—and suggest—something more than "Richard is brave," otherwise we would regard the two as synonyms and have only the sound of the words to justify a choice between them. There is some added significance in the word *lion*, however slight.[7] The other metaphor is even more difficult to justify as mere substitution. The context would partly determine its meaning—if approval, there are suggestions of speed, panache, or even elegance in "powerboat ride" that are lost in a prose paraphrase; if disapproval, suggestions of riding roughshod, leaving everyone behind, flamboyance, or arrogance are equally difficult to pin down in prose.

A strong metaphor does indeed save many lines of prose, but the reasons for choosing metaphor rather than prose have as much to do with impact as economy. Impact on the imagination is especially important in religious language, since "belief in God depends to a small extent on rational argument, and to a larger extent on our ability to frame images to capture, commemorate, and convey our experience of transcendence."[8] The persistence of substitution views does, however, help to explain the bias against metaphor in some theological writing, as when "metaphorical knowledge" is described as "only intuitive awareness" and con-

trasted with "real knowledge."[9] For a substitution view implies
that there is something shifty about metaphor, since the intersecting image is supposedly only a stand-in for what the speaker or
writer "really means" but chooses not to say. What follows is intended to help release the specter of substitution theory from its
theological haunts and lay it to rest.

"Metaphor is that figure of speech whereby we speak about
one thing in terms which are seen to be suggestive of another."
Janet Martin Soskice's definition uses the word *metaphor* in a use-
fully precise way to describe a particular use of language, whether
in speech or writing.[10] Metaphors are not, then, mental events.
We may intersect different situations wordlessly in our minds, but
the word *metaphor* is best used for any language that results. Similarly, metaphors are not physical objects. To say that daffodils are
metaphors of rebirth is to use the word in an unnecessarily wide
sense, where *symbol* will do perfectly well. Similarly, a cartoon may
intersect different visual images and encourage us to make un-
looked for connections, but it is better to say so in those terms
than use the word *metaphor*. In appreciating a poetic metaphor,
such as Emily Dickinson's

> *A Narrow Wind complains all day*
> *How someone treated him*

we can draw out meanings by seeing the wind as animate, personal, and "whining." But all such drawing out is ultimately
language-linked: "A metaphor may prompt us to non-linguistic
recognitions and comparisons, but of equal if not greater importance are the linguistic associations to which it gives rise."[11]

Metaphors can take different syntactic forms, for example:

- the smoke *danced* in the chimney (verb)
- the trees bowed in the *dance* of the seasons (noun)
- *dancing* waters surrounded the canoe (participle)

Metaphors can be wider than the individual word. The context often establishes whether a particular sequence is metaphor or
literal speech. "That's a cold coal to blow at" is a literal statement,

but not if it replies to another speaker who says, "I hope the king will forgive the rebels." To speak of "blossoms of smoke" could mean "gray blossoms," "billowing smoke," or "a feeling of emptiness," according to context.

Few metaphors can be extended beyond a sentence or two, because too much extension makes it hard to hang on to what the metaphor is about, and because a metaphor continued on and on becomes tedious, unless it is rich enough to be developed into an allegory. Yet a great allegory, like Bunyan's *Pilgrim's Progress*, succeeds not only because it is an extended metaphor (the Christian life as a pilgrimage), but because the story itself captures the imagination with its description, characterization, and tension.

The two images or ideas acting together in a metaphor are sometimes explicitly stated, as in:

• War is a game of chess.
• People are wolves.

The fact that both subject (war/people) and intersecting image (a chess game/wolves) are fully presented in such metaphors has prompted the suggestion that metaphors have two subjects, not one, the subjects in this case being "war and chess" and "people and wolves," respectively. Yet the context will usually make it clear that the speaker is dealing not with warfare *and* chess, but with warfare alone (with chess as one way of seeing it), or with human beings (with wolf qualities as one way of speaking of them). The reverse metaphors ("this chess tournament is an all-out war" or "every wolf is a person to me") would almost certainly occur in contexts whose main concerns were chess and wolf behavior, respectively. Moreover, a two-subject theory collapses when it runs into metaphors such as:

> *When by my solitary hearth I sit*
> *and hateful thoughts enwrap my soul in gloom.*
>   (Keats, "To Hope")

This is clearly about the poet's state of mind and cannot have two subjects, since the intersecting image is not fully presented. The word *enwrap* does not present us with another subject, but only hints at possible images—a man wrapped in a blanket, or perhaps a cloak. Similarly, in

> *A stubborn and unconquerable flame*
> *creeps in his veins, and drinks the streams of life*[12]

the subject, on inspection, is a lethal fever, but it is unstated and has to be inferred from the two intersecting images; one of these images is a raging fire (unconquerable flame), and the other (creeps, drinks) suggests such images as a prowling, predatory, thirsty animal, but leaves them unstated. The metaphor has one subject matter (the fever affecting the man under discussion), but two matrices are interacting in the utterance, namely:

- matrix A: the fever and its effects (the subject)
- matrix B1: the consuming flame (main intersecting image)
- matrix B2: suggestions of something that creeps and drinks life's streams dry (secondary intersector)

Both elements in matrix B intersect with matrix A, but B2 is secondary because it depends syntactically on B1 and can't be expressed without it. The examples show that the two different images or thoughts active together in metaphor may, but don't have to be, explicitly presented in words, and that a metaphor has one subject, which subject and intersecting image together depict and illuminate.[13]

The impact of such strong metaphors invites us down the false trail that sharply distinguishes metaphor from simile, on the grounds that metaphor intersects two situations, whereas simile only puts them side by side. Some similes lack the impact of metaphor, but not all do. Similes such as "The sun is like a golden ball" and "These biscuits taste like cement" are certainly prosaic, but so is the metaphor "cement biscuits." Some similes are striking and suggestive. When Gustave Flaubert says that "Language is like a cracked kettle on which we beat out tunes for bears to dance to, when all the while we long to move the stars to pity" (*Madame Bovary*), the impact is not increased by dropping the word *like* and making the statement a metaphor. When Amos says that the Day of YHWH will be

> as if *a man were running headlong from a lion*
> *and a bear met him,*
> *and when he got into his house and leaned against a wall*
> *a snake bit him* (Amos 5:19)

it would be difficult to turn the statement into a metaphor without misunderstanding, for one would have to say something like "In that day a man will run headlong . . . ," which would be taken as literal prediction. Yet likening "the Day of YHWH" to this terrifying sequence of "danger-flight-safety-terror-death" has an intersecting impact on the imagination, especially if, as seems likely, the "Day" was a yearly festival with joyful associations.[14]

What, then, are the differences between metaphor and simile? Soskice suggests that similes can be of two kinds: comparison of similars (sun-golden ball) and of dissimilars, and that the latter have the same effect as metaphor. Thus, "metaphor and simile share the same function and differ primarily in their grammatical form."[15] Though her discussion corrects any false antithesis between simile and metaphor, the conclusion is not completely accurate. Not all similes can be expressed as metaphor (see the Amos example, above), and as Soskice goes on to show, metaphor can sometimes extend language in ways barred to the most striking simile. Moreover, popular perception often sees differences between them: where God-talk is concerned, some who reject the metaphor "God our mother" will accept the simile "God, you are like a mother to us." This suggests that differences in function remain. To base judgments on the dissimilarity between two matrices does not do justice to the before-and-after effect of a good simile or metaphor, namely, its power to make us see connections where none had been seen before. Sometimes, what was obviously dissimilar becomes unforgettably connected.

What I mean by the before-and-after effect is that some things about a metaphor or simile are impossible to tell in advance. One is the extent to which the imagery can be made vivid. I call this its degree of *development*. Another is the number of points of contact that can be made between the two matrices, which may be described as the degree of *correspondence* between them.[16] In Hosea 13:8 there are not many ways in which the living God can be seen as a mother bear. Rage, grief at the loss of Israel's loyalty, and terrifying retribution are the main points of correspondence. Yet the image can be presented briefly, or developed with imagery of snarling, clawing, and rib crushing.

The immediate impact of a metaphor or simile depends on both development and correspondence; whether it has occasional use or lasting value depends more on the further correspondences that can be elaborated. When a united family is said to be like oil running down Aaron's beard, the correspondence is only in terms of the oil's fragrance and would be nonsensical if extended to its greasiness and volatility (Psalm 133:2). But the church seen as the body of Christ turns out to have many points of correspondence. It can suggest the variety of function by which different members stay in organic unity (1 Cor. 12:12–21), the relative importance of the humbler members (1 Cor. 12:22–27), the interdependence of the members (Rom. 12:4), the subordination of all the body to its head (Col. 1:18), and the need for steady growth to maturity (Eph. 4:13–16).

Such a metaphor can be called a *model*, because of its capacity to go on generating insights, as in recent suggestions that while the body of Christ has clear boundaries, it is a spiritual body, like Christ's risen body, cosmic in scope, which should be governed by the mutual concern of all members for each other (1 Cor. 12:25), not by hierarchies, bureaucratic rules, or any other forms in which some have power over others.[17] It is a characteristic of imaginative language that some intersections suggest many correspondences and others do not, and the only way to find out is to make the metaphor and see where it goes. Before I coined the metaphor of the chairperson's powerboat ride, I could not have worked out its possibilities for development and correspondence, nor compared them with the potential of a different metaphor, such as "the chairperson *piloted* us through a long and difficult agenda."

What Metaphors Can Do

Metaphors can organize thinking, encourage a transfer of associations and feelings between the matrices they intersect, extend language, generate new insights, and move us at a deep level by their appeal to the senses and imagination. Some of these qualities are shared with simile, whereas others belong to metaphor alone.

For example, the philosopher Max Black invites us to consider the metaphor "Man is a wolf," for which a nonsexist version might be "The human race is a pack of wolves." To understand either metaphor, we need to know what in our culture are the most common associations of "wolf/pack of wolves," what Black calls their "system of associated commonplaces." These probably include carnivorousness, treachery, and ferocity. Other cultures might have different associations. Thus, in a culture in which wolves are regarded as reincarnations of dead ancestors, the statement would have a different meaning and might not be regarded as a metaphor at all. Black points out that the metaphor—if we accept it—organizes our thinking by highlighting human traits that can without undue strain be talked about in wolf terms, and by pushing others into the background. The organizing power of metaphor has already been noted in Chapter 3, in the discussion of Nazi propaganda using metaphors that made Jews seem less than human. If the metaphor succeeds, it also encourages us to transfer feelings and attitudes from the intersecting image to the subject, thus feeling about human beings what we feel about wolves. [18]

In making Black's metaphor nonsexist, I have altered its meaning slightly. The plural form "pack of wolves" may be to "the human race" what "wolf" is to the supposedly generic "man." Yet "pack of wolves" shifts us to our system of associated commonplaces for wolf packs, which will be different, because the new metaphor highlights the collective aspects of wolf behavior: whereas before we pictured a single wolf, now we see an organized group, working together to find, corner, and kill prey. Since wolves typically hunt in packs, the new metaphor is arguably an improvement. Nonetheless, to change a metaphor even slightly will probably change its meaning. Changing our God-metaphors means changing our understanding of God. The question, then, is what are the changes and can they be justified?

Metaphors (though not similes) can also extend language. They not only name something new (which can be done by other forms of extension, for example, naming something after its discoverer or place of origin, as in "volt" from Signor Volta and "sherry" from the town of Xeres), but do so in a way that suggests further possibilities. To call one electrical phenomenon an "ampere" commemorates the discoverer but does nothing more.

To name another as a "current" suggests that it can be damned, that it flows, that it can have higher or lower "pressure," and so on.[19]

The power of some metaphors to suggest new associations is shown in an example with which Soskice illustrates her definition. When W. H. Auden says, in his poem "1st September 1939," that

The unmentionable odor of death
offends the September night

he is not speaking about a literal smell, or speaking of smell and meaning something else, but speaking of forebodings of war in terms appropriate to odor. In other words, he is "speaking of one thing (the odor of death) in terms which are seen (if we understand the metaphor) to be suggestive of another (forebodings of war)."[20]

This explanation does not exhaust the power of Auden's metaphor. Words such as *offends* and *unmentionable* come from the language of prudery and suggest a distaste at something too indelicate to be spoken of, reinforced by *odor*, a more refined word than *smell*. In context, "the unmentionable odor of death" might suggest rotting corpses in World War I trenches, the indecency of this, and war as morally disgusting or distasteful. Similarly, the simple metaphor "writhing script" can suggest a number of associations to the hearer or reader: synonyms, such as *squirming* and *twisting*, but also images, such as snakes in movement or people in pain. As Soskice remarks, "It is the capacity of a lively metaphor to suggest models that enable us to 'go on' which gives the clue to the richness of metaphorical description."[21]

Sometimes metaphors say something that cannot be said in any other way. To put it more precisely, metaphor can be cognitive, bringing us new knowledge. Soskice deals convincingly with objections to this view, then gives a clinching example from Virginia Woolf's novel *To the Lighthouse*: "Never did anybody look so sad. Bitter and bleak, half-way down, in the darkness, in the shaft which ran from the sunlight to the depths, perhaps a tear formed; a tear fell: the waters swayed this way and that, received it, and were at rest. Never did anybody look so sad." The subject, what is being spoken about, is someone's deep and private grief. Yet to say only this is to fall short of the metaphor's power of description, when it is read and reread. The most sensitive paraphrase hardly captures it. The intersecting image (something like a shaft with water deep down inside it) does not by itself suggest grief, but only speaks of grief in union with the subject. The subject matter is barely captured by the word *grief* (even less by the word actually used, *sad*). It is not by itself the meaning of the metaphor, for if the intersecting image is removed, all we have is the sentence "Never did anybody look so sad," which cannot do what the complete statement does. This particular mental state is accessible only through this particular union of subject and intersecting image. What is here described and depicted is identified uniquely by this metaphor. "It is in this way that metaphor is genuinely creative and says something that can be said adequately in no other way, not as an ornament to what we already know, but as an embodiment of a new insight."[22]

Writing the above leads me to make a further suggestion, for the reader to check against experience: a creative metaphor or simile is difficult to analyze, and analysis remains incomplete. Yet analysis does not leave the imagery lifeless, like a frog dissected in a laboratory, but returns us to it with enhanced appreciation.

Understanding God-Talk

To quote one eminent biblical scholar, George Caird, "All, or almost all, of the language used by the Bible to refer to God is metaphor (the one possible exception is the word 'holy')." Caird also states that most such language is anthropomorphic, enabling us to speak of God in language drawn from our experience of the human body, senses, and personality. In speaking of God, he says, we begin with the familiar situations of home and community and derive from them metaphors to illuminate the activity of God.[23] If all Christians agreed, we could move on without further ado.

Some, however, disagree. When considering "the enigma of God-Language," Donald Bloesch says that the crucial question is whether such language gives "true knowledge" or "merely a symbolic awareness" of the ultimate reality we call God. He goes on to say that "analogical knowledge" is real knowledge, whereas metaphorical knowledge is "only intuitive awareness or tacit knowledge." (The terminology is unclear, but I quote it in fairness to its author.) Later, he argues that words such as Father, Son, and Lord, applied to God, "are derived not from the experience of human fatherhood or sonship or lordship, but from God's act of revealing himself as Father, Son and Lord." Speaking of the Trinity, he argues that "the Trinitarian names are ontological symbols based on divine revelation rather than personal metaphors having their origin in cultural experience."[24]

Bloesch's contrast between "true knowledge" and "symbolic awareness" is unclear and makes no sense if applied to something expressed in language, since language itself is a symbolic system and there is nothing "mere" about it. It may simply be another way of expressing his second distinction, between "metaphor" and "analogy," which *is* thought to be detectable in language. By "analogy" Bloesch does not mean an extension in meaning creating no sense of surprise (see beginning of this chapter), but a meaning drawn from Thomas Aquinas. In Bloesch's account of Thomas, we cannot speak literally (univocally) of God. We can use metaphors, but metaphorical words are dissimilar to what is described (that is, God). "While there may be a suggested likeness between the sign and what it signifies, there is no conceptual knowledge." With analogy, on the other hand, there is said to be a partial resemblance between our words and the transcendent reality to which they point.

Bloesch claims that his distinction is visible in such statements as "God is my rock, my fortress," which he calls metaphor, and "God is my father, my lord," which is said to be analogy. Yet all four statements are linguistically identical, for each has an image (rock, fortress, father, lord) that intersects with the subject (our understanding of the word *God*). It is true that different words for the divine might have different connotations for different speakers, and that part of the meaning of "God" for us is given through other metaphorical images. Nonetheless, the four pieces of language all work in the same way. There is of course a difference in the degree of correspondence involved. "Rock" enables us to say fewer things about God than "father." Yet this does not set God-metaphors apart from others, since all metaphors show different degrees of correspondence, impossible to predict before the metaphor is first made. We may, if we wish, go on to make theological judgments based on these differences, but those judgments have to be made on other grounds, not because God-talk works differently from non-God-talk.

It is important to establish this, because Bloesch goes on to argue that some names for God are revealed as definitive, whereas others are not. For example, he argues that though beyond human gender, God chooses to relate to us in a masculine way, thus making the Bible's male metaphors for God unchangeable. His main evidence seems to be that in the Bible male images of God are overwhelmingly more frequent than female images. Yet a majority vote cannot settle the question, since the Bible itself makes no comment on this frequency and was in any case formed by and in a patriarchal society.

How the Bible exercises its claim on us will be discussed in Chapter 5. My point here is that whether or not we agree with such claims, they cannot be settled by appeal to the workings of biblical language. God-talk, in and outside the Bible, is not a special type of syntax or word use with a halo around it: God-metaphors and God-similes work in the same way as other metaphors and similes.

Bloesch's other important contrast is between divine revelation and human experience. He argues that some names for God as Trinity come not from human experience but from divine revelation, and his discussion seems to suggest that the revelatory nature of these names is visible in the very language used. I shall support my previous point, and test this claim, by looking at some biblical images of God and the connection between human language and human experience.

Hosea is one of the earliest Hebrew prophets whose work has come down to us. His oracles abound in powerful metaphors and similes, some of which have already been considered. Two of his God-images were quoted at the beginning of this chapter. Hosea 13:7–8 reads:

> *So now I will be like a panther to them,*
> *I will prowl like a leopard by the wayside;*
> *I will meet them like a she-bear robbed of her cubs*
>   *and tear their ribs apart.*
> *Like a lioness I will devour them on the spot,*
> *I will rip them up like a wild beast.*

Some of the Hebrew text is uncertain, but the bear image is sound. As previously noted, it combines a simile with a metaphor. Angry female bears were so familiar to the prophet's contemporaries that this image became proverbial:

Your father and the men with him are hardened warriors
and savage as a bear in the wilds robbed of her cubs. (2 Sam. 17:8)

Better face a she-bear robbed of her cubs
than a stupid man in his folly. (Prov. 17:12)

In speaking of God in terms appropriate to an enraged and bereft mother bear, the prophet is drawing on human experience of bears. He is not speaking of God in terms appropriate to hermaphrodite sprigbyths from the planet Aurelia, and if he were, he would not be understood by Hebrew-speaking Israelites in the eighth century before Christ, or by us. The image is highly developed ("tear their ribs apart," cf. Dan. 7:5) and has a powerful impact amid similar intersections of Israel's covenant God with dangerous, prowling, fierce wild beasts. Though there is limited correspondence between subject and intersecting image, this does not entitle us to conclude that Hosea here gives us no revelation of God, or knowledge of God. Such a view would not be Hosea's, since he uses the form of the prophetic oracle.

Nor can it be said that the metaphor gives no conceptual content, if by that we mean more generalized statements that help us to understand and think about God. If we want conceptual content, this image can be linked with others presenting the living God as awesome, unpredictable, even dangerous—a mighty wind, tongues of fire, holiness blazing in a bush or dazzling in the temple—and we can use the network of such imagery to form concepts of God. Such concepts will be a corrective to the more homely connotations of imagery drawn from personal relationships, as is also the case with Hosea 5:12–14:

But I am [like] a festering sore to Ephraim,
*　and rottenness in the bones to the house of Judah.*
So when Ephraim found that he was sick,
*　Judah that he was covered with sores,*
Ephraim went to Assyria,
*　he went in haste to the Great King;*

> *but he has no power to cure you,*
>   *or to heal your sores.*
> *Yes, indeed, I will be fierce as a panther to Ephraim,*
>   *fierce as a lion to Judah—*
> *I will maul the prey and go,*
>   *carry it off beyond hope of rescue.*

Here again there are two intersecting images, each drawn from human experience and expressed in a combination of metaphor and simile that illustrates their frequent similarity of function. God is imaged as a festering sore, weakening the body, foul, rotten, and pervasive, and as a lion or panther, pouncing, mauling, tearing apart, and carrying off the prey: destruction comes ferociously from without and insidiously from within. The subject is YHWH, Israel's husband-lover (Hos. 2–3), God of Exodus and Covenant. The shocking metaphors of divine activity as creeping disease and ferocious attack are not Hosea's most important models for understanding and knowing God, but it is difficult to see how they can be less *revelatory* than his metaphors of God as husband-lover and motherly parent.[25]

The ways in which language reflects distinctively *human* experience are easily illustrated. In everyday speech we use up-and-down language without a second thought. "I'm feeling *up*, my spirits *rose*, my heart *sank*," we say. "After the party last night the children were as *high as kites*, but I'm feeling really *low* this morning—in fact, I've *hit rock bottom*." These are not literal statements about our distance from the earth's surface, but descriptions of emotional states. Why does it seem so natural to talk this way and see happiness as "up" and sadness as "down"? The most plausible explanation is that these metaphors or analogies[26] have their basis in human experience, where a drooping posture goes with weakness and depression and an upright one with well-being. In sickness we sit or lie down, whereas in health we stand erect. In other words, the language reflects our experience as bipeds living in a gravitational field.

The same applies to another up-and-down metaphor, where having control is "up" and being subject to someone else's control is "down." So we say without any sense of strain that Joan has control *over* her daughter, whereas Peter is completely *under his mother's thumb*; that President Kennedy was assassinated while he was at the *height* of his power, but President Nixon *fell from power*; that Britain's power is *declining* and Japan's is *rising*. Such language is probably drawn from the experience of physical combat, where the victor stands triumphant and the vanquished collapses beneath. Physical height is certainly associated with power and status. The same man introduced to different groups of students was rated taller when thought to be a professor than when introduced as a fellow student,[27] while advertising frequently shows women in such postures as "the bashful knee-bend" in relation to male authority figures.[28]

Such language makes sense to us because it is drawn from specifically human experience. A deep-water creature, living under enormous pressures, for whom to go upward would be dangerous and to go high up would mean death, would speak differently of "up" and "down." In such a creature's language, "I chased them up and I was under them all the way" would mean "I won, I had the advantage." "I'm feeling really low today" would signify well-being, and seabed doctors would reach for the antidepressants when their patients said, "I'm on the up and up." A spherical being in zero gravity would have no language for "up" and "down." It would be mystified by Isaiah's vision of the Holy One, "high and lifted up," but would probably well understand what it meant to be cast into outer darkness.

Another set of metaphors is derived from our experience of having only two eyes in our head, facing in our direction of movement, so that we easily see what lies "in front of us," but cannot without turning see what is "behind us." So we most commonly conceive of time as a line along which we move. We wonder what lies *ahead* of us tomorrow. Of future events we say that we *can see it coming*, or that we can't. Of an unpleasant event we say that we are *trying to put it behind us*.[29]

The basis of this metaphor is our physical shape, which gives us a definite "front" and "back." If we had eyes all around our head, or walked sideways, our metaphorical system for time would be different. If we were sentient crabs, time might have a left-right orientation, so that we saw past and future, if at all, out of the corner of our eyes, as we scuttled from one day to another and listened to our neighbor's forebodings that "the right-side year will be like a great slippery rock; I can feel it in my claws."

These examples illustrate my claim that all human language, including metaphors and concepts, arises out of the specifically *human* experience of being mammalian bipeds breathing air and living in the earth's gravitational field. It is difficult to see what other basis it could have for us to understand it. Thus, when the prophet says to God, "Thou hast cast all my sins *behind* thee," his experience of God as forgiving is what God reveals to us, but that experience is expressed in an orientational metaphor drawn from the human experience of being creatures with eyes in the front of our heads (Isa. 38:17). Paul's metaphor of the Christian life as a foot race in which, forgetting what is behind him, he presses on toward his goal (Phil. 3:12–14) has the same basis. Revelation is not disembodied, but incarnational: if God reveals Godself to us, it has to be in language drawn from the particularities of our physical makeup and our political, economic, and cultural experience.

I have spent some time looking at Donald Bloesch's arguments because they arise out of a widely shared concern to safeguard belief in divine revelation, plus a less widely held conviction that it is possible to demonstrate *how* revelation occurs. I believe in revelation, but the impossibility of demonstrating it does not make me anxious. It would be nice if the language of the Bible had its grammar and syntax unmistakably illuminated by divine laser light, but that would also diminish the need for faith and a trusting response to God.

As it is, to set divine revelation against human experience is a false opposition. Divine revelation cannot be made except through human experience, and it leaves no distinctive mark on the language. If God reveals Godself to us as mother, father, son, friend, judge, rescuer, light, wind, fire, and even "love," the meanings of these metaphors will be modified by the meaning that "God" has for us overall, and especially by what we know of God in Jesus; but we can only make sense of such names if we can relate them to human experience, including biblical human experience and our own. Human language has to come from human experiences rather than, say, the experiences of angels or rational fish.

Bloesch makes a similar distinction when discussing the Trinity. He argues that the traditional trinitarian titles (Father, Son, Holy Spirit) are "ontological models based on divine revelation" and thus different from, and superior to, "personal metaphors originating in cultural experience." The problem is that his distinction is not visible in these names, which are all metaphors, derived initially from human family life and the intangibility of wind and breath. Bloesch's distinction comes perilously close to the view that if God said, "I am Galumphy, nardy, ablodic, and murbing in every respect," and we could establish this beyond doubt as divine revelation, we would have to say that we believed it and adore, even though we could make no sense of what was thus "revealed."

Bloesch's view is only tenable if we put the Bible in a separate box from other uses of language and argue that human experience is here uniquely overruled by divine intervention. This is a widely held view, but there is nothing in biblical God-language to support claims that its metaphors, similes, concepts, and analogies come from anything other than the culture and experience of the human writer or speaker. Faced with the marvelous variety of biblical God-images, we are bound to make judgments as to which reveal more, and which reveal less, and what patterns emerge from the mosaic. We may legitimately look for *theological* guidelines (such as our understanding of Jesus' life, death, and resurrection) to help us make these judgments. We do not, however, find an explicit ranking of names and metaphors in biblical language itself.

Biblical God-Talk

In their own way, biblical voices know that all naming of God is indirect. In the most anthropomorphic passage, Moses is not permitted to see God's face, only his back (Exod. 33:23). Isaiah of Jerusalem sees YHWH enthroned, but describes only the skirts of his robe (Isa. 6:1), whereas Isaiah 31:3 implies that God is by nature not flesh but spirit. Ezekiel sees a human form, with "what might have been brass," glowing like fire from the waist upward, and "what looked like fire with encircling radiance" from the waist downward, "like a rainbow in the clouds on a rainy day," and says of it, with threefold reticence, that it was "the *likeness* of the *appearance* of the *glory* of YHWH" (Ezek. 1:27–28).

Biblical voices are more at home with imagery than definitions, but their approximations to the latter keep a wide distance between human and divine. God does not vacillate as human beings do (1 Sam. 15:29). Human judges may be corruptible (for example, 1 Sam. 8:3), but the judge of all the earth will do what is just (Gen. 18:25). God's love is everlasting (Ps. 100:5), though Israel's disperses like morning mist (Hos. 6:4).

Having established this distance between human and divine, biblical voices nonetheless draw on a great variety of human experiences to depict God's nature and action. From our experience of nature and the animal world come images of God as a sun, whose voice is like a thunder or a mighty torrent, whose spirit is like the wind, and whose justice and wisdom are like the deep ocean and an irrigating river. God is a rock, a spring, a shield, a fortress, or a devouring fire, who pounces on Israel as a panther, lion, leopard, or bear, carries them on eagles' wings, and protects them like nestlings. From human life God is depicted as a potter, builder, farmer, shepherd, hero, warrior, doctor, judge, midwife, bird-catcher, woman in labor, king, husband, and father. In language drawn from the human body, God is said to have a head, face, eyes, eyelids, ears, nostrils, mouth, voice, arm, hand, palm, fingers, foot, heart, bosom, and bowels.

Such expressions need careful evaluation, since some are dead metaphors and linguistic conventions like "to the face of," meaning "before," and "in the eyes of," meaning "in the estimation of." But the language of action, also drawn inescapably from human experience, is even more important. It can be said that God sees, hears, speaks, calls, whistles, wounds, heals, and fights; or rescues, guides, guards, makes and unmakes, plans, appoints, and sends; or shows patience, generosity, jealousy, anger, regret, hatred, pleasure, and scorn.[30]

God-language in Second Isaiah

From the Babylonian exile comes a useful case study, in the outstanding work of a Hebrew poet-theologian who emphasizes the distance between God and humanity yet depicts God in a host of images drawn from human experience. At the beginning of his work, "Second Isaiah" (Isa. 40–55) asks, rhetorically, "What likeness will you find for God, and what form to resemble his?" (Isa.

40:18). It is not only carved images that are inadequate, for nothing and no one can be likened to God or set up as God's equal (40:19–25). The prophecy ends with the conviction that God's thoughts and ways are as high above ours as heaven is above earth, which does not mean a moon shot's length or a galaxy away, but— in ancient picture language—an almost infinite distance, which even Babel builders cannot hope to cross (Isa. 55:8, cf. Gen. 11:1–9).

In between, the prophet uses a variety of metaphors and similes to speak of God's nature and action. The incomparable God, for whom no likeness is adequate, can be freely described as tending the flock like a shepherd, carrying the lambs, and leading the ewes to water; as measuring the waters and the heavens, and weighing the mountains in a balance; as one who sits enthroned on the vaulted roof of earth, and in whose sight the inhabitants are like grasshoppers; as stretching out the skies like a curtain or tent; and as the creator, the first and the last, who tells what will be, calls the pagan Cyrus, and gives breath to all earth's people. This sublime creator also goes out like a berserk clansman rushing into battle and cries out like a woman in labor, whose birth giving lays waste mountains and hills, leading the blind on their way and turning darkness into light before them. God is the maker, the helper, Israel's king and ransompayer, carrying Israel from birth to old age, the one and only God, who makes light and creates darkness, whose own hands founded the earth and formed the expanse of the sky, the husband who acknowledges Israel once more as wife.[31]

Second Isaiah states that God has no human or earthly likeness, yet uses a great variety of metaphors and similes to show what God is like. The invisible God cannot be represented in graven images, but is freely depicted in linguistic images. This is typical of biblical God-language. Elsewhere it occurs without comment. Here it appears in the close-knit work of an articulate prophet, and it is reasonable to assume that he knew what he was doing. The apparent paradox needs interpretation, but it is noteworthy that Second Isaiah does not appear to find it paradoxical.

Second Isaiah illustrates the prime function of biblical God-language, which is to affect the imagination and evoke an active response. The biblical experience of God is not in concepts that are argued and reasoned about (though people do think and reason in its pages), but of the Holy One who encounters us and whose reality impinges on us. Like all good metaphors, biblical images "strike the imagination with a sense of intuitive certitude. . . . The image does not defend itself; no mediating interpretation stands between it and the mind."[32]

Kingship Language

Like other metaphors, biblical God-images can also organize thinking and make it possible to gain new knowledge. In the early stages of Israelite kingship, we find Saul holding court in Gibeah, sitting under a tamarisk tree on a hilltop with his spear in his hand and his retainers standing round him (1 Sam. 22:6). The court soon moves to a permanent palace, where the military bodyguard gives place to a permanent council of advisers and secretaries.

This human experience of kingship enables Micaiah-ben-Imlah to speak of God's will and purpose. In his vision, he sees YHWH seated on a throne with the host of heaven in attendance on his right hand and on his left. God discusses the earthly situation with his counselors. One says one thing, and another says another, and then a spirit comes forward and offers to go and entice King Ahab to make a disastrous attack on Ramoth-Gilead, to fulfill YHWH's decree of disaster on him (1 Kings 22:19–24).

Linguistically, this is metaphor, even though Micaiah would probably not make our distinctions between literal and nonliteral.[33] The *subject* is God's action and purpose, and the *intersecting image* is the workings of the Israelite king's council. The metaphor makes it possible to think and speak in a complex yet vivid way of God's sovereignty, purposive actions, and intervention in Israel's history. Envisioning the members of the heavenly council as spirit beings enables the prophet to suggest *how* God's purpose will be fulfilled, since a command leading to action is an early experience of cause and effect. The image also presents God as the divine king ruling the earthly one, thus cutting Ahab down to size.

This metaphorical language is not an emotive ornamentation: it does what we might try to do more abstractly, namely, understand and know God. It does not carry conviction merely because it is a powerful image, but in this instance becomes an arena for argument, when Zedekiah-ben-Kenaanah accepts the image of the heavenly council, but claims that the lying spirit has passed from him to Micaiah.

The image of the divine king with his heavenly advisers had a long history in Hebrew thought, but changed with changing times. In the great powers of Assyria and Babylon, the supreme monarch delegated powers to provincial governors and satraps. Israelite theologians, using this more complex imagery, were able to develop a coherent account of monotheism, as in Deuteronomy 32:8–9:

> *When the Most High parceled out the nations,*
> *when he dispersed all humankind,*
> *he laid down the boundaries of every people*
> *according to the number of the Sons of God;*
> *but YHWH's share was his own people,*
> *Jacob his allotted portion.*

The Most High is God, and the Sons of God are angelic satraps, appointed to rule over each nation. But no angelic deputy governs Israel, which has the direct rule and protection of the one true God. The imagery is drawn from the organization of world empires and enables this Hebrew theologian to assert the worldwide sovereignty of YHWH; distinguish between the operation of that sovereignty in Israel, where it was recognized, and pagan nations, where it was not; and do justice to the political power of pagan gods without admitting their divinity. This metaphorical system, drawn from and recharged by changing human experience, enabled Israel to develop its knowledge of God.[34]

Yet having given Israel tools to articulate its faith and experience of God, the institution of kingship was not left unchanged. There was two-way traffic between subject and intersecting image. God was imaged as king, and monotheism thus articulated and developed; but if *God* was king, then the impassioned loving justice of YHWH, who defends the poor and weak and rules with equity according to Covenant, must become the standard by which Israel's earthly kings are judged (for example, Jer. 22:13–17), the ideal to which they must aspire (Ps. 72), and the foundation of messianic hope (Isa. 11:1–9).

Conclusions and Issues

Imaginative language eludes attempts at control and definition, and this is both exhilarating and problematic. A good metaphor impacts on the imagination and suggests new possibilities. In the free space between sender and receiver, its full range of associations can neither be predicted nor prescribed. There is no point in pontificating about what metaphors like "God as father" *ought* to mean. There can be no dogmatized or delimited set of approved meanings once such metaphors enter the public domain. If a God-metaphor becomes problematic for a significant group of people, it is pointless and patronizing to tell them that they ought to understand it differently.

The problematic aspect of imaginative language is not that it eludes control and precise definition, but that it sometimes subverts thought. "The trouble with metaphors is that they have a strong pull on our fancy," says Monroe Beardsley. "They tend to run away with us. Then we find that our thinking is directed, not by the force of the argument in hand, but by the interest in the image in our mind."[35] We need precision and clear thinking, not to *govern* imaginative language, but as an equal partner to it. Sallie McFague puts it pithily: "Images feed concepts; concepts discipline images; images without concepts are blind; concepts without images are sterile."[36] One important issue is how a proper partnership between reason and imagination can be achieved in theological work. At present, the relationship is patriarchal. Theology is done by specialists and abstraction prized above imagination. Concepts are seen as the prison warders of metaphors, since the warders both try to control the prisoners and treat them as a suspect, antisocial, and hostile population.

The preceding discussion points to an important distinction. It parallels the distinction between metaphors and concepts, and I shall call it the distinction between *devotion* and *reflection*. In the devotional mode, which occupies a significant part of worship, we open ourselves to the impact of God through a variety of media, including language. The best God-metaphors are those that move us deeply and enable us to encounter or be encountered by the dynamic dance of incandescent love that Christian experience names Trinity. In the reflective mode, whether in discussion, study, dialogue, debate, or weighing what the preacher has just said, we stand back from the world, ourselves, and even our language in order to consider, question, and reason. This distinction is important, and I shall return to it.

If biblical language is not a Turin shroud marked by divine laser light, we have to find nonlinguistic reasons for deciding which metaphors of God reveal more than others, and how different God-metaphors and images relate to one another. Two comments are appropriate. One is that images of God in language must not become idols. However hallowed by tradition, however enriching and suggestive, however profoundly they move us, our metaphors and names for God are not themselves God. We should no more bow down and worship mental and linguistic images of God than the graven images forbidden in the Bible, or the idols of money and success. The fact that many Christians do seem to regard their God-language as directly describing God suggests that much educational and homiletic work needs to be done.

The other point is that the meaning of God-metaphors, and their revelatory value, change over time. Metaphors that once generated important insights lose their capacity to surprise us and change their meanings as society changes. Metaphors of divine kingship once permitted crucial moves toward monotheism and set standards for Israel's government. Yet for a contemporary society to image God as an all-male absolute ruler makes God a patriarchal idol, is out of tune with our knowledge of the universe, and does not adequately portray God's love in Jesus Christ. I shall develop these points in Part III.

What the best God-metaphors do (though they may do more) is express the impact God has on us and point to important qualities of relationship. If I speak of "my mother, Mabel," I can communicate two inseparable yet distinguishable aspects of her: her unique personality (appearance, voice, London accent, temperament, and life story) and the quality of relationship we have with each other, her supportive *mothering* of me.

If I then speak of my friend Angela as a "motherly person" and tell you no more, I am pointing to one aspect of her temperament and giving—I hope—reliable knowledge of her. But I am doing so only by linking her with other experiences of "motherliness," not by a description that shows who and what she uniquely is.

If I speak of God as my Mother, or as like a mother, I am using language closer to Angela-talk than Mabel-talk. I am (I hope) giving reliable knowledge of God, but the metaphor or simile cannot pin down who and what God uniquely is. Even if I pile metaphor on metaphor and call God rock, water, fire, father, sister, midwife, friend, what I am describing is God's impact on us and qualities of relationship we can experience with the divine. My best language will be like a finger pointing at the moon, and I shall be foolish indeed if I confuse the moon with my finger. To say that God "literally is our Mother (or Father or Friend)," or to claim that God must be thought of and addressed in no other way, would be to misunderstand how metaphors and similes work. If it meant anything, it would mean we were making metaphors into idols.

If our experience of God changes, new metaphors will be needed to express new qualities of relationship, and this is exciting and risky because changing a metaphor changes its meaning. To take a secular example, if we think of the nation as the *body politic*, one implication is that if the ruler (its head) is cut off, the body will die, which means that rebellion is out of the question. If we see it as the *ship of state*, on the other hand, it is our right and duty to depose an incompetent captain.[37]

An example of a God-metaphor ripe for change is found in Hosea 2:2–23, a metaphorical series with the common intersecting image of the relationship between a loving husband and an unfaithful wife, the subject being the relationship between YHWH and Israel. When I realize that I live in a society in which men subordinate women and that God does not intend this or wish it to continue, Hosea's imagery presents problems. For it was drawn from human experience in a patriarchal society and assumes a relationship in which the husband rules the wife, and is entitled to punish or forgive her, because she is destined for subordination. Such assumptions give a distorted model for relationships between women and men, and it is doubtful whether they can helpfully model God's love relationship with us.

Some theologians ask us to "demythologize" such metaphors, by which is meant translating them into contemporary philosophical categories. Others speak of "remythologizing," intending to retain the impact and vividness of metaphor, but substituting new metaphors for old. The first suggestion is a blind alley, for the

Bible is mistreated if its imagery is filtered into abstractions. The second suggestion has unfortunate terminology, since for many people the word *myth* is inseparably associated with "falsehood." I prefer to look for a *reimaging*, innovative yet faithful to the revelatory roots of the original. In Hosea 2:2–23, for example, we could retell the story with God as the faithful wife and the church as the unfaithful husband, since the original metaphor has a positive image of one partner, committed to the other, whose love endures hurt and disloyalty, and who longs to mend the broken relationship. In subsequent chapters I shall suggest guidelines for reimaging and share examples.

Part III

Knowing and Naming Anew

The Gallery exhibit on the following pages is an indispensable introduction to this section. Through the literary convention of an extraterrestrial observer, it shows that the metaphor system of divine kingship still dominates the God-language of contemporary worship.[1] Chapter 5 shows how close this God-image comes to the patriarchal idol sketched out earlier (see the Gallery following Chapter 2) and suggests warrants and guidelines for reimaging. Chapters 6 to 8 explore new names and metaphors, looking at God and creation, the maleness of Jesus, and the experience of God as Trinity. The final chapter suggests some consequences for faith and practice, and the Epilogue revisits the language of divine kingship and asks how it is best dealt with if retained.

Gallery: The Roq:un Fragment—An Extraterrestrial Looks at Earthly Hymnody

On the bus to London airport I became aware that my neighbor was not human. Though indistinguishable in a crowd, there was something about the set of the shoulders and the sharply defined nose that gave a strong impression of alienness. We struck up a conversation and discovered that we were both bound for New York, that "her" name was Art-Xela, and that "she" (our pronouns don't really fit) was an anthropologist from the planet Roq:un, many light years from Earth.

Art-Xela's project was a survey of Earth's major religious faiths, the current phase being English-speaking Christianity. She admitted to being tired and depressed, having spent the previous two weeks reading the first 328 hymn texts in a recent British hymnal. By contrast with our best theology, which to Roq:unian eyes seemed profound and beautiful, the way we name and praise God in worship appeared crude and one-sided. As we touched down in New York, Art-Xela made an extraordinary gesture of friendship by giving me the transcript of her most recent transmission home.

So it was that I came to possess a copy of the Roq:un Fragment. Though limited to British hymnody, it is doubtful whether research elsewhere would show significant differences. Be on your guard: Art-Xela may even now be in your congregation.

Note: The fragment is a memorandum to home base on Roq:un (the "q:" is a Roq:unian sound approximating a tongue click and a gulp; pronunciation of other symbols is uncertain). Gender on Roq:un is a fluctuating system untranslatable into Earth concepts. The form "G-d" is Art-Xela's rendering, since Roq:unians do not pronounce divine names.

Sol III Cultic Survey—Unasked Partword No. 6001

FROM: Art-Xela Irrt"Serrett II, Seeker.
To: Gre-Ble-Ipsn"eh-Petsã, Collector, Airo"eP City 250-61B,
        Roq:un

Embraced Sister-Son,

The air of Sol-III flows heavily round me. I am obliged to walk or use human transport, even when unobserved, and my spirit aches for the free air of home. Wearily I complete my introductory survey of the G-d worshipped by British Christians. I am discouraged; please Empathize.

Previous researchers gave high cloudsong about the Christian conception of G-d, reporting that the divine beauty was seen as "trinity"—one g-dhead in three coequal, distinct, yet united centers of personhood, whose wings hovered over creation at the beginning, and who creates all life forms on Sol-III. The human species, in its two fixed genders (see Partword 0005), is believed to be created, as a partnership, in the likeness of the Divine Complexity. These advanced conceptions, arising from a species so limited in gender possibilities, excited my appetite for more knowledge.

Imagine, then, my disappointment at the true outlines of the terrain. My enquiry hovers over hymnody, alighting on three branches of evidence: a recent British hymnal, the most frequently chosen hymns in a popular television program, and ancient prayers, creeds, and praises still frequently used in Christian worship.

Hymns and Psalms—a Methodist and Ecumenical Hymnbook is the most recent denominational hymnal published in the British Isles, with 823 hymnic entries, plus canticles and psalms (Methodist Publishing House, London, England, Sol-III year C. E. 1983). The book's structure is:

Part 1—G-d's Nature	Hymns 1–328 (Total—328)
G-d's Being and Majesty	1–20
The Eternal Father	21–73
The Eternal Word	74–278
The Eternal Spirit	279–328
Part 2—G-d's World	Hymns 329–432 (Total—104)
Part 3—G-d's People	Hymns 433–823 (Total—391)

Time prevented me circling over the entire work. I therefore limited observation to the 328 hymn texts of Part 1. Since they account for over one-third of the book and sing directly about G-d's
nature, they probably give an accurate small view of the whole.

Names, Titles, and Pronouns

I began by sighting and gathering all the names and titles for
G-d,[1] leaving the standard title names ("G-d," "Jesus," "Holy
Spirit," etc.) aside, as it difficult to be sure what picture of G-d
they suggest.[2]

I looked first at the First Person of the Christian Trinity and
found that many hymns make no distinction between the First
Person and the g-dhead as a whole. The images for the First Person seem to stand for the g-dhead par excellence, the basic or
original image of G-d, to which was added the belief that the
Second Person is also G-d, as is the Third Person. For example,
seven occurrences of "Father" clearly refer to the whole g-dhead,
not the First Person alone.

I found 290 different names for G-d the First Person. However, 14 are found only once, another 8 twice only, and a further 5
occur thrice each. Though G-d can be called Formless and Eternal (once), Friend, Light, and Defender (twice), and Sun or Wisdom (three times), such beautiful names are marginal to human
understanding. I found only 4 Loves, 6 Makers, and 7 Shep-
herds, but 12 Almightys, 34 Kings, 91 Fathers, and 87 Lords.[3]

Two aspects of this catch the eye. First, though the human
species lives in two fixed genders, G-d is seen only in images
from the male. The score is: male images of G-d—76.5 percent,
female images—none. Second, the great majority of names are
associated with males who wield power over others—no less than
81 percent. The First Person of the Trinity, and the whole
g-dhead, is seen as a male being who rules over everything.[4]

Names and titles for the Second Person of the Trinity are
more numerous and varied, 816 in all. In trinitarian *theology* a
distinction is made between the eternal, soaring, dynamic Word,
the Second Person of the Trinity, far beyond the shackles of human gender, and the Word's grounded manifestation as "flesh" in
the male human, Jesus of Nazareth. Such distinctions leave no
trace on hymnody, where the Second Person is seen and spoken
to as male.

There is a beautiful variety in some of these names. G-d in
Jesus is Wonderful, the Way, Bridegroom, and Crown (one each);

Feast, Heart, Rock, and Spring (twice each); Joy, Friend, and Truth (3–6 times); and Light (12), Life (11), Lamb (21), and Love (16). Even so, there is a similar concentration on maleness and on power understood as the strength to rule over others. I gathered 105 Saviors, but also 140 Kings and 262 Lords. Male titles accounted for 64.5 percent of the total, and titles of power as rule for 62 percent. There were surprisingly few names and titles for the suffering, humility, and peaceful equality of Jesus—what Earth theologians call servanthood. Since this is said to be centrally important, I expected to find many references to it and at first thought that some must have gone undercover. Yet, turn and whirl as I might, I could only find 174 names that clearly spoke of this—a mere 21 percent of the whole.[5]

When humans speak of the Third Person of the Trinity, they almost breathe Roq:unian air. The Spirit is the Breath of God, the Dove, Guest, Comforter, and Guide.[6] The Third Person is often spoken of in terms of *activity,* given adjectives like Gracious, Truthful, Mighty, and Loving, or designations like Spirit of life, truth, power, health, faith, refining fire, light, purity, or grace. However, the Spirit is always spoken of as male, as we shall see.

I next surveyed the pronouns used for G-d. The English language is limited to three pronoun forms: feminine (female gender), masculine (male gender), and neuter (ungendered). Christian theology has ascended to the recognition that G-d is genderless yet "personal" (that is, more than what humans know as personality, but never less). Thus, the neuter pronoun is considered inappropriate for G-d. If female and male humans were really believed to be created as an equal partnership in the divine image, one would expect to find both feminine and masculine pronouns chosen for divine action. This is not so. In the 177 texts carrying pronouns, there are 1,423 pronouns for the divine. One is neuter, none are feminine, and 1,422 are masculine. The First Person of the Trinity has 432, the Second has 950, and the Third has 41 (40 masculine, 1 neuter).

We know that human languages (like our own) draw on the experience of their speakers and blow powerful updraughts or downdraughts on thought and behavior. The fact that the genderless Trinity is prayed to and depicted in exclusively male images and pronouns must give humans a hooded or one-eyed vision of G-d.

Of the three Persons, the Holy Spirit is the least likely to be seen in terms of human gender. Yet a striking feature of these texts is the way the Spirit becomes masculinized. The Holy Spirit section has 49 hymns, of which 13 carry pronouns. There is one text in which the Spirit is neuter; one with the Holy Spirit and Christ, both masculine; one with the Holy Spirit and the Father, both masculine; four with all three Persons of the Trinity, all masculine; and six with the Holy Spirit alone, all masculine. There are approximately five other texts where the Spirit is given male plumage, either by the use of male titles (Lord, Father of the Poor) or by close association with the Father and Son, where phrases like "Spirit *of* the Father" and "Spirit *of* the Son" suggest that the Spirit is their male or masculine essence.

Metaphors for G-d

To glide only over titles and pronouns might be misleading, since the texts have many rich *metaphors* for G-d and divine action. I therefore studied all 328 texts for the main metaphors used. Noting that many depict G-d as a kingly figure, receiving homage, I listed all such metaphors, whether well developed, less developed, or presupposed.[7] As with the titles and pronouns, the most frequent metaphor is of God as a dominant male, a king who rules and gives commands. Approximately 190 hymns (60 percent of those giving G-d images) have strong imagery of rule, and many others presuppose it.

Thus, though there are other rich metaphors, the dominant metaphor system is KINGAFAP—*the King-G-d-Almighty-Father-Protector. God is pictured, worshipped, and encountered by the human imagination as follows.*

A Powerful King, seated on a high throne, receives homage and tribute from prostrate, beseeching subjects and praise from human and angelic choirs. The King rules by word of command, and his decrees protect his subjects and stabilize the cosmic order. The King is all-powerful, awesome and terrifying, yet also merciful. As King, he is also Father, meaning that he is the origin of all things, humanity's lordly and merciful male parent, and the Father of his own Son (see below).[8] The King is mighty, sometimes called All-mighty. His power is shown in making the world by a word of command, and by triumphing in battle over enemies. The "enemies" are supposed to be evil tendencies in each human, but human antagonists often claim that G-d is on their side in human wars. The King is also the supreme Judge, with power of life and death over his subjects, but it is believed that his last word is mercy and love.

The King has a son, the Crown Prince, who sits beside him. At his father's bidding, the Prince steps down from his throne and surrenders his royal power and privileges. He descends to earth and is born as a male human child. When he grows up he shows the King's love, cares for outcasts, announces the King's advent to the chosen people, is betrayed to the authorities and crucified. The crucifixion is often depicted as a battle with sin, death, and the devil. The Prince Royal lies dead, but is lifted up to life by his Kingly Father. There are two versions of what happens next. In a few hymns the Prince takes his human experience of humility and suffering forever into the being of G-d. This is a minority view, for in most texts the impression given is that the Prince *leaves behind* his suffering, humiliated, humble state, comes back to the throne, and waits till he can return to earth with supernatural power, fight and slay his enemies, and receive tribute and homage from everyone.[9] He is often portrayed as a Judge who will come with awesome power at the end of the world.

Meanwhile, *the King and Prince (Father and Son) send their Spirit down to earth,* to help their followers and occasionally do good in the world as well.

A minority of texts explore different images. "As the bridegroom to his chosen" (30) has twenty different similes exploring what the Second Person means to the believer. "Lead, kindly light" (67) sees G-d as a light guiding the believer, one step at a time, over "moor and fen . . . crag and torrent, till the night is gone." In "Now the green blade riseth" (204), Jesus' death and resurrection are explored through the metaphor of a seed buried in the ground, which grows "like the risen grain." Some of the greatest hymn writers soar above KINGAFAP even as they echo it. Charles Wesley sings of G-d's "sovereign grace" for which the believer's heart is the "throne," but then upsounds the divine love in metaphors that would bring an answering song in the altitudes of our own planet, calling it "immense and unconfined" and "infinitely wide," as it "extends" and "never ends" ("What shall I do my G-d to love?"—46). Elsewhere he speaks of the love that "reigns" throughout the universe in terms of the oceans so characteristic of his planet: it is "ceaseless, unexhausted love," a "vast unfathomable sea where all our thoughts are drowned" (48). Yet such explorations are rare and do not challenge the dominance of the KINGAFAP metaphor *system.*

Other Sources

To determine whether this limited picture of G-d is a crosswind, or part of the main airstream of Christianity, I alighted briefly on two other sources.

"Songs of Praise" is a television program presented every seven earth days on the major national network, BBC-1. Large groups of Christians gather to sing the favorite hymns of some of their number, who explain their choice. Whereas *Hymns and Psalms* shows what its compilers think Methodists want to sing, a program such as this indicates which hymns are most popular among the main flock of British Christians. I obtained the 137 hymns most frequently chosen in a ten-year period (approximately 1976–85).[10] There were well-developed KINGAFAP metaphors in 46 of the texts, visible but less developed examples in a further 21 and evidence that the KINGAFAP system was presupposed in 34 more. In other words, 75 percent of the most popular hymns express or presuppose the KINGAFAP system. Clear alternative images are found in only 26 (19 percent), of which 5 are about the Holy Spirit.[11]

How did the human species come to worship the divine Trinity in terms of this one dominant metaphor system, so male-centered, so permeated with language of domination? Until quite recently, most human societies were ruled by male monarchs (kings). I assumed that early Christians would inevitably think of G-d in terms of their powerful human ruler, that kings themselves would encourage this, and that the experience of kings causing things to happen by giving orders to subordinates would make it possible to conceive of G-d creating the universe in like manner, by uttering a Word of command.

A glance at some ancient Christian hymns and prayers confirms my hypothesis and shows how ancient is the KINGAFAP system.[12] The Gloria in Excelsis sees Jesus Christ seated at the right hand of his Father, the Heavenly King, Almighty G-d, giving mercy and peace to his earthly subjects. The Apostles' Creed speaks of G-d the Father Almighty, whose only Son is born, suffers, is crucified, goes down to the dead, rises again up to heaven, sits at the Father's right hand, and will come again to judge living and dead. The Nicene Creed elaborates the same story, but says more about the Son's eternal relationship with the Father, and the Spirit as "proceeding" from them both. The Te Deum shows all creation giving homage to the Father-King, "of majesty unbounded," and of Christ "the king of glory," seated at his Father's right hand.

Conclusion

The continuous flightline between ancient and modern texts shows how tenacious is religious tradition, here as elsewhere. Yet viewing the cirrostratic beauty of trinitarian theology, and the obstinate peacefulness of Christianity's divine Nestling, a more varied pattern of metaphor should have been cultivated before now. If KINGAFAP was one metaphor system among many for encountering the divine, humans could appreciate its beauty without being grounded by its limitations. Its exclusiveness suggests that it mirrors the pattern of male dominance over females in human society.

> Let Thought take Wings,
> Art-Xela &c.

5

Dethroning Patriarchal Idols

To see and worship God through the eyes of a flawed maleness is a serious problem for Christian faith, because it puts us in danger of worshipping an idol. If our images of God are defective, it is no defense to argue that though we use male-dominance metaphors, we really think differently, since systematic language use is never "mere metaphor," but slants and angles thinking and behavior.

Nor can we excuse defective worship-talk by pointing to the greater sophistication of our theologies. As I have argued earlier, there are important differences between the devotional and reflective modes, the former being what much of worship aims for. In the devotional mode—in a heartfelt hymn or prayer, say—we open ourselves to the impact of God on us, and much of that encounter happens across the bridge of language, though it has other bridges (music, dance, color) and depths that language cannot express.

In reflection we can stand back, to some extent, from the maleness of the classic trinitarian metaphor of Father and Son. In devotion, we turn toward God and meet God *as* "Father-and-Son": there is a direct encounter with that particular imagery, and with whatever associations it has for us. Our associations may be modified by learning what the metaphors have meant in the past, but are also affected by the way "father" and "son" resonate in our personal stories and relationships, and by the fact that the metaphors are male rather than female. It cannot be otherwise: what makes those metaphors *personal* is not just the "personhood" of God, but their echoing of human relationships. Extraterrestrial birdlike beings mating in threesomes while in flight might have a beautiful system of personal metaphors for the Trinity, but their names would not resonate in our imagination as much as those drawn from our own human relationships.

The Roq:un Fragment (see Gallery preceding this chapter) shows how the metaphor system of divine kingship dominates the God-language of Christian worship. As noted earlier, I call this system KINGAFAP (the King-God-Almighty-Father-Protector) because although some hymns stress one theme rather than another, protection, fatherliness, kingship, and omnipotence belong together in its most elaborate expressions, and in the "story line" of early Christian creeds.

Earlier in the book, I asked what kind of god a patriarchal society would worship and drew a sketch based on the analysis of patriarchy in the opening chapters (see the Gallery following Chapter 2). The KINGAFAP metaphor system does not completely conform to that sketch, since the divine King-Father is not always impassive, but gives an overall impression of deep, caring, everlasting love. At its best, KINGAFAP arouses wonder. When the shock of the original metaphor ("commanding king" intersecting with "suffering slave or servant") is retained, the news that the divine, all-powerful King could graciously accept us, humble himself, and die for us has continuing imaginative power.[1]

Yet the dominant picture in hymnody is of a god who suffers as a temporary measure. Because it is cast in story form, there has to be a *sequence*. Because the story line stays within the KINGAFAP system, the sequence is: leaves throne, suffers, comes back to throne. The weakness lies in the final part of the story: most expressions of it get so caught up in celebrating the Prince of Life's triumph over death and sin that they separate the humiliated from the exalted Christ. There are few hymns where the descent of the Prince-Son of God is seen as the permanent surrender of kingship and control.[2]

In other respects KINGAFAP bolsters patriarchal society and closely fits my sketch of a patriarchal god. The King has complete control of everything, makes the universe by word of command, and is the ultimate overseer or mon-arch, at the top of the cosmic pyramid. Human beings relate to him as to a powerful superior, by submission and obedience. Though often mitigated by a note of gladness and freedom, and by emphasis on the Holy Spirit as enabling and empowering, it is still a patriarchal over-under relationship, so ingrained in consciousness that it may be difficult to see how God could relate to us differently.

KINGAFAP has built-in overtones of coercion: kings *rule* and maintain their rule against enemies by force of arms. Sometimes the paradox of fighting against sin with "weapons" of love is maintained; frequently it is lost in the patriarchal fascination with control and conquest. Transcendence is expressed in terms of distance: God may suffer for us on earth, but is essentially invulnerable, inaccessibly above us in heaven.

Above all, God is imaged exclusively in male and masculine terms. Metaphors drawn from "feminine" qualities or female experience are few and far between and, if used, are coopted into the maleness of divine nature. It is important, for men in particular, to dwell a while on this. We grew up with it, and it probably seemed natural to meet God in and through this imagery. Of course it did: only recently have some begun to question it, and they have mostly been female. Envisaging divine energy in male terms is easy for us; we can identify with that image of God, and it quietly supports the predominance we take for granted (and feel to be under threat) in our society.

What gives the game away is not the maleness of the imagery, but its drive for hegemony. Not content with being part of a mosaic of divine metaphors, it tries to take over the floor. By nature, it must bid for control. "God *is* King," it whispers. "It says so in the Bible, and in the great Christian creeds. There is no other way laid down by which we can encounter God or God encounter us." To admit that there might be other ways, equally valid, would dethrone the patriarchal idol. Kings can't be one king among many: it goes against their nature.

God and Creation

Some of KINGAFAP's limitations are built in, others are contextual. Envisaging God as the King of creation has both sorts of limitation. Built into the metaphor is the idea of the King's absolute and detailed control of his realm: a king who loses control of his realm rules no more, and deserves no honor. Until recently, this image of God sat quite well with our knowledge of the universe.

As long as the cosmos was seen as running according to well-defined rules, we could assert faith in God as the kingly rule maker, however hidden his scepter and sword. It is impossible to reconcile KINGAFAP with evidence of randomness and chance. An unkinglike creator might say, "Let there be randomness," and enjoy surrendering control; but kings can't afford uncertainty. The metaphor of God the King no longer fits with God-given knowledge of the universe; we need other metaphors to express God's relationship with chance and change.

KINGAFAP is also problematic because of changes in the context in which it is used. The divine King's original subjects could not alter the fundamentals of human life. It made good sense for them to worship God as the King on whom they relied utterly—to send the rain in season, keep back the chaotic forces of nature (expressed and symbolized in Hebrew thought by the sea), govern nature and history, and bring human life on earth to its appointed end. The God-King could be trusted to keep the cosmic order intact, "while the earth remains," and the rainbow was a sign of that promise. There was no possibility of the human species destroying the fabric of life on earth. The birds, beasts, and fish may have been ours to govern, but not the water, soil, and air. Faith that God was in control and would protect humanity against chaos was an affirmation of trust in a loving creator, in a world often threatened with chaos and destruction, both political and natural.

Today, though we still depend on the seamless fabric of air, earth, and water, most of the conditions of human life can be modified by human action, and human actions can "by stealth or conflagration, snuff out all life, and put an end to birth."[3] It is tempting, but mistaken, to draw on the Bible's end-of-the-world imagery, either to claim that nuclear holocaust could be God's will, or that God won't allow it to happen. The first claim draws on KINGAFAP, but empties divine kingship of the loving care that is its central feature, in favor of a male god-tyrant who turns against humanity and remains invulnerable to the pain and tragedy of a "spoiled, aborted, barren earth."[4] The second draws on KINGAFAP to deny the evidence that through the process of history, the divine Spirit has given human beings the power either to destroy their planetary home or tend it. The KINGAFAP metaphor system cannot deal with this new reality; we need new language to express God's love and human autonomy.[5]

KINGAFAP and Kingship

"Kings are justly called gods, for they exercise a manner or resemblance of divine power on earth." The speaker is King James I of England (James VI of Scotland) in the seventeenth century. He goes on to compare God's power to create or destroy, and judge all yet be judged by none, with the absolute power he himself claimed. As one God rules the world, said John Hayward in 1603, one master governs the family, and one head governs and controls the human body, "so it seemeth no less natural, that one state should be governed by one commander." Others drew a different conclusion: if God is king then all are set free from human lordship. "We are of such a kingdom whereof not man but God is our king," said Paul Bayne. To Gerrard Winstanley, Christ was the great leveler, who had cast out kingly power to make England a free commonwealth. The Quaker James Parnel declared, "Amongst us there are no superiors after the flesh, but Christ is the head. . . . Here God alone is the king and he alone is honoured, exalted and worshipped."[6]

KINGAFAP's record is ambiguous. If God is King, opposite conclusions can be drawn: either all are free and equal under God's authority, or all should obey the human monarch God has appointed. The Hebrew prophets made messianic kingship language a judgment on existing kings and the expression of hope for a just social order. Jesus, the servant free from servitude, created a community calling God "Father," which must therefore renounce the human hierarchies whose rulers have themselves lauded as "benefactors" (Matt. 20:24–28, Luke 22:24–27). Early Christians risked persecution for confessing that Christ was "Lord" and praying *for*, rather than *to*, the emperor.

Yet when Christianity won the emperor's recognition, its KINGAFAP vocabulary suited perfectly the Hellenistic philosophy of kingship. God is the King of earth and heaven, said the former. As God is to the cosmos, so the king is to the state, and the divine Logos indwells the king, helping him to be a good shepherd to his people, said the latter. The cult of emperor worship was refocused on Christ, who in return crowned the emperor as his earthly deputy and validated his rule. Christ "assumed the outward marks of imperial rank; he was the ruler who sat on a throne adorned with jewels and purple cushions, who wore the royal halo, whose foot and hand were kissed, who was surrounded with a heavenly cortege of palace officials." In retrospect, "the Christ of the Eastern Church looks all too like the Hellenistic king, exalted to heaven to become the ideological basis of the Christian Empire; and the Christ of the Western Church looks like one who died to seal the authority of the patriarchal family as a model for the organization of church and state."[7]

One factor in KINGAFAP's political "ups and downs" is the social position of those who appeal to it. When Christian groups are excluded from political power, divine kingship stands against unjust authority and champions the oppressed. When they join the power structure and see themselves as stabilizing it, the same metaphor system becomes "a language to sacralize dominant authorities and to preach revenge against former enemies."[8]

As in the previous section, KINGAFAP's problems are both contextual and built in. The fundamental associations of KINGAFAP are rule, authority, command, and a response of submission and obedience. To see God as the *liberating* sovereign—as do Jesus and others before and since—is a radical departure, an injection of new meanings not easily absorbed. In its original context, the metaphor of the "crucified king" had the shock of the unexpected, as is clear from Paul's sense of the foolishness of the cross in 1 Corinthians 1, where he contrasts human wisdom and power with God's wise folly and empowering powerlessness. A crucified messiah was a stumbling block to Jews and an absurd contradiction to educated gentiles. When that shock wears off, or is lost, the patriarchal pyramidism of the metaphors reasserts itself: it is neither marginal nor optional, but central to their normal usage in patriarchal society.

The Almighty King in Wartime

Christian praise to *"Almighty* God" may sound harmless in peacetime, but it becomes problematic in time of war. G. A. Studdert-Kennedy was a British army chaplain in World War I. Beloved by the front-line soldiers, he worked out his theology in poetry and essays written amid shellfire, mud, and ministry to the wounded and dying. His experiences made him question traditional ideas of God's omnipotence. If God really is a god of power and might, then the German emperor (Kaiser Wilhelm II) was right to claim that God was on his side. "If God be absolutely Almighty, then He *is* with him, and was when he declared war." For a God of dominating might must value domination and want us to worship conquest and control. If God is indeed "Almighty," the Kaiser is God's true worshipper: "He believes in power, patiently makes himself powerful, and then puts power to the test. If he loses, then it must be because he is not powerful enough, and must set to work again. In the end power must prevail, for that is God's will in the world."[9]

Studdert-Kennedy's experience of war, and of God's love in Jesus, together convinced him that "Almighty God" is an idol. "I want to kill the Almighty God and tear Him from his throne," he writes. "Human strife is not God's method, but His problem. . . . War is the crucifixion of God, not the working of His will."[10] As with kingship, so with might, different conclusions can be drawn from the King-God's complete power over all things. Either "Almighty God" is unloving, and supports human domination and the spilling of blood in war, or he is both all-loving and all-powerful. But if so, he has the power to intervene and prevent the Nazi holocaust or Hiroshima, so that when he fails to do so, his might or his love must be in doubt.

A few lines cannot plumb the depths of this, but one comment is relevant to this book. The problems of God the Almighty and Omnipotent arise inexorably within the KINGAFAP metaphor system, which combines a patriarchal assertion of power-as-control with the contradictory claim that God is revealed in Jesus of Nazareth as self-giving love. Every metaphor has its limits; it is a common experience to hear someone say that a metaphor is being pressed too far. If this problem is insoluble within the KINGAFAP metaphor system (as I believe it is), we should ask how far it is a problem about *God*, and how far a problem that arises when the KINGAFAP system is the only source of our thinking about God. If we coin other metaphors, no doubt other problems will arise; but maybe, also, this particular problem will be seen in a new light.

Studdert-Kennedy also suggests that a commanding God goes with a submissive Christ, bowing to the will of his incomprehensible Father. I would go further and suggest that within the KINGA-FAP system, the all-powerful God-King *needs* a submissive Son, and that both are distortions. Thinking about the biblical experience of God, our earliest theologians came to the conclusion that the three "persons" of the godhead must be coequal. Christian worship can never express this while it is dominated by the KINGAFAP system. For in that system, though fathers and sons can reach adult equality, there is a built-in inequality between a king and the prince that KINGAFAP cannot resolve. If trinitarian faith is to be more adequately sung and experienced, we need new metaphors to express the equality, mutuality, and dynamism of trinitarian relationships.

Guidelines for Innovation

I have argued that our traditional picture of God is, in large measure, a patriarchal idol; shown that KINGAFAP is the dominant metaphor system of Christian worship; and begun a critique of it. Yet all the while we face a mountainous problem: this metaphor system permeates the Bible and the great Christian creeds. The patriarchal idol is no local infection we can treat with the antibiotics of traditional theology. It permeates the central symbol system of Christian faith, the very language that bears Christian revelation.

Faced with this problem, some claim that the KINGAFAP system, being biblical, must be accepted as normative. Others say farewell to the Bible and Christian tradition, as being irredeemably patriarchal. My hunch is that many Christians are unhappy with such choices and would like to find a way forward that is innovative yet recognizably faithful to Christian revelation.

Finding such a way means making choices within the Bible and Christian tradition and explaining and sharing them. In my understanding, the language and imagery of the Bible have a classic claim on us. We do not decide to speak of God in any way we like, without reference to that tradition. The Bible has to remain our indispensable point of reference, because it records the Jewish and Christian discovery of, and wrestling with, the true and living God.

Yet the Bible's language and imagery cannot control or restrict us, for three reasons. First, biblical language reflects the experience of its time and culture, which was, among other things, pre-scientific, largely rural, and unquestioningly patriarchal. Our experience and context are different. Second, all revelation is impeded by sin, and one of the sins of the society through which our classic revelation came is that it was a patriarchal society, with a continuing tussle between KINGAFAP power-talk and a questioning and critique of it. Finally, as that sentence suggests, the biblical tradition itself is marked by frequent self-criticism and innovation. By the present-day activity of God, as Holy Spirit, the biblical story should itself offer guidelines for deciding which God-metaphors are fitting, unfitting, illuminating, and misleading. One of the oldest things we know about God is that God does new things.

In a book trying to develop a line of argument, it is convenient to set out guidelines and illustrate them. This format does not mean that reason and reflection come first, or that they rule over imagination and creative work. As a hymn poet, I revitalize images and invent new ones. The guidelines are partly clear before a given prayer or hymn is written, partly clarified afterward, and partly realized in the act of creation. Creative work is an equal partner with conceptual work, and each helps the other. My guidelines, and how adequately I follow them, will be fully apparent when the work is done. What follows now is a sketch of guidelines that have emerged as I tack to and fro between hymn writing and theological reflection.

My first guideline comes from the Bible's apparently contradictory attitude toward images. Central to the Hebrew-Christian encounter with God is the conviction that the living God cannot be represented in any three-dimensional shape or form. God is beyond our imaging and our imagination.[11]

Yet this conviction is accompanied by the use of a considerable variety of God-images in the shapes and forms of language. I have already noted this apparent paradox and pointed to Second Isaiah as a classic example. Biblical faith forbids tangible graven images, but revels in a variety of intangible linguistic ones. Since the Bible does not itself interpret this phenomenon, we have to make sense of it as best we can. My provisional interpretation is that graven images (statues, paintings, and the like) were suspect because they are more fixed and final than linguistic images. They also seem to locate and limit God, and as such were felt to be incompatible with God's holiness, unboundedness, and presence in and beyond all things.

Linguistic images are more fleeting and leave room for the imagination. We cannot speak of God except in images or negatives, and the latter have never been sufficient for Hebrew-Christian experience. In the best-known hymn of this type, negatives such as "immortal," "invisible," "inaccessible," "unresting," and "unhasting" are only satisfying in counterpoint with the KINGAFAP language of "Almighty," "victorious," "Father of glory," and "Ancient of days."[12]

No image is adequate. To select one image and bow down to it is idolatrous. If we draw on a variety of God-images and let them balance, enrich, and clash with one another, we shall be following the instincts of biblical faith and the methods of many biblical voices.[13] Allowing God-images to *clash* is important, because it reminds us that we are approaching that which is beyond all images.[14]

Another important clue is the way biblical God-images function. Though biblical voices think with their imagery, as for example in their imagery of kingship (see above, Chapter 4), the main purpose of the linguistic image is to express the impact of the living God on the person who speaks. God is beyond all imaging, but God's holy and impassioned otherness strikes sparks from the anvil of our imagination and experience, and those sparks register linguistically as similes and metaphors.

It therefore seems true to biblical faith to use *strong and vivid* God-images, in considerable *variety*. Then we can let each image have full impact on our imagination before moving on to another, which may connect or clash with it.

My second guideline is the liberating *direction* of divine action in the biblical record. I am not talking of automatic upward progress, for new moves can be followed by the reassertion of old ways. Nonetheless, it is fair to speak of a direction of divine action, seeking to undermine and overthrow patriarchal structures. God meets us as one who loves with awesome passion, persistent and searching, yet never manipulative or coercive. The King abandons his throne, calls his disciples friends, and washes their feet. The Spirit creates a community uniting gentiles and Jews, slaves and free citizens, in which there is a brief glimpse of women exercising leadership with men.

These moves toward a community based on mutual love rather than authority structure are antipatriarchal, as is God's repeated option for the poor, downtrodden, excluded, and oppressed. This begins with the choice of a small, enslaved people in pharaoh's Egypt. It continues as the prophets assert the covenant rights of the poor against the oppression of kings, merchants, and corrupt judges. It is a central theme in the ministry of Jesus, as he welcomes and makes friends of people excluded or subordinated in his own society and issues God's open invitation to them. It finds expression in the church, in both preaching and practice, for several centuries.[15]

It would be consistent with this liberating direction of divine activity to speak of God in metaphors that suggest dynamic energy, creating community, affirming the equality of all human beings, and persisting in active, uncoercive love. Since God makes an option for the oppressed and excluded, and meets us in our oppressed or impoverished neighbor, many powerful God-metaphors are likely to come from the experience of subordinated, oppressed, and excluded people in our own time.

The liberating direction of divine activity is my warrant for reimaging, for the biblical tradition is itself self-critical and innovative. Its keynote is not "Look back and do what the fathers did," but "Behold, I am doing a new thing." There is continuity, of course, since a new thing always needs precedents from the past. But there is also discontinuity, creativity, and exploration. To intersect "suffering servant" with "triumphant messiah" was one such innovation, and the record shows others. Being true to that liberating, innovative feature of biblical tradition means not photocopying what Jesus and the first disciples said and did, but pushing forward in the direction they point. If what they said and did was right in their own context, what is right for us will in some ways be different, because our context is different.

To put it parabolically, when we encounter the world of the Bible, we are like a group of explorers moving through an uncharted land. One day we find a trail and explore it. We deduce that it was made by a bygone people, detect where it began and where it ended, and trace a number of parallel paths, with side trails arriving at dead ends. Despite uncertainties, the general direction of those bygone explorers is clear, and we become convinced that the old trail is crucially important to our own quest.

There is no certainty about the exact course we should take if we move on from where they left off. Yet move on we must, since being true to the old explorers means pushing on in the direction they were taking, not settling down at their last campsite.

My third guideline is the doctrine of the Trinity. New imaging should aim to be consistent with it, because it is a unifying core of Christian tradition, based on the scriptural experience of God, to which almost all Christians can relate. Trinitarian experience is unique to Christianity. Though formed within the KINGA-FAP metaphor system, it broke through it, to see God not as a single, isolated being, the mon-arch, but as a complex, coequal unity in relatedness. The Christian experience of God as Trinity is implicitly antipatriarchal and a rich resource.

Parent Me, O Great Sustainer?

My first guideline puts question marks against a common move toward "inclusive language," in which supposedly neutral terms are substituted for masculine ones, and "Father" becomes "Parent," the "Son of God" becomes "Child of God," "Lord" and "King" become "Sovereign One," and "Father, Son, and Holy Spirit" become "Creator, Redeemer, and Sustainer." The aim is to move beyond male God-images and avoid the controversy that would be inevitable if monarchic language was abandoned, or female metaphors set alongside male.

The aims are commendable, but monarchic language does not cease to be patriarchal if kings turn into sovereigns instead of queens. Jesus the child of God suggests a continuing infant-parent relationship and loses the possibilities of coequality available (despite its masculinity) in "Son and Father." "Creator, Redeemer, and Sustainer" are functions of each person of the Trinity (the First Person is all three at once, as are the Second and Third), so the formula collapses God's distinctive threesomeness into a single being performing three functions. There is good evidence that the secular use of supposedly neutral imagery does not in fact move us away from sexism in language,[16] which suggests that in many minds "Sovereign" may be just as masculine as "Lord." Most important of all, biblical imagery is vivid and related to experience, not bleached and faded by jargon. "Parent me, O great Sustainer, as I traverse the alienating institutions of industrial society" is no substitute for "Guide me, O thou great Jehovah, pilgrim through this barren land."

I cannot deal with the problem of biblical translation, but suggest that for other aspects of worship there are two complementary ways forward. One is to make a point of using a much greater variety of names and titles for God, following the guidelines suggested above. Experiment and innovation will eventually suggest alternative metaphor systems that model the living God more helpfully than KINGAFAP. Poets, worship leaders, and systematic theologians have important work to do, in dialogue with each other.[17]

The other way forward is to raise the issue of patriarchy in our congregations, ensure that the nature of God-talk is better understood, and explore alternatives. As I argue in Chapter 6, encountering God in female terms is, for us, and in our particular era, an essential part of that exploration. *How* we encourage that encounter is important. It is wrong to do so, patriarchal fashion, by imposing it from the top or dumping radically new God-language on an unsuspecting congregation in the middle of worship. Yet it is important to face controversy, not hope to go on avoiding it. The impassioned resistance to the very idea of speaking of God in female terms is linked with patriarchal culture's disvaluing of the "feminine." If the structure of patriarchy, and its disvaluing of the "feminine," are brought to light, I suspect that some will reaffirm the patriarchal order, but that many will be willing to follow the implications of their conviction that women and men are created as coequals in the image of God.

As one writer suggests, a congregational study could help everyone move forward by encouraging women to describe their experience of motherhood, childbirth, nurturing, and lovemaking and ask how their experience helps us to know God. Men could be encouraged to express their perceptions of women in their lives and search for "feminine" attributes within themselves. Women and men could write prayers, poetry, and hymns searching for new ways of naming God. A final step would be to introduce female imagery (in simile form if metaphor is felt to be too direct) in worship, drawing on the work of several members of the congregation.[18]

Conclusion

I have suggested three guidelines for reimaging God that can claim innovative faithfulness to biblical tradition: the importance of variety, and of strong images that both balance and clash with each other; the liberating direction of divine love, which moves toward freedom and community by a continuing option for the excluded and oppressed; and the experience of God that led to the doctrine of the Trinity. In the following pages I follow these guidelines and reflect further on them, while sharing some of my own attempts at reimaging.

Gallery: Songs of God and Creation

Bring Many Names*

Bring many names, beautiful and good;
celebrate, in parable and story,
    holiness in glory,
    living, loving God.
Hail and Hosanna,
bring many names:

Strong mother God, working night and day,
planning all the wonders of creation,
    setting each equation,
    genius at play:
Hail and Hosanna,
strong mother God!

Warm father God, hugging every child,
feeling all the strains of human living,
    caring and forgiving
    till we're reconciled:
Hail and Hosanna,
warm father God!

Old, aching God, grey with endless care,
calmly piercing evil's new disguises,
    glad of good surprises,
    wiser than despair:
Hail and Hosanna,
old, aching God!

Young, growing God, eager still to know,
willing to be changed by what you've started,
*　　　quick to be delighted,*
*　　　singing as you go:*
Hail and Hosanna,
young, growing God!

Great, living God, never fully known,
joyful darkness far beyond our seeing,
*　　　closer yet than breathing,*
*　　　everlasting home:*
Hail and Hosanna,
great, living God!

We Are Not Our Own*

We are not our own. Earth forms us,
human leaves on nature's growing vine,
fruit of many generations,
*　　　seeds of life divine.*

We are not alone. Earth names us:
past and present, peoples near and far,
family and friends and strangers
*　　　show us who we are.*

Through a human life God finds us;
dying, living, love is fully known,
and in bread and wine reminds us:
*　　　we are not our own.*

Therefore let us make thanksgiving,
and with justice, willing and aware,
give to earth, and all things living,
*　　　liturgies of care.*

And if love's encounters lead us
on a way uncertain and unknown,
all the saints with prayer surround us:
We are not alone.

Let us be a house of welcome,
living stone upholding living stone,
gladly showing all our neighbors
we are not our own!

Are You the Friendly God?*

Are you the friendly God, shimmering, swirling, formless,
nameless and ominous, Spirit of brooding might,
presence beyond our senses, all-embracing night,
the hovering wings of warm and loving darkness?
If hope will listen, love will show and tell,
and all shall be well, all manner of things be well.

Are you the gambler-God, spinning the wheel of creation,
giving it randomness, willing to be surprised,
taking a million chances, hopeful, agonised,
greeting our stumbling faith with celebration?
If hope will listen, love will show and tell,
and all shall be well, all manner of things be well.

Are you the faithful God, watching and patiently weaving,
quilting our histories, patching our sins with grace,
dancing ahead of evil, kissing Satan's face,
till all of our ends are wrapped in love's beginning?
If hope will listen, love will show and tell,
and all shall be well, all manner of things be well.

Name Unnamed*

Name Unnamed, hidden and shown, knowing and known: Gloria!
  Beautiful Movement,
    ceaselessly forming,
    growing, emerging with awesome delight,
  Maker of Rainbows,
    flowing with color,
    arching in wonder,
    energy flowing in darkness and light:
Name Unnamed, hidden and shown, knowing and known: Gloria!
  Spinner of Chaos,
    pulling and twisting,
    freeing the fibers of pattern and form,
  Weaver of Stories
    famed or unspoken,
    tangled or broken,
    shaping a tapestry vivid and warm:
Name Unnamed, hidden and shown, knowing and known: Gloria!
  Nudging Discomforter,
    prodding and shaking,
    waking our lives to creative unease,
  Straight-Talking Lover,
    checking and humbling
    jargon and grumbling,
    speaking the truth that refreshes and frees:
Name Unnamed, hidden and shown, knowing and known: Gloria!
  Midwife of Changes,
    skillfully guiding,
    drawing us out through the shock of the new,
  Mother of Wisdom,
    deeply perceiving,
    never deceiving,
    freeing and leading in all that we do:
Name Unnamed, hidden and shown, knowing and known: Gloria!

Dare-devil Gambler,
risking and loving,
giving us freedom to shatter your dreams,
Life-giving Loser,
wounded and weeping,
dancing and leaping,
sharing the caring that heals and redeems:
Name Unnamed, hidden and shown, knowing and known: Gloria!

Who Is She?*

Who is She,
neither male nor female,
maker of all things,
only glimpsed or hinted,
source of life and gender?
She is God,
mother, sister, lover:
in her love we wake,
move and grow, are daunted,
triumph and surrender.

Who is She,
mothering her people,
teaching them to walk,
lifting weary toddlers,
bending down to feed them?
She is Love,
crying in a stable
teaching from a boat,
friendly with the lepers,
bound for crucifixion.

Who is She,
sparkle in the rapids,
   coolness of the well,
living power of Jesus
flowing from the scriptures?
She is Life,
water, wind and laughter,
   calm, yet never still,
swiftly moving Spirit,
singing in the changes.

Why is She,
mother of all nature,
   dying to give birth,
gasping yet exulting
to a new creation?
She is Hope,
never tired of loving,
   filling all with worth,
glad of our achieving,
lifting all to freedom.

6

Bring Many Names

Bring many names, beautiful and good;
celebrate, in parable and story,
holiness in glory, living, loving God.

In this chapter I shall seek alternatives to KINGAFAP by drawing on the creative work of workshop participants, highlighting alternative biblical metaphors, thinking afresh about God and creation, and naming God in female terms.

My aims and methods partner the work of systematic theologians. In *Models of God*, for example, Sallie McFague explores the metaphors of God as Mother, Lover, and Friend, calling them *models* because they have sufficient correspondences to generate many new insights. She asks what sort of divine love these metaphors suggest; what activity, work, or doctrine are associated with each, and what each implies for human life and conduct. She aims to develop a reasonably comprehensive and unified understanding of the relationship between God and creation, and her method is to look at each metaphor systematically, through the lens of traditional questions about the meaning of creation and salvation, revelation and incarnation, sin and evil, the Christian life, church and sacraments, and the nature of human existence.[1]

My aim is to find new ways of naming and praising God in worship, and my methods combine those of poet and theologian, with special attention to the writing of hymn texts. The creative process includes times of waiting, inspiration, and crafting, informed by theological concerns. Experiment is essential, since the only way to find out about metaphors and similes is to make them and see where they lead, and how well they can be expressed in different types of liturgical speech: some metaphors of God can be spun into verse easily, whereas others are more at home in story, preaching, and prayer.

Success or failure are initially measured by whether congregations and hymnal editors want to sing or say what is thus written, then by whether or not the words have staying power for worshippers and provide an image quarry for preachers and theologians. Each of the next three chapters highlights one of the guidelines worked out previously, while drawing also on the others. In this chapter the emphasis is on variety; in the next, on God's liberating direction in Jesus; Chapter 8 looks for more adequate metaphors of trinitarian faith.

I. Drawing on "People's Theology"

Given encouragement, and a participatory framework,[2] most people can be verbally creative. While teaching a preterm course at a seminary near Chicago, I asked the thirty people present to "brainstorm" images of God and used the resulting names as the basis for a hymn whose first stanza incorporates some of their expressions of mystery and wonder:

> *Are you the friendly God, shimmering, swirling, formless,*
> *nameless and ominous, Spirit of brooding might,*
> *presence beyond our senses, all-embracing night,*
> *the hovering wings of warm and loving darkness?*
> *If hope will listen, love will show and tell,*
> *and all shall be well, all manner of things be well.*
> ("Are You the Friendly God?" Gallery preceding Chapter 6)

I am not sure whether the hymn needs to be in question form: it was cast that way on the assumption that novel thoughts are more easily accepted if presented as possibilities rather than statements. The last line of the refrain picks up a serene expression of confidence from the thirteenth-century mystic Julian of Norwich to counterbalance the novelty of some of the preceding imagery.

At another workshop I asked the fifty people present to take one or two God-names from the Chicago list and write a brief prayer to develop the metaphors they had chosen. To discourage prolixity and enable everyone to work quickly, I specified a length of only one or two lines. After ten minutes we had fifty diverse offerings, many well crafted and innovative. As each prayer was read aloud, there was a silence of concentration and receptivity; many said afterward that they were surprised and moved by the creativity of their companions. I offered to write a hymn, using their work as a basis, and over the next three days shared something of the writing process, and the reshaping, crafting, and ordering needed to recreate the material in stanza form. The completed work was sung on the final day of the workshop and is printed above (Gallery preceding Chapter 6).

One of my contributions was the recurring refrain "Name Unnamed, hidden and shown, knowing and known." The name God gave to Moses at the burning bush had the consonants YHWH (Hebrew vowels were not written). It was originally spoken freely, but a sense of God's holiness eventually made people reluctant to pronounce it, and the word *Adonai* (Governor) was substituted. This was then rendered into English as LORD.

The original name YHWH has no gender reference and probably means something like "Being-Becoming." The translation LORD, while faithful to later Hebrew usage, moves from the indeterminate sense of the original into the male-dominance world of KINGAFAP. "Name Unnamed" is an attempt to reverse that process, express what happened to the divine name, and delight in the impossibility of pinning a label on God. The hymn therefore begins and ends with this, and continually returns to it. Set against this reticence is a pageant of developed metaphors, including "Beautiful Movement," "Maker of Rainbows," "Weaver of Stories," "Straight-Talking Lover," "Midwife of Changes," "Daredevil Gambler," and "Life-Giving Loser." Though some lines are my own, the hymn as a whole is drawn from God-metaphors coined by different groups of people. My experience suggests that many people welcome a more varied vocabulary for naming and praising God and can themselves contribute to it.

II. Highlighting Neglected Metaphors

Here is the first stanza of a biblically grounded hymn:

> *God of many Names*
> *gathered into One,*
> *in your glory come and meet us,*
> *Moving, endlessly Becoming.*
> *God of Hovering Wings,*
> *Womb and Birth of time,*
> *joyfully we sing your praises,*
> *Breath of life in every people.*
> *Hush, hush, hallelujah, hallelujah!*
> *Shout, shout, hallelujah, hallelujah!*
> *Sing, sing, hallelujah, hallelujah!*
> *Sing, God is love, God is love!*[3]

"Hovering Wings" draws on the Hebrew text of Genesis 1:2 and suggests the Spirit moving over the void at creation. "Breath of life" is another biblical metaphor for the Holy Spirit. "Womb and Birth of time" is new coinage, but echoes biblical references to God as giving birth (for example, Isa. 42:14–16). "Moving, endlessly Becoming" interprets the experience of God in Exodus 3:13 and Ezekiel 1:4–28.

None of these God-metaphors is based on KINGAFAP. They remind us that KINGAFAP is not the only way the Bible sees God, and they offer reassurance as we step into paths less well known. The hymn suggests that there are many and varied ways of naming God, and in its variety follows the first guideline in the preceding chapter. My hope is that each singer will find something illuminating, since different metaphors speak to different people. The third stanza has a similar blend of old and new images, with repetition of key phrases:

> *God of Wounded Hands,*
> *Web and Loom of love,*
> *in your glory come and meet us,*
> *Carpenter of new creation.*
> *God of many Names,*

> *gathered into One,*
> *joyfully we sing your praises,*
> *Moving, endlessly Becoming. . . . Hush, hush, hallelujah.*

Another text explores biblical imagery associating God with darkness.[4] The imagery is valuable in itself and may help to undermine the racist contrasts already mentioned.[5] The first stanza celebrates the darkness of God:

> *Joyful is the dark,*
> *holy, hidden God,*
> *rolling cloud of night beyond all naming,*
> *Majesty in darkness,*
> *Energy of love,*
> *Word-in-Flesh, the mystery proclaiming.*

The last three lines take a trinitarian form, but are passing allusions, not a metaphor system permitting elaboration. The First Person is suggested by a residual KINGAFAP reference ("majesty in darkness"), the Third by "energy of love," and the Second by the Scripture reference "Word-in-Flesh." The middle stanzas take us to the darkness of the stable, "as with exultation, Mary, giving birth, hails the infant cry of need and blessing," and to the "dark coolness of the tomb, waiting for the wonder of [Easter] morning":

> *Never was that darkness*
> *touched by dread and gloom:*
> *darkness was the cradle of the dawning.*

The final stanza returns to the imagery of the first, with additional metaphors expressing wonder and praise:

> *Joyful is the dark*
> *depth of love divine,*
> *roaring, looming thundercloud of glory,*
> *holy, haunting beauty,*
> *living, loving God.*
> *Hallelujah! Sing and tell the story!*[6]

III. God and Creation

"In no other religion does God not only create matter, but also accept it into the divine life itself and remain in this loving relationship for all eternity."[7] We know that creation is good, and that God delights in it. I therefore begin by affirming the goodness of creation, the body, and the material world. One aspect of that goodness is God's decision to make human beings dependent on the biosphere of planet earth for our existence, while giving us a degree of freedom. By memory, imagination, and reason we can put one foot outside the limitations of time and space, and over a period of time make changes in the conditions of our lives. We live in time, and in a universe where there are real changes and real moves forward.

Patriarchal thought sees this in terms of superiority and inferiority, whereby each positive step is higher than what has gone before. Yet the complex relies on the simple, as the present grows out of the past. The human mind depends not only on other human beings, but also on stimuli from nature. Without "warbling birds, blossoming cherry trees, sighing wind, and speaking humans, there would be no source of signals—and thus no intellects." We belong, cell and brain, to an intricate, changing cosmos.[8]

Patriarchy deludes us into thinking we are free *from* nature, whereas we can only be free *within* nature. The idea of dominating the universe from a remote height is an illusion.[9] We need imagery that expresses our gratitude for water, soil, and air, "large gifts supporting everything that lives," for "priceless energy, stored in each atom, gathered from the sun," and especially for God, who has woven nature's life "into a seamless robe, a fragile whole," which we tamper with at our peril.[10] The hymn "We Are Not Our Own" (Gallery preceding Chapter 6) expresses this understanding in simple metaphors. We are the product of a long process of evolution, "human leaves on nature's growing vine." We cannot live in isolation. On the contrary, "past and present, people's near and far, family and friends and strangers *show us who we are.*" God finds us through the human life of Jesus, and we respond "with justice, willing and aware." We seek justice among human beings as part of a wider concern, whereby we "give to earth, and all things living, liturgies of care."

How should we envisage God creating all things? The KINGAFAP metaphor of creation by the King's word of command expresses the conviction that God is beyond nature and distinct from it. Its weakness is that it also suggests remoteness, an invulnerable God "above it all." More peaceable creation-metaphors name God as potter, weaver and spinner, for example:

> *Spinner of chaos, pulling and twisting,*
> *freeing the fibers of pattern and form.*
> ("Name Unnamed," Gallery preceding Chapter 6)

Yet these do not change the basic model. God is still the one who manipulates or wishes into existence something separate from Godself. Such metaphors cannot express the equally important conviction that the Holy One indwells and permeates all things. We may do more justice to God's love if we also see God as moving deep *within* matter as it emerges and explodes into innumerable galaxies ("Beautiful Movement, ceaselessly forming, growing, emerging in awesome delight," as "Name Unnamed" puts it), or enclosing the entire cosmos deep within the divine life, yet giving it birth into its own space and freedom. I shall return to such metaphors later in this chapter.

"Let There Be Randomness?"

I said earlier that for the Creator to say, "Let there be randomness," is incompatible with patriarchy, because it suggests a God who delights in relinquishing control of creation. One of the hymns in the Gallery expresses this idea in question form:

> *Are you the Gambler-God, spinning the wheel of creation,*
> *giving it randomness, willing to be surprised,*
> *taking a million chances, hopeful, agonised,*
> *greeting our stumbling faith with celebration?*
> ("Are You the Friendly God?" Gallery preceding Chapter 6)

The hymn is based on creative work by several people and is an exploration of an idea then new to me. The metaphor "God the

Gambler" has been suggested by people in different workshop settings and presumably reflects their experience of life and understanding of creation. I have heard what follows dismissed as "process theology," but have never understood why labeling should be an excuse to avoid listening. Understanding how the universe could have elements of the uncontrolled is important for postpatriarchal faith, and at this point "process" theologians have helpful suggestions.

If I understand it correctly, an element of randomness is built into the physical universe. We live in a world marked by a mixture of order and randomness, freedom and necessity, creativity and routine.[11] Once we have taken off our patriarchal spectacles, there is no reason why the will of a loving Creator should be expressed by controlling and determining everything. It would be more appropriate for love to want spontaneity and surprise. In personal relationships, we are often surprised by what the other person thinks or does, and part of our surprise is due to ignorance: we do not know them sufficiently well to predict what they will do or say. Yet even when we know them intimately, there is a precious element of spontaneity, which is lost only if mistrust creeps in, or one person dominates or controls the other.

If God creates the universe with a certain degree of randomness and creates human beings capable of relatively free choice,[12] God will effortlessly know all the possible ways randomness can operate and a free person behave. But there is an important distinction between what is *actual* and what is *possible*. When two people meet, God knows every possible way they might begin their conversation, including the odds against Welsh sheep farmers conversing in Arabic, or Americans saying "Guten Tag" instead of "Hi!" When they actually speak, God knows what they have said, and of course knows that speech the instant it is formulated in their mind, before it reaches the larynx and is uttered.[13]

But it makes no sense to say that God knows what they will say *before they know it*, for that is to obliterate the distinction between the actual and the possible. If God knows everything I do before I know I am going to do it—and knows it as a certainty rather than a possibility—then I am being deluded. I think I am free, but am really no more than an unusually complicated puppet, for

> *. . . if, made like some android race,*
> *though warm with flesh and blood,*
> *our happy self, with smiling face,*
> *was programmed to be good,*
> *and had no freedom, seeing wrong,*
> *to choose it, or say no,*
> *our praise would be a puppet-song*
> *and love an empty show.*[14]

I'm not exaggerating the freedom I have. In God's eyes I am no doubt very predictable, and my capacity to surprise God is limited. Yet God is love, and love includes both the capacity to be hurt by my blindness, denial of gifts, or rebellion and the capacity to be gladdened, delighted, and surprised by some small, unexpected loving act or flowering of the creativity given me. The joy in heaven when one lost sheep is found is not just for the angels: it is a delight deep within the life of the Trinity and must contain a note of surprise, because the point of the story is that it could have ended differently: the sheep could have insisted on staying lost. But no! Praise be! It is found.

Perhaps God might pretend to give us freedom and the universe randomness? That cannot be, for pretense is not God's nature. God is faithful. Faithfulness is a keynote of divine love, and God's perfect love never puts on an act with anyone or anything. Deep within God's love, from all eternity, is a decision to create beings capable of achieving relative freedom, whose actions, though often predictable, will sometimes surprise.

Equally characteristic of love is an expectant attitude toward the other. It is a kind of knowing that is the opposite of being a know-it-all. A mother whose child brings her a baked clay cup made at school in the image of umpteen others will not need to *pretend* to be delighted and surprised. She *will* be delighted and surprised, because the predictability of the offering is unimportant compared with the child's delight and the creative potential it signifies. If that comparison holds true, it follows that God is far more able to be delighted and surprised by us than we can imagine. God "greets our stumbling faith with celebration," and the celebration includes a divine surplus of delight, as God celebrates the potential in the actual. As we take our first stumbling steps, God celebrates our potential to walk, run, leap, and fly.

Similarly, God is far more able than us to be delighted and surprised by other life forms, precisely because God knows them and their possibilities infinitely better than we do. Listen to the select group of people who spend years observing animals in the wild, and you will usually find that their delight in what they study grows with their knowledge, and that their sharpest pleasures come from the spontaneous and unexpected.

Since God is love, it makes sense to see that perfect love as delighting in the randomness of creation and the spontaneity of living things. Perfect control casts out spontaneity. Perfect love invites it. Controlling omniscience makes God a divine know-it-all, bored with the tedium of our utterly predictable "freedom." Loving omniscience combines effortless grasp of infinite possibilities with childlike joy whenever positive things occur unexpectedly. God looks at creation and is delighted with its goodness, and with the results of its God-given randomness. " 'The morning stars sang together for joy.' And God, who made it possible for them to sing but did not write the score, is delighted."[15]

What I'm getting at can be expressed in two contrasting images, drawn from a hymn containing four personal images of God:

> *Old, aching God, grey with endless care,*
> *calmly piercing evil's new disguises,*
> > *glad of good surprises,*
> > *wiser than despair:*
> *Hail and Hosanna,*
> *Old, aching God!*
>
> *Young, growing God, eager still to know,*
> *willing to be changed by what you've started,*
> > *quick to be delighted,*
> > *singing as you go:*
> *Hail and Hosanna,*
> *young, growing God!*
> ("Bring Many Names," Gallery preceding Chapter 6)

Delight and grief, joyful and agonized surprises go together. Human and animal pain, and the awful evils that haunt our century, are not explained away by seeing God as capable of surprise and delight. I cannot answer the questions that arise, but suggest they now take a different form. The KINGAFAP question is "Why does the all-controlling God allow these things to happen?" which I have already suggested is unanswerable within that metaphor system. If creation implies God's option for a degree of freedom and randomness, the question now is "Why does God, who loves, relinquish control in this way, knowing far better than we do the possibilities for radical evil that may then be actualized?" Within that framework, any attempt at an answer must be in terms of whether the divine risk is, or is not, justified. The monarchical model sees the crucial divine activity as the redemption of rebellious subjects, to whom other life forms and creation itself are an unimportant backdrop. This alternative sees God's crucial activity as creating a world with staggering possibilities for good and evil, out of a love that knows the possible costs and is willing to become involved as "God with us."[16]

In the devotional mode of Christian worship, the reality of good and evil, and God's fearful choice to allow freedom, have to be contemplated, carried as a burden in prayer, or felt as an ache unhealed. So great are the evils of our time that they overwhelm our capacity to mourn. "The horrors of our century have *iced the wells of grief.* We greet each new atrocity with frozen disbelief." Yet we know that evil comes from human possibilities, "not from alien galaxies, but from our inner space":

> *and Auschwitz and Hiroshima*
> *intrude on every prayer*
> *with shades that whisper, "Where is God?—*
> *If only God were there!"*

The hymn recalls the myriad ways in which human beings kill one another and asks how love could justify our "terrible free will." A stanza already quoted argues that without the freedom, "seeing wrong, to choose it or say no," there can be no genuine praise and love. The hymn continues:

> *Pol Pot and Stalin* are the cost
> of every willing prayer
> *that chooses justice, love and trust,*
> *and hopes that God is there.*

And God is not an analyst,
observing gain and loss,
but loves us to the uttermost,
and suffers on a cross,
for love comes, not like Heads of State,
in power and glamor known,
but as a loser, desolate,
in anguish and alone.
   Golgotha and the empty tomb
   enlighten every prayer,
   when faith discovers, "There is God,
   and all of God is there."[17]

One of the hymns in the Gallery preceding Chapter 6 deals with another concern, namely, how does God end all things if creation implies a surrender of control? In the KINGAFAP system, the divine mon-arch, having begun everything by word of command, retains total control of space-time and ends it in the same way. If the act of creation implies a relinquishment of total control, how does God cope with the resultant possibilities for evil and bring about the new creation, which is God's hope and longing? The devotional mode cannot resolve that problem, but expresses our faith that God, who started it all, knows how to cope with it while it goes on and moves within and ahead of all things, outlasting and outwitting evil and failure, and bringing about new creation through all the possibilities that God effortlessly knows and we cannot. The hymn expresses it thus:

Are you the faithful God, watching and patiently weaving,
quilting our histories, patching our sins with grace,
dancing ahead of evil, kissing Satan's face,
till all of our ends are wrapped in love's beginning?
   If hope will listen, love will show and tell,
   and all shall be well, all manner of things be well.

Creation in a Nuclear Age

The future is henceforth overshadowed by the knowledge that human actions can end life on earth. Among the possible futures for

for earth that God knew from the beginning, God knew that this possibility might become an actuality and took account of it. From now on, we are responsible to one another, to all the generations that might possibly be born during the natural life of our planetary home, and to God, for the care of planet earth.

What image of God best expresses this? I was prompted to ask that question by Gordon Kaufman's book *Theology for a Nuclear Age*,[18] in which he criticizes earlier conceptions of God, expressed devotionally in the KINGAFAP system, and argues that we need new concepts to take account of our new situation.

Kaufman suggests two key verbs for understanding God's relationship to humanity. As our "ultimate point of reference," God *relativizes* and *humanizes* us. Nothing exists for itself, or has meaning only in and of itself. Everything exists *in relation to God*, and so is partial and incomplete till fulfilled in that relationship. God also humanizes us, meaning God wishes to bring human life to its most humane fulfillment in a society brimming with freedom, justice, health, and peace. God calls everything about us into question, yet is completely good and loving in the quest to actualize the highest possibilities for humanity on this earth.[19]

Well and good, but can these ideas be translated into worship-talk? "O God our Relativizing Humanizer" is not an inspiring beginning to a prayer. As I read Kaufman, two complementary metaphors come to mind: God as Questioner and Lover. They can be elaborated, checked against Kaufman's analysis, and used in worship. They may say more or less than Kaufman intends—but that is the way with metaphor.

When we encounter God, we know that everything in us exists in relationship to God. To be relativized is to be called to account and given the most searching critique. So God is our ultimate Questioner, who will not let us go or let us be, but intimately knows our best possibilities as individuals and as a species, so cannot rest content with less. On an individual level, our divine Questioner meets us as our

Straight-Talking Lover,
  checking and humbling
  jargon and grumbling,
speaking the truth that refreshes and frees,

while as individuals, societies, and the whole human species, we can voice the same awareness by singing "We Are Not Our Own" (for both hymns, see Gallery preceding Chapter 6).

Because we are created beings, our divine Questioner cannot help "putting us in our place," if once we open ourselves to question (though God never forces us to). When we accept our place as God's created beings, we find immeasurable gladness and freedom. Yet the divine Questioner is also our Lover, who loves the material world, delights in human achievement, and calls us out of limited hopes, false submission, arrogance, and despair. As Lover, God is vulnerable to us, capable of being hurt beyond our imagining by individuals, societies, or the human species: it is not only our individual acts that hurt or delight, but our collective achievements, failures, goodness, and wickedness. As the Lover of humankind, God is also capable of being delighted by us beyond our wildest hopes.

In saying this, I am rejecting as a patriarchal error the tradition that so emphasizes God's transcendence that there is no possibility of God *needing* anything from humankind. If God is love, without pretense or facade, then God does need us, and it is pointless to argue whether this is by choice or necessity.[20] As Sallie McFague observes, "Neither the covenantal God of the Hebrew Scriptures who pleaded with Israel to be his faithful partner nor the compassionate God of Jesus of Nazareth who healed the sick and cast out demons is an unmoved mover or an absolute monarch entirely outside the circle of need." Until we understand the need God has for us, we may lack the will to take responsibility for planet earth. Our response to God our Lover is to care for the earth God loves, since the Lover of creation is not interested in netting individual souls from the stream of time, but in saving, making whole, the entire estranged cosmos—of which our embodied selves are an integral part.[21]

This understanding of God as Lover finds expression in the following hymn:

Great Lover, calling us to share
your joy in all created things,
from atom-dance to eagles' wings,
we come and go, to praise and care.

To express the nature of that love, the hymn needs to voice awareness of our capacity to end human life on earth. Yet this must be
set in the context of our ultimate safety in God's love. The former
must not drown eternal hope, nor the latter diminish planetary
responsibility. So the hymn holds them together, then sings of the
divine quest on planet earth:

> *Though sure of resurrection-grace,*
> *we ache for all earth's troubled lands*
> *and hold the planet in our hands,*
> *a fragile, unprotected place.*
>
> *Your questing Spirit longs to gain*
> *no simple fishing-ground for souls,*
> *but as life's story onward rolls,*
> *a world more joyful and humane.*
>
> *As midwives who assist the birth,*
> *we give our uttermost, yet grieve*
> *lest folly, greed or hate should leave*
> *a spoiled, aborted, barren earth.*
>
> *Self-giving Lover, since you dare*
> *to join us in our history,*
> *embracing all our destiny,*
> *we'll come and go, with praise and care.*[22]

God joins us in our history, decisively and wholeheartedly in
Jesus Christ, and continues with us by the Holy Spirit. Immanuel
is "God with us" to the end of time. This does not mean that
God's being is emptied into our human story, so that the end of
the story would be the end of God. It does mean that if we leave
"a spoiled, aborted, barren earth" on which myriad human possibilities remain unrealized, this will be a real and terrible loss for
God, as well as for us. Our Lover can make golden garments out
of burnt straw and transfigure our incomplete human story into
light. But even so, the loss of all the possibilities for humanity,
which God effortlessly knows and longs to see actualized, would
be a loss whose pain we cannot fathom. If we love our Lover, it is
not a loss to be made light of.

    This can be expressed in another metaphor, which may or
may not transpose into hymnic form. God is not the omnipotent

stage manager, author, and theater owner, standing outside the action of our human play, who will ring down the curtain if we stray from the script, or call the fire brigade if we set fire to the theater. If we vandalize the stage or burn down the theater, God will not smile indulgently and magically produce another theater in which to restart the play. Whether there are other theaters for other plays in other galaxies or universes, we do not know. We do know that this planet is our theater and that for us, the human race, there is no other.

The author and theater builder has been deeply involved in the drama from its beginning and has even risked becoming one of the human characters. In that character, God lived out, onstage and entirely within the confines of our human story, a life giving the most profound clues for the future possibilities of our play. In our own century God has shown us that we are coauthors of the script, and that the playwright has placed the remainder of the play in the hands of us, the actors. God's presence is not withdrawn, but remains, as always, a questioning and loving presence, not a controlling presence. As the playwright, manager, and theater owner who risks such a surrender of control, God has become deeply vulnerable to us. If we destroy the stage and the theater, one of God's most cherished projects will be ended, and that ending will be a disaster for God, as well as for us.

Since we are indissolubly linked with other people in the biosphere of planet earth, on the loom of history in space-time, our first thought will be of God as the Lover of creation, planet earth, and all humankind. In this respect, the hymn just quoted may be inadequate, since I am not sure that its interpretation of "Lover" ("calling us to share your joy in all created things") gives a clear enough *communal* reference. As McFague points out, we need communal, relational metaphors, and she is careful to speak of God as the Mother, Friend, and Lover of the world, or of creation. In future hymn writing I shall try to express this more clearly. Yet it is in the nature of personal metaphors to suggest one-to-one relationships; the most we can do is highlight their cosmic and communal meanings, speaking where possible of God as Mother of creation, Lover of humankind, and Friend of planet earth, and letting one-to-one meanings flow from that source.[23]

In calling God "Lover," I am following the logic of saying that "God is Love," but pushing against the church's resistance to

God-metaphors felt to have sexual overtones. This resistance is irrational and selective, since God as "Father" and Christ as the church's "husband" are full of male sexual meanings that custom makes us overlook. The word *lover* reminds us that God is not aloof, but *longs for and desires us,* and that it matters how we respond. It is personal, yet not specified in terms of gender: God as Lover may be she or he to you, or neither in particular.

Perhaps by using the word we can free it for wider meanings. There are many levels of loving, and their most important aspect is not sex or desire (important as they are), but *value.* To love another is to value that person deeply and show it; the most wonderful thing about being loved is to find oneself valued, treasured, and prized by another, with an intensity that gives a joy and security beyond measure. Lovers can't justify their love. In the end, the perceiving of such value cannot be accounted for: it is in the eye of the beholder. Love also endures, is faithful through all barriers, and continues to find the beloved valuable, even when no one else does.[24]

Here is a hymn that tries to express God's profound valuing of human beings. Though communal meanings are important, it seems to me right that God's valuing of us should be expressed in terms of a one-to-one relationship with each individual in the corporate "us" of the congregation. The hymn begins from the story of Paul's conversion in Acts 26:1–18:

> *All-perceiving Lover,*
> * sensing each disguise,*
> *kindly you uncover*
> * bruised and aching eyes.*
> *Wake us into wonder*
> * at your dawning day.*
> *Halt us with your thunder*
> * on our stubborn way.*

Two obstacles to our Lover's call are then suggested. They are obstacles for people of either gender, though patriarchal society so forms us that women are more likely to experience "false submission" and men more likely to live "in unfeeling walls":

Armored with our work-load,
   in unfeeling walls,
reaching for your love-road
   as the Spirit calls,
guide us as we fumble
   for the open air.
Show us, though we stumble,
   how to feel and care.

Let no gift lie fallow
   in self-bruising blight,
hiding in the shadow
   of another's light.
Let your new commission
   touch our every choice,
free from false submission
   as we find our voice.

The final stanza adds other metaphors to amplify the meaning of God as Lover and speaks of salvation as the fulfillment of God-given potential. Though not the whole truth about sin and salvation, it is a neglected truth worth singing about:

All-perceiving Lover,
   good and guiding star,
helping us discover
   who we really are,
Life-creating Wisdom,
   always you amaze.
Fit us for your freedom,
   fill us with your praise![25]

IV. Meeting God as She

The metaphor of God as Lover has three advantages: it has precedents in Christian tradition, is fully personal, and is open to a wide variety of interpretations, since a lover can be young or old, sexual or nonsexual, of the opposite gender or one's own. Yet it does not lessen the need to name God in metaphors from human gender. In real life, there are no unsexed, ageless, vaguely humanoid lovers. Lovers and loving friends are called Tracy, Bill, George, Waltraud, Xavier, Maria, Dimza, Natasha, or Jean-Pierre, and what makes the general term *lover* meaningful is its capacity to remind us of the people who have loved us and received our love. We shall only move beyond patriarchal idols if we name God with a variety of personal terms from human relationships, both female and male. At this stage in our relationship with God, naming God in female terms is a priority, because it tilts our world from its patriarchal axis and enables us to meet the living God anew.

What is a man doing coining female metaphors for the living God? Not, I hope, trying to take over, show women how to speak, or any such patronizing maneuver. If I'm right, none of us is confined to one gender's experience: I can reach for the feminine in myself, just as women can reach for the masculine in themselves. If I speak of God in female terms, I'm not speaking from a woman's experience, but from my own. My perspective is limited, but that goes for all of us. What I do will be of most value if it helps the exploration of others.

Since "Father" is the most deeply rooted male metaphor for God, "Mother" may seem the obvious alternative. In discussions about naming God in female terms, people often assume that "Mother" is the only term available and stick in that groove. "Mother" is certainly an important metaphor evoking diverse and complex reactions. To some it suggests nurturing, security, and the memory of an unconditional love. To others it calls up the memory of utter dependence on an all-powerful figure and concern lest our relationship with God continue in perpetual babyhood. I suspect that to most of us it evokes mixed feelings.[26] Because it strikes echoes from our deepest personal relationships, "Mother" is just as ambiguous as "Father." To focus exclusively on God as Mother would not do justice to the multitude of ways in which God can be known and would exchange one parental authority image for another. Though I shall name God as Mother, it is equally important to meet her as Sister, Midwife, and She.

Speaking to God in female terms may prove to be revelatory, liberating, daring, or frightening, but is unlikely to pass unnoticed. By speaking of God as She and naming the whole being of God anew, we are going against the grain of the society that has formed us. Since that society downgrades and disvalues what it labels "feminine," naming God as She means facing that down-grading head-on and hoping to break through it. Here is part of a Jewish Sabbath prayer for women. Saying it is a step forward in our adoration of God and affirmation of women made in God's image:

> *Blessed is She who spoke, and the world became.*
> *Blessed is She.*
> *Blessed is She who in the beginning gave birth.*
> *Blessed is She who says and performs.*
> *Blessed is She who declares and fulfills.*
> *Blessed is She whose womb covers the earth.*
> *Blessed is She whose womb covers all creatures . . .*
> *Blessed is She who lives forever, and exists eternally.*
> *Blessed is She that redeems and saves.*
> *Blessed is Her Name.*[27]

Speaking of the Womb of God makes some people uncomfortable. Donald Bloesch argues that such metaphors (his example is "Womb of Being") suggest that God is wholly contained within creation.[28] He couples this concern with an attack on anything that could be called Goddess worship. It is risky for two men to debate the meaning of giving birth. From what women say about it, some experience the child as a separate and distinct being from well before birth, while others are more aware of the continuity between mother and child. Yet both experiences point toward separation. If the universe is God's "child," the image suggests God's profound involvement in the act of creation, whereby the universe is held within God's being, but then "comes forth," is "born" into its own time and space—in this case a space-time that God, in giving it birth, freely allows it to have. The divine Mother is not coterminous with the child, or in symbiotic union with it, however close the bonding may be. In the eleventh century Hildegard of Bingen had a series of prophetic illuminations, visions that she and others set down on paper in the form of paintings. One is of the whole universe as a sphere *within* the body of God. God effortlessly surpasses and contains it, enfolding it deep within God's being.

To speak of God as the Mother of Creation seems to me a beautiful image, entirely consistent with Christian faith in God who surpasses and contains all created things, yet expressing in a new way God's profound care for creation and involvement with it. There are in fact two contrasting images, drawn from the same experience. The universe can be imaged as *born from God*, in a great labor of love that creates it as intimately coming forth, yet separate from the creator. Or the universe can be imaged as effortlessly *contained within God*, perhaps while it awaits birth as new creation. Bloesch's objection probably springs from an awareness of the genetic continuity between mother and child; to him the metaphor suggests that the universe is of the same substance or nature as God. One may take this as a reminder that this metaphor, like all others, has limited correspondences. This is a problem only if it is idolized and used in isolation.

Bloesch's other objection is that to speak of God as Mother is to go back to the religions that monotheism superseded. He speaks as if the idea of seeing God in female terms is automatically a bad thing and needs no further discussion, or as if calling God Mother, or Sister, or She must mean the same in the twentieth century as in ancient Near Eastern societies three thousand years ago.

This is prejudiced and unreasonable. What it means *now* to speak of the living God as She, and talk to her in female terms, cannot be decided by appeals to what it may have meant in another time and place. It might be argued that the gods and goddesses of the ancient East were forces or aspects of nature, not the creators of nature. But if so, we have moved on. The idea of worshipping a deity who is only part of the universe, and has no existence beyond it, is today a nonstarter. We *know* that God is both infinitely close to us and infinitely beyond the whole universe She has made. To speak of God as the Mother who carries the universe within Herself, or gives it birth into its own space and freedom, explicitly denies that God can be reduced to natural forces or nature itself.

What female metaphors are likely to do is create a culture shock, because the downgraded and disvalued feminine and female are being seen, at last, as fitting ways of imaging and adoring the divine. If we use female images, we must make sure that they are being *revalued into equality*. Otherwise all that will happen will be the incorporation of a devalued femaleness into the godhead. Though I have called the Holy Spirit "She" in the odd hymn text, such a move now seems mistaken if it suggests a female Spirit alongside a male Father and Son. For that would give the divine Trinity a two-thirds male majority, in a context in which we already have difficulty naming and adoring the Spirit as a fully coequal Person.

It is a mistake to introduce metaphors of gender division into the being of God. Ideas of a Mother-Father God with Jesus Christ as its (their?) Son, are problematic because they suggest *two* parents (thus making quaternity instead of trinity) and reinforce patriarchal stereotypes, since the "Mother" aspect of God can be seen as subordinate to the "Father" aspect. If we speak of God in female metaphors, they must apply to the whole of God, not to a "feminine" aspect alongside "masculine" aspect.[29]

With these provisos, let me share a few attempts to enjoy and value female God-language from my own experience and perspective. My first such attempt began thus:

> *Dear Sister God,*
>   *you held me at my birth.*
> *You sang my name, were glad to see my face.*
>   *You are my sky, my shining sun,*
> *and in your love there's always room*
> *to be, and grow, yet find a home,*
>   *a settled place.*[30]

I chose "Sister" because I was not yet ready to name God as "Mother," and out of respect to what sisterhood means to many women. The imagery of the first four lines was drawn from personal experience: my daughter is two years older than my son, and when he was born she held him in her arms and was indeed glad to see his face. When they were young, it often seemed as if he looked on her as his "sky": the word suggests to me an overarching environment of space and light, love just "there" as we grow. The assurance that "there's always room" is a profound gift; I experience it as a woman's gift, though some men also give it. Since I have no sister, the word has no negative associations for me— though others have told me it is ambiguous for them ("If you knew my sister you wouldn't have written that!"), which strengthens the case for variety.

Where can such a hymn go from this beginning? I first developed "Sister" in terms of a listening love, which encourages meeting and sharing, "as sighs and hurts too deep for words" are heard and accepted by others. Then it seemed important, in a Christian hymn, to ask how our Sister's love is expressed in Jesus. I chose the phrase "in Christ your love rings true" to express this and showed that love undermining all our pyramids:

> *Directors, boards and bosses lose their sway*
> *Your service, free from servitude,*
> *draws out a love that, strong to give,*
> *can struggle, suffer, care and live*
> *a better way.*

Finally the hymn looks forward in hope of making a better earth in God's company, "where all can grow, and know that life is good," and "none exploit, *or win, or lose*," as all explore "the promised land of personhood."

I have begun to use pregnancy-birth imagery in other contexts, because it is beautiful and appropriate. A hymn on Hebrews 11 notes how we sometimes "laugh at hope," as Sarah did, "yet bear, like her, a promise past conceiving, of justice, joy, shalom and kingdom-come," for:

> *Within the womb of every best tradition*
> *the Spirit moves, and cannot be ignored.*
> *We feel the kicking of our inner vision*
> *and sing, "My soul shall glorify the Lord!"* [31]

The imagery is drawn directly from the Scripture passage, linking it (by that final line) with Luke 1:44–55, to express both passages' hopeful faith.

In Psalm 22:9 God is seen as the midwife "who drew me from the womb, who laid me at my mother's breast." This image is picked up in the hymn "Name Unnamed" (Gallery preceding Chapter 6) and joined with the metaphor of God as Wisdom, seen here (as in Hebrew thought) in female form:

> *Midwife of Changes,*
> *skillfully guiding,*

> *drawing us out through the shock of the new,*
> *Mother of Wisdom,*
> *deeply perceiving,*
> *never deceiving,*
> *freeing and leading in all that we do.*

Reversing the image, the human race takes responsibility with God for the fate of the earth. The fruits of knowledge have scattered their seeds, and humankind has sown and reaped them, so that we are now, "as gods, with open eyes, for shame or glory freed"

> *. . . and share, as midwives to our God,*
> *the pain of giving birth*
> *to faith's fulfillment, mercy's child,*
> *new heavens and new earth.*[32]

Pain is a man's word, chosen by one standing outside the experience of childbirth. Women have since told me that it is misleading to reduce their birthing experience to that one word. Giving birth is experienced in different ways, and "excitement," "fear," and "damned hard work" are some of the descriptions that accompany it. It might be better to speak of God's "work of giving birth," and let people add their own interpretation.

A further step was the writing of "Who Is She?" (Gallery preceding Chapter 6). The first stanza came easily, but I had to wait a year before I could complete the hymn.

> *Who is She,*
> *neither male nor female,*
> *maker of all things,*
> *only glimpsed or hinted,*
> *source of life and gender?*

In these opening lines it seemed important to say clearly that God is "neither male nor female," but the "source of life and gender," so that the feminine pronoun is not literalized. Were I to use masculine pronouns for God, I would now try similar qualifications, so that *male* God-talk is presented as equally inadequate and provisional. The hymn then names God as Mother, Sister, and Lover and moves on in trinitarian form. The First Person of the Trinity is God, "mothering her people, teaching them to walk, lifting weary toddlers, bending down to feed them" (Hos. 11). The Second Person is Love incarnate,

> *crying in a stable,*
> *teaching from a boat,*
> *friendly with the lepers,*
> *bound for crucifixion.*

When I first wrote this, it seemed too much of a metaphor clash to envisage the divine She becoming present in a male human. The clash now seems less striking and makes me aware that it is equally startling for a divine He to become incarnate, a surprise until recently masked by the patriarchal coziness of a male-imaged God becoming "Man."

The hymn moves on to speak of the divine She as Holy Spirit, "sparkle in the rapids, coolness of the well, living power of Jesus flowing from the scriptures," and "water, wind and laughter, singing in the changes." Finally, in an image of birth written after women's critique of my earlier "pain" image, the hymn asks:

> *Why is She,*
> *mother of all nature,*
> *dying to give birth,*
> *gasping yet exulting*
> *to a new creation?*
> *She is Hope,*
> *never tired of loving,*
> *filling all with worth,*
> *glad of our achieving,*
> *lifting all to freedom.*

Our Mother here shows a love that enables and frees, and is the opposite of possessiveness, a thought that also informs the following prayer:

God our Mother, you give birth to all life, and love us to the uttermost. Your love surrounds us and feeds us. Within your love we find our home, our joy, our freedom. You open the world to us, and give us room to change and grow. As you love us, so you love all your children. Help us, dear Mother God, to catch something of your love: your delight in others' uniqueness, your care for their well-being, your grief at their suffering, your patience and forgiveness, your energy and hope. We praise you, we thank you, we love you, through Jesus, our Savior.[33]

If this prayer is used without the word *Mother*, it attracts no adverse comment. I take this to mean that the qualities it expresses are *human* qualities, attainable in principle by both women and men. Put alongside 1 Corinthians 13, its language is not far removed from the language of Saint Paul.

It is a mistake to use female God-names only with qualities our culture labels "feminine." We face difficult choices. Part of the joy of speaking to God as Mother, Sister, or Wise Woman Friend is that it enables us to know God in terms of what those experiences mean to us; yet part of that meaning is drawn from the way mothers and sisters and wise women are formed by patriarchal culture. Giving them feminine stereotypes neither revalues the feminine nor helps us break out of the patriarchal mold.

Sallie McFague discusses this problem and suggests that the metaphor of God as Mother should be built not on stereotypes of softness, tenderness, and sentimentality, but on the female experiences of pregnancy, birth, and lactation. God our Mother does not judge her children as products measured against standards of perfection, but loves them with a sense of kinship, as the offspring of her own body. Yet she is no soft touch. The female experience of gestation, birth, and lactation engenders not passivity but active defense of the young. Our Mother is a just yet impassioned judge. She longs to see a just ordering of our planetary household, on terms beneficial to all. Her anger is not provoked by affronts to her majesty or her creatures' failure to meet a moral standard, but bursts forth when the offspring of her own being are denied food, shelter, and fulfillment.[34]

To meet such anger would be to meet a female strength both fierce and daunting, because it springs from impassioned, empathetic love. It gives a new dimension to God's "wrath" and is already imaged in the biblical metaphor of the mother bear robbed of her cubs (see Chapter 4). I have not yet put this insight into hymnic form, but it excites and moves me, not least because I have fleetingly experienced God in this mode. What I have done is reverse conventional stereotypes, as in the hymn quoted at the beginning of this chapter:

> *Strong mother God, working night and day,*
> *planning all the wonders of creation,*
> *setting each equation,*
> *genius at play:*
> *Hail and Hosanna,*
> *strong mother God!*
>
> *Warm father God, hugging every child,*
> *feeling all the strains of human living,*
> *caring and forgiving,*
> *till we're reconciled:*
> *Hail and Hosanna,*
> *warm father God!*

V. Bag Lady God

One other female God-metaphor needs consideration. At workshops in the United States, sessions of creative imaging have led several people to picture God as "the Bag Lady." The name is American, but the person she represents can be met in many cities outside the United States. She is a woman, prematurely aged by her outdoor life, who lives on the streets and carries everything she has in bags. Sometimes she stacks them in a supermarket cart and trundles it from place to place.

To think of God as a Bag Lady means taking both God and bag ladies seriously. She is our Mother, our Sister, the Christ in our neighbor. She has the waywardness of Holy Spirit. The whole Trinity meets us, once again, in the last and the least. So we can't use her as a charming metaphor. Bag ladies should not be sold as dolls in toyshops. Using the metaphor means loving the real bag lady, as one in whom God meets us.

What does she say, Bag Lady God? Here she comes, shuffling along. Her eccentricity, mumbling, and unpredictable moods, her deep suffering, are broken mirrors of divine life. "I am here," she says. "We are here. God. Yes. The one you look askance at. I make you uncomfortable, don't we all? We disturb you, yes, you don't know what to say to me. Ha!"

She has no easy message for us. She is discomfiting, and we often get no sense out of her. In worship we might best meet her nonverbally, through the medium of dance. She is unpredictable Holy Spirit, but also our divine Questioner. "What sort of society makes us come to you like this?" she asks. "Look at your society through our eyes, and what do you see? I am Bag Lady God, pushing my cart full of treasures and rubbish. We are not here for you to patronize, or ignore, or discard, or do good to."

Suffering God, Bag Lady of our cities, you come to us in our neighbor. But we cannot bypass her, as if you were hiding behind her—for you are deep in her uniqueness, in her mumbling voice, her straying hair, her care-worn hands. Help us to love our neighbor as she is, and because she is.

Lover of Creation, you come to us in our neighbor who is exploited, discarded, and despised. Yet you are never the object of our charity, to whom we can graciously do good. You are our Mother, and in her face is your image. In her speech you call and claim us, as one crucified and risen from the dead. In her coming it is you who disturb us, Spirit beyond our control. Bring us to repentance and lift us with good news. Help us to know you, and hear your gospel call.

7

A Male for Others

The experience of salvation through Jesus means more than all the explanations of it.[1] Each time we run around the problems and explanations, we have to "touch base" on the fact that women and men are met, attracted, called, and freed through him.

The maleness of Jesus is one such problem. It fits snugly into the KINGAFAP metaphor system and seems almost essential to it. I suspect that men take it for granted, because a male savior is "one of us." We can feel our way into the problem with some simple questions. How would we feel about praying to a female Savior? What would it mean for us if a woman had been crucified for our sins? How would it feel to be taught, from boyhood, that God became Woman for the salvation of all women, but that this includes men, even though—in the apt phrase—it just "goes without saying"?

Asking myself these questions, I found a residual prejudice: the idea of God becoming incarnate in a woman startled me more than the idea of God becoming incarnate in a man. A crucified woman moves me profoundly (I have seen and touched her sculpture), one reason being the shock of seeing an overly familiar image of divine suffering transposed into the other gender. Beyond that, I realize that if God's Anointed One was a woman, then however deeply saved and called I was by her life, death, and resurrection, I would always be aware that she was she and I was he. Her femaleness would highlight the differences between us and would be (potentially or actually) an obstacle to faith.

171

I then begin to see why the maleness of Jesus is a stumbling block for many women, because "he is not like us."[2] The stumbling block is not only his maleness, but what maleness means in patriarchal society. In that society he easily seems, and easily becomes, yet another oppressive male symbol. Because men are dominant in patriarchal society, a male Savior can be presented as an intermediary *who has power over women*. He can be seen as blocking or restricting access to the throne of grace. Women can be excluded from priestly or ministerial functions, or assured that their honored place is as subordinates, as church helpers rather than church leaders.[3]

The justice of that critique prompts me to ask questions about Jesus' maleness, from my own viewpoint, as a man becoming aware of patriarchy. What would a patriarchal Jesus be like? Was Jesus like, or unlike, a patriarchal male? Granted that his maleness is a problem, how can we deal with it, or live with it?

Starting with the last question, if God was to become incarnate as an individual human being, that person would have to be—as each individual human life is—unique, gender-specified, and timebound. This is the "scandal of particularity," which has been a problem ever since educated Greeks were mind-boggled by the announcement that salvation could reach them through the absurd figure of a crucified Jew. In all sorts of ways, we try to smooth the sharp edges of that scandal. Yesterday's Anglo-American Christians hung flaxen-haired Anglo-Saxon pictures of Jesus in their Sunday school rooms, which today's sophisticates smile at, but don't often take down. The visual message is that Jesus was really a white man, not olive-skinned; a Jew, yet somehow not *really* Jewish.[4]

Now we face another aspect of that scandal: the maleness of Jesus. It is sometimes suggested that although the historical Jesus was male, the timeless Christ, God's Anointed One, is beyond female and male. But this doesn't solve the problem, since the image of the timeless Christ can only reach us through the memory of the historical Jesus. In classic trinitarian theology, it is valid to speak of the eternal Word-Wisdom, the Second Person of the Trinity, beyond the limitations of human gender, who becomes incarnate in the male human being, Jesus of Nazareth. But that doesn't diminish the maleness of Jesus, nor alter the fact that our knowledge of the Second Person comes through that male human life.

Again, it is not helpful to argue that Jesus is revealed to us as the ideal mixture of masculine and feminine, an androgynous figure. Even if we had clear evidence that Jesus had both "feminine" and "masculine" qualities, labeling them as such and putting them inside one body would still keep them apart and leave unchallenged the society that stereotypes them as superior masculine and inferior feminine. Moreover, if Jesus is both female and male in one body, he's not like us, but a special case, equally distant from both sexes.

The Woody Allen Factor

Instead of trying to escape from the particularity of Jesus of Nazareth, I shall begin by accepting it, then asking how it is problematic. Most of the Woody Allen films I've seen live and breathe New York. Emily Bronte's novel *Wuthering Heights* is set in Yorkshire, England. James Joyce is unmistakably a Dubliner. From their particularity, they reach a universal audience, and do so because of their particularity, not in spite of it. What they reach out to is not the universality of abstract principles, but the empathy and solidarity human beings can have with one another, in grief, laughter, failure, striving, and hope, communicating person-to-person across class, culture, time, and gender.

The more faithful we are to the limited locale we know, and the more deeply we reach into our own experience and culture, the more we become luminous to people whose language, thought-world, and experience are different. We become luminous when we accept our limitations, explore and delight in what we know, and abandon pretensions and posturing.

This is what God does in Jesus of Nazareth, and it is part of the humility of incarnation. It does not mean turning inward and shutting out other voices, for the more we open ourselves to the experience of others, the more our own is illuminated and enlarged. When Jesus told a gentile woman that his mission was to the lost sheep of his own people, he was accepting both his own Jewishness and the specific, urgent, and geographically limited need to announce God's nearness to the Jews in Judaea under the procuratorship of Pontius Pilate. When she took his metaphor about a household's food going first to its own children and elaborated its implications ("even the dogs get the scraps"), he listened and responded with a messianic act of healing to her daughter, an outsider. Perhaps she helped him sense the wider meaning of his mission.

My hymnic exploration begins by accepting everything about Jesus that makes him particular and unique, including the fact that he was a first-century, Aramaic-speaking male Jew.

> LORD, *thank you for the Jews*
> *who first revealed to us your Name:*
> *for Peter, Martha, Paul, for John, and Mary Magdalen*
> *who prayed, "Your Kingdom come," in synagogue and home,*
> *and found you as they knew and loved*
> *a Rabbi out of Nazareth.*[5]

However puzzling it may seem, it is through that particular human story that God reaches us. In the following Advent hymn, the story touches present needs and is illuminated by future hopes, as the Spirit blows on us "from worlds already new":

> *Who comes?—a child, delivered on a stable floor.*
> *His mewing, newborn cry is all that God can say*
> *of hunger, thirst and aching need*
> *where Jesus lives today.*
> *Come, singing Fire of truth, compassion, right,*
> *and scorch our hardened apathy*
> *till love is new and bright.*
>
> *Who comes?—a Jew, declaiming from a prophet's scroll.*
> *His messianic cry is all that God can say*
> *of freedom, health, and saving hope*
> *where Jesus lives today.*
> *Come, singing Breeze from worlds already new.*
> *Blow in and out of weary minds,*
> *till faith is singing too.*
>
> *Who comes?—a man, in dying moments on a cross.*
> *His God-forsaken cry is all that God can say*
> *of searching, scarred, redeeming love*
> *where Jesus lives today.*
> *Come, singing Light from new creation's dawn,*
> *where trees of healing deck the streets*
> *and joy is newly born.*[6]

A Liberating Direction

One way Jesus speaks to us from his own time is in his attitude toward women. In Luke 8:1–3 we meet Jesus moving from town to town and village to village, proclaiming the good news of the kingdom of God: "With him were the Twelve and a number of women who had been set free from evil spirits and infirmities: Mary, known as Mary of Magdala, from whom seven devils had come out, Joanna the wife of Chuza, a steward of Herod's, Susanna, and many others. These women provided for them out of their own resources."[7] In the time of Jesus women were thoroughly subordinate to men. Men counted as members of a synagogue congregation; women did not. It was customary for a rabbi to ignore a woman in public, even if she was a close relative. For several days a month a woman was "unclean" and to be avoided. Law, doctrine, and all matters of faith were for men, and the devout man daily prayed:

> *Praise be to God that he has not made me a gentile,*
> *Praise be to God that he has not made me a woman,*
> *Praise be to God that he has not made me an ignorant man.*

The innermost courts of the Jerusalem Temple were for men only, the court of the women being five steps below and outside.

In the family, a woman's value was bound up with childbearing, and "barrenness" was a terrible stigma, since it was her duty to produce sons to carry on her husband's name. A husband sleeping with another man's wife was committing adultery against her husband, not against his own wife. He was offending another man's honor by misusing his property, not offending his wife's honor by being unfaithful. Divorce was overwhelmingly a husband's right, and the only disagreement was whether he was entitled to divorce his wife at will, or only if he could prove she was at fault. In legal cases, a woman's eyewitness testimony was unacceptable: women did not count as reliable witnesses.

Against that background, Jesus' attitude toward women is consistent with his whole ministry: he valued, called, and moved alongside the poor, outcast, discarded, and subordinated people of his time. He drew Mary of Bethany into the circle of disciples to listen to his teaching, which was probably (as elsewhere) in question-and-answer form. Called "Rabbi" by many, he spoke to women in public, even when they were strangers, and discussed the deepest matters of faith with a Samaritan woman at a well. He accepted the touch of a woman made "unclean" by a decade of menstrual problems and welcomed the nameless woman who touched his feet (an intimate gesture, then as now) and another woman who anointed him with precious oil.

In particular, he went about the countryside not only with male disciples, but also with a large group of women (Mary of Magdala, Joanna, Susanna, "and many others"). They had come to salvation not by being called away from home and occupation (as the male disciples were), but by an experience of healing (being "set free from evil spirits and infirmities"). They were women of means—perhaps widowed and (as sometimes happened) inheritors of property. These women provided for the whole group "out of their own resources." The sharing of goods and possessions in the early church was not a new invention. One of its origins is recorded here, in this large group of sharing women. Perhaps they provided the expensive embalming oils they took to the tomb on Easter morning and the one-piece garment Jesus wore to the cross, which was valuable enough for soldiers to gamble for it.

Two of the women stand out. Joanna is listed as the wife of Chuza, a steward of King Herod. A woman from court society, she joins Jesus and his traveling group after an experience of healing, an extraordinary act while her husband and master is still living. Perhaps hers was one of the healings that made Herod hope Jesus would perform a miracle for him (Luke 23:8).

Mary of Magdala is not the reformed prostitute of legend. That character is a fabrication, made by adding her name to two stories of unnamed women who anointed Jesus, and the similar story of a different Mary (John 12). The real Mary came from the town of Magdala, had money or property of her own, had been overtaken by a severe mental illness ("seven demons"), and had come to salvation through a healing that, by analogy with other recorded healings, would have included Jesus speaking lovingly, a healing touch, a command to the demons to depart, and an experience of wholeness, of coming to her true self: as deep an experience as Peter's, but different.

In the half dozen lists of women around Jesus that have come down to us, the other names vary, but Mary of Magdala is always there and always first, indicating that she was prominent in the group. In all four gospels she is the first witness to the resurrection. In Mark 16:9 she tells the men the good news and (because she is only a woman) they don't believe her. In Matthew's account an angel tells her and "the other Mary" to tell the disciples that Jesus is raised and will meet them in Galilee. They then meet Jesus and clasp his feet. He tells them to go and tell his brothers the same news (Matt. 28). In Luke (23:55–24:11) she is one of a group of women who receive the good news from angelic visitors and tell the male apostles, who dismiss their report as nonsense. In John Mary meets Jesus, who tells her not to cling to him, but to tell the disciples that he is ascending to God. Later, they get their own vision, behind locked doors (John 20:11ff.).

The accounts suggest that something remarkable happened here, at odds with patriarchal society and an embarrassment to the male disciples, whose vision and conviction come after the good news they receive (and disbelieve) from Mary and other women. As Paul said of the crucifixion, so one may also say of the resurrection: "the foolishness of God is wiser than *men*."

When I invite people to look at Jesus' encounters with women, in the context of his time, and ask how they would describe his behavior *in that context*, the responses fall into two categories. Many people are impressed by the interpersonal qualities: compassion, respect, taking women seriously, and accepting women as full human beings. Others notice the probable effect of such behavior on his contemporaries. Though not apparently "illegal," and thus not cited as one of the reasons for crucifying him, his behavior toward women was unconventional, controversial, radical, shocking, even revolutionary.

We honor the incarnation by seeing Jesus in his historical context and trying to follow the direction in which his life points us, not by pretending his decisions were made in the twentieth century and that all we need do is make exact copies of them. Following his liberating direction means accepting that our context is different from his and asking what, in our stage of patriarchal society, can lead us toward intergender relationships characterized by mutual compassion, respect, taking each other seriously, and accepting each other as full human beings, joint reflectors of God's nature and life. We shall know we are moving in the right direction if our God-names and unpatriarchal relationships are as challenging now as Jesus' behavior was then.

Maleness Renewed

In many ways Jesus beckons us by showing human qualities not tied to gender.[8] Yet he is still a male human being. The liberating direction of his ministry is the liberating direction of a man, a male person, working within patriarchal society. If I, as a man, now look at him again, a new dimension appears, as when a photograph springs into life as a hologram.

A Jesus upholding patriarchy would be a strong and commanding leader. He would either come from the upper reaches of society or be a "self-made man," go-getting and upwardly mobile. He would be tough and victorious, with awesome charisma, a man whom other men would follow to death or glory. He would weld them into a brilliant military force or political movement, with himself as leader and a clear chain of command. He would be a superb manager, knowing every face and name, sensing exactly when to hire and fire, inspiring devotion to himself and the company, with a control so effortless that no one would question his leadership. Or again, he might be the supreme intellectual, astonishing us with his detachment, control of emotion, and reasoning power. He would probably be all these things rolled into one, the perfect polymale. As such, he would reaffirm my dominant place in the patriarchal scheme of things. He would meet women with effortless charm and gallant attention, his predominance unquestioned as the perfect man on whom every woman can adoringly depend.

At every point, Jesus gives a different portrait of manhood. He rejects the claims of his family in favor of a group of assorted followers whom he has the nerve to call mother, brother, and sister. He displaces the authority of the fathers with his own interpretation ("You have heard it said . . . but I say to you"). He calls God "Abba," but won't let us call any *man* father or have grades and titles among ourselves. He leads a rainbow coalition of the dispossessed, but rejects the revolutions of patriarchy, where the oppressed win power and take revenge on their oppressors. Patriarchal heads of state have themselves honored and called "benefactor," he says, "but it shall not be so among you." Among us, the greatest are known as such because they act like servants, and their service is the offering of free spirits, not an Uncle Tom mask of smoldering servitude.[9]

Jesus does not merely fail to uphold patriarchal norms or take a different direction. His whole ministry *undermines* those norms and gives us a vision of a different kind of society. He demonstrates the revolution in relationships he aims for by himself becoming a servant. The significance of this is that "unlike women, he did not have to be a servant. He had power and access to power." But he renounced it and "modeled in his own being a dramatic assault on male privilege. Who but a man could credibly teach and model such a revolution in relationships by giving up power? Only a man could do that, because only men had power."[10]

Reading that comment from Diane Tennis is like seeing distant lightning. There is an instant flash of relief: the maleness of Jesus has a positive value! Only after several seconds do we hear the thunder: the positive value in Jesus' maleness is that he calls his male followers to go and do as he did. Christian men are to give up male power and privilege and, by so doing, undermine the power and privilege of other patriarchal males.

Here is an important theme for preaching and prayer. Looking again at a popular phrase in 1960s theology, Jesus the "free man" is not a genderless humanoid, but a free *male*, a "male for others." Reared in a patriarchal society, something sets him free from patriarchal drives and expectations. He seems free from all fear of authority, so that when he questions established rules he does not appear as an adolescent rebel but as an adult seeing with clarity and confidence.

We have few clues to Jesus' "inner life," but the temptation stories focus on one point of growth and development. In a struggle with archetypal male temptations,[11] he becomes free from the male need to have power over others. It is liberating to find this recorded as a temptation, something that was seductive and had to be faced and overcome, for that shows Jesus as a true human being, a believable male. At the beginning of his public work he feels, resists, and sets aside the temptation to try and win power over others, whether by raising an army or by miracles of feeding and flight.

Instead, he goes in a new direction. When he takes on the role of servant, this does not mean he wants his disciples to be good servants of existing authorities. Instead, they are to be a community of equals, calling no human being "father" or "rabbi," and setting aside the hierarchies in which some lord it over others (Matt. 23:1–12, Mark 9:30–37, 10:41–45). What he shows and asks for is precisely described in the following lines:

> *Dear Sister God,*
> *in Christ your love rings true.*
> *Directors, boards and bosses lose their sway.*
> *Your service, free from servitude,*
> *draws out a love that, strong to give,*
> *can struggle, suffer, care and live*
> *a better way.*[12]

Another aspect of Jesus' freedom is the way he deals with his gifts and powers. The gospels preserve the memory of a man with superb command of language and extraordinary gifts of healing and leadership. He acts as one called by God and therefore entitled to call others into discipleship, to reinterpret past laws and declare sins forgiven. Because we see him as God-filled, it is easy to underestimate how perilous it is for anyone to have such a high and heady calling. Compared with other men who have felt the call of destiny, his way of handling it stands out. In patriarchal society, the good man with a sense of destiny sometimes ends up like Napoleon. More often he leads others into guru-centered good works: the hospital with its indispensable saintly founder; the industrial mission revolving round its charismatic leader; the anti-poverty campaign whose organizer can't surrender control. The leader may end up as a guru against his best intentions, or because he cannot resist other people's need to make him so.

Measured against these familiar experiences, Jesus shows how to accept that one has great gifts and a high calling, yet live without self-delusion or arrogance. He neither denies his gifts nor endlessly proves himself by putting them to the test. He resists his disciples' needs for a "strong leader," without rejecting them or (with one exception) causing them to defect. He is truly free—to be himself and to empower others.

His encounters with women show similar freedom from convention, taboo, and patriarchal authority. As Dorothy L. Sayers memorably states it, he was a prophet-teacher who never treated the female sex as "the women, God help us" or "the ladies, God bless them . . . who rebuked without querulousness and praised without condescension; who took their questions and arguments seriously; who never mapped out their sphere for them, never urged them to be feminine or jeered at them for being female; who had no axe to grind and no uneasy male dignity to defend."[13]

Two gospel titles for Jesus express something of his freedom. The first is his own choice: "servant." In taking this role, he comes to us, as a free male, and gives up male power in a way that does not embarrass or paralyze us, but challenges men to give up male power and be free for others as he is:

> *Great God, in Christ you call our name*
> *and then receive us as your own,*
> *not through some merit, right or claim,*
> *but by your gracious love alone.*
> > *We strain to glimpse your mercy-seat*
> > *and find you kneeling at our feet.*
>
> *Then take the towel, and break the bread,*
> *and humble us, and call us friends.*
> *Suffer and serve till all are fed*
> *and show how grandly love intends*
> > *to work till all creation sings,*
> > *to fill all worlds, to crown all things.*
>
> *Great God, in Christ you set us free*
> *your life to live, your joy to share.*
> *Give us your Spirit's liberty*
> *to turn from guilt and dull despair*
> > *and offer all that faith can do*
> > *while love is making all things new.*[14]

In this action, Jesus represents the whole being of God and God's whole way of dealing with us, so that we can also say:

Praise the God who changes places,
leaves the lofty seat,
welcomes us with warm embraces,
stoops to wash our feet.[15]

The other title is "friend," drawing on John 15:12–15, where Jesus calls us "not servants but friends." Masters and servants have an over-under relationship. Masters don't take servants into their confidence: to do so undermines their authority. Friends confide in each other, and the relationship is two-way. Everything we can say about Jesus as our true friend we can also say about what it means for us to be God's friend, and friends to each other. A true friend is one who confides in us, acts as our equal not our superior, speaks the truth in love, and loves to the point of self-sacrifice. The metaphor of God, or Jesus, as friend has been rightly revived in recent theological writing.[16] As friend, Jesus shows us how God means to be "God with us," as Questioning Lover and Loving Critic:

True friends
like us to tell our joys and our fears
and need us to hear their plans and ideas.
Jesus says, travel with me,
and we'll be friends for ever.

True friends
show that they care, when life gets us down.
They never play boss, or push us around.
Jesus says, travel with me,
and we'll be friends for ever.

True friends
say what they think (and sometimes it hurts),
but stay on our side when we're at our worst.
Jesus says, travel with me,
and we'll be friends for ever.

True friends
don't make us pay for all that they give.
They even will die, so others can live.
Jesus says, travel with me,
and we'll be friends for ever.[17]

Jesus and the Father

Jesus is a man following a liberating direction in his behavior toward women. As a male for others, he calls other men to surrender patriarchal power and humbly search, with women, for new patterns of coequal relationship. He also teaches his disciples to call God "Father" and himself speaks of God as "my Father." Knowing God as "Father" is at the heart of his ministry and mission.

It is not, therefore, surprising that any proposal to speak differently to God, especially the suggestion that God can properly be addressed in female terms, leads swiftly to the response that "Jesus called God Father and taught his disciples to do the same," implying that this settles the matter.

It doesn't, of course, because the response is a condensed argument, freeze-dried for instant use, of which only the first term has been stated. Reconstituted, the full argument runs something like this:

- Jesus taught his disciples to pray "our Father" and himself called God "Father." (Fact)
- What Jesus said and did is authoritative for us. (First claim)
- The way it is authoritative is as a rule book that we must follow precisely, without change or deviation. (Second claim)
- In calling God "Father" and teaching his disciples to do the same, Jesus was also teaching them and us that God may never be spoken to in female terms. (Third claim)
- Therefore, Jesus has given us a binding rule that we must speak to God in personal metaphors only if they are male not female, and only if the word *Father* is predominant. (Conclusion)

The conclusion is only warranted if all three claims hold true, but the second and third claims are untenable. They come from reading a prejudice into the text, not reading evidence out of it. The second claim is contradicted by Jesus' ministry, which is not rule-based, but God-centered and love-directed. He teaches with mind-teasing parables, not mind-closing edicts. He overturns the rule mentality of the Pharisees by offering God's overflowing, immeasurably generous love precisely, openly, and deliberately to the very people who did not, or could not, keep the Law of Moses. The Gospel of John presents him as commanding us to love, but this language is itself paradoxical, since love breaks through laws even when guided by them. Paul correctly interprets Jesus by announcing a gospel of justification by grace through faith, not by works of the Law.

The third claim misreads the gospels and makes nonsense of the incarnation. Speaking to his first-century Jewish disciples, Jesus said, "When you pray, say 'Our Father . . . ' " This is not at all the same as saying, "When all future Christians pray, they may only speak to God in terms of male authority figures." Seen in its historical context, what Jesus said is a statement with depth and motivating power. Wrenching it out of that context, and treating it as a paragraph in an eternal rule book, means disvaluing the incarnation and saying that God did not, after all, fully accept the limitations involved in being among us as a male Galilean prophet-rabbi, "crucified under Pontius Pilate" two thousand years ago. For one of the unbreachable limitations of human existence is our inability to predict the remote future, or know even approximately what will happen a century after our time. The Word-made-flesh experienced all those limitations, and in doing so revealed the glory of divine humility and God's complete integrity with us.

To accept God's self-revelation in the incarnation means that we stop looking for Christ the eternal rule giver or demigod disguised in human clothing and take him utterly seriously as the person he was. His authority stems from his particularity. Accepting him as authoritative means understanding and valuing what his teaching and practice meant in his own specific historical context, and then asking how we, in our twentieth-century context, can be faithful to his intent and direction.

The context in which Jesus called God "Father" was partly ancient Hebrew Scripture (our "Old Testament") and partly the customs of his own time. In Hebrew Scripture God is called "Father" only fifteen times, and the title conveys a sense of God's absolute authority combined with loving tenderness and the conviction that God is the creator of all things. By the time of Jesus, God could be spoken of as the Father of an individual Jew, whereas previously God was only seen as Father of the people or nation.

Jesus calls God "my Father," showing his awareness and conviction of a special relationship with God. His communion with God as "*my* Father" is the source of his authority. I said earlier that something set him free from the drives and norms of patriarchal malehood. The gospels speak of this "something" in two ways: his anointing by the Holy Spirit, at baptism and thereafter, and his special relationship with God as Father.

The Aramaic words Jesus used, and their meaning, are in dispute. We cannot be sure that *Abba* was the only word for "Father" that Jesus used, or that it meant something more childlike than other names. Rather than hang arguments on one word, it is safer to look at the *character* of the God whom Jesus knew as "Father."[18] The word *Abba* is useful, even if linguistically inexact, because for contemporary English speakers it is free from the heavy baggage of associations that cluster around "God the Father." We learn Abba's character from the explicit teaching of Jesus, from the way he dealt with people he met (since in doing so he claimed to represent God's active love), and from the conduct he asked of his disciples (since this is meant to mirror and respond to God's love).

Thus, Mark 1:40–2:17 might suggest (as it did to one seminar group) that Abba is indignant with the ways society treats outcasts; is willing to remove stigmas that separate and divide; feels empathy deeply for the hurting, sick, and outcast; is available when called on; breaks cultural barriers; and wants table fellowship with all people. To another group, Matthew 23:1–39 suggested that Abba loves integrity; helps people carry their heavy loads; loves the ones who are humble; does not like hypocrites; loves justice, mercy, and good faith more than precise keeping of the law; and is disgusted with greed and self-indulgence. Mark 5:21–43 suggested that Abba is a healer of women (a daughter, a woman, and a little girl); is approachable by crowds; is compassionate; cuts through distractions and doesn't get sidetracked. Matthew 5–6 (the Sermon on the Mount) depicts Abba as one who seeks relationships; is consoling and has a gentle spirit; is merciful, pure, and righteous, a peacemaker willing to suffer; has a generosity knowing no bounds; is unconditional love; longs to see reconciliation between human beings; is beyond our ken but with us always; does not discriminate in giving nature's gifts; and is not hypocritical.

Even from this quick glance at a few passages, it is clear that what Abba/Father meant to Jesus is a rich, complex characterization not tied to the maleness of the word *father* or to patriarchal notions of fatherly authority. Jesus taught his disciples to pray "our Father" not to make them idolize a word, but to help them focus a relationship. He called God "Father," and taught his disciples to pray "our Father," in the context of his particular mission within first-century Palestinian Judaism. His mission was centered on the announcement that God's active rule ("kingdom") was at hand. He proclaimed that kingdom not as the dominance of God Almighty, but as the governance of Abba. "In this kingdom," as Jürgen Moltmann observes, "God is not the Lord; he is the merciful Father. In this kingdom there are no servants; there are only God's free children. In this kingdom what is required is not obedience and submission; it is love and free participation."[19] The rule of God as Abba is prefigured and demonstrated by Jesus, as he calls the weary and heavy-laden to himself, brings the poor the joyful news that the kingdom is theirs, treats subordinated women as equal human beings, and offers friendship and gracious acceptance to Zacchaeus before he shows any sign of repentance.

In other words, Jesus knew and named God as Abba/Father in the context of a patriarchal society, but in such a way that the patriarchal order was itself called into question. Being faithful to him, therefore, means naming and praising God in ways that point us toward the loving community he inaugurated, and call our patriarchal order into question.

In Jesus' time, women had no hope of emancipation from male control, and to name God in female terms was not an option. It would have been an incomprehensible break with the past. "Father" was close enough to past usage to be accepted, but Jesus' characterization of Abba was innovative enough to provoke new insight. At that moment in history, seeing God in terms suggestive of a male head of household who risks himself in costly acts of unexpected love was a clear way of signaling radical change, from over-under relationships to a community of equals with only one Abba.

Our moment in history is very different. Naming God as Father is still one important way of meeting God as our caring, loyal, and forgiving parent. Yet that name no longer has the power, *in our context,* to subvert patriarchal norms: indeed it is angrily invoked in defense of them. In Western societies at least, women have made their first strides toward emancipation. For the first time in Christian history, women are gaining access to theology as a public forum for seeking to understand our faith, and many are ministering with full status in Christian churches. In our context, naming God in female terms is in line with Jesus' intentions. By demonstrating the equality of women and men, and the fitness of women to image the living God for us, it calls our own patriarchal society into question as nothing else can.

When Jesus knew God as his own personal "Father," he was, no doubt, expressing his experience and vocation in the most appropriate imagery that "came to mind." The metaphor of God as Abba was not "mere metaphor." Though we have no means of knowing, it is fair to assume that it was, for him, an obvious and inescapable choice, imparted in one or more moments of insight, as the baptism and transfiguration stories suggest.

Nonetheless, what Jesus was doing in linguistic terms was coining the metaphor that most accurately portrayed the quality of relationship he experienced. As already noted, that quality of relationship is not conveyed only by the word *Father.* It is visible in everything Jesus said about God, in his encounters with women and men, and in the life-style expected of his new community. The seminar groups previously quoted suggest that Abba's attributes include caring, self-giving, gracious, trustworthy, vulnerable, noncoercive, persistent in love, peacemaking, seeking justice, loving the enemy, including the excluded, love never tired out, and love outrunning the worst evil and sin.

What metaphors and similes best express that caring, self-giving, spontaneity, and vulnerability *for us?* If we let our imagination loose on that question, new images of God will be released, sparked by the contact between twentieth-century experience and the gospel record. The test is not whether they verbally imitate the patriarchal framework in which Jesus lived and moved two thousand years ago, but whether they are in tune with the qualities of relationship he experienced with God.

Some of the hymns already quoted point in that direction. Abba is "warm father God, hugging every child," but also our "strong mother God, planning all the wonders of creation." Abba's care and self-giving reach us in the "ever-seeking Lover" whose grace brings us to rebirth. Abba is our Nudging Discomforter, waking our lives to creative unease; our Straight-Talking Lover, speaking the truth that sets us free; and the Weaver of all our stories, quilting our histories, patching our sins with grace. Abba is the Mother of creation, caring for her people, making human-kind God's midwife, helping to bring new possibilities to birth on this planet. Abba is the Spirit, seeking peace and justice. Abba is vulnerable and self-giving, the Lover of creation who joins us in our history, the Life-Giving Loser, wounded and weeping, whose love heals and redeems.

As in Chapter 6, the key word is *love*. The Gospel and Let-ters of John, and Paul in 1 Corinthians 13, were correct in taking love as the essential revelation of God in Jesus. The revelation of God as self-giving suffering seeking love comes to us in patriar-chal forms, but is not bound by them. Love is embodied in Jesus as a beginning, not an ending, so that the love of God may dwell in more and more people and move through all human history.

Open-Ended Incarnation

The incarnation is open-ended. If we make incarnation in Jesus the be-all and end-all of God's indwelling human life, the partic-ularity of this one male human being is a stumbling block to faith. If God's embodiment in Jesus is a stepping stone to the outpour-ing of the Spirit on all flesh (Joel 2, Acts 2), and God's indwelling all human beings, the maleness of Jesus becomes less obtrusive, and God's love is seen as dynamic, moving, and developing through space-time.

From early times, Christian theology got caught up in the problem of explaining how Jesus could be divine and human. The understanding of "divine nature" and "human nature" available at the time made it inevitable that the incarnation would be seen as a problem of how two distinct "essences" could be united in a hu-man being without one overpowering the other. Orthodox theology arrived at the doctrine of the "hypostatic union," in which the di-vine nature and human nature in Jesus were seen, paradoxically, as inseparable but distinct.

This statement of faith prevented Jesus from being seen as just a good man whisked up to heaven, or as God dressing up and pretending to be human. But because it saw the union of human and divine from the viewpoint of divine choice, it diminished the freedom of the human male, Jesus of Nazareth, to accept or reject his messianic vocation. Though the doctrine intended to preserve that freedom, the way it was formulated pushed it into the background. The doctrine of the hypostatic union also focused "incarnation" exclusively on this one male person. It implied that God was fully here, therefore in no one else, not that God was fully here, in order to indwell many others.[20]

Though I cannot explain here how a doctrine of incarnation can still be intellectually coherent, I shall take it on faith and look at a neglected aspect of biblical tradition. John 14–15 is an important source. In the Upper Room discourse, Jesus tells his disciples that believers will do greater things than he has done and promises that the Spirit will dwell in and with his disciples. The metaphor of the vine and the branches states that the fruitful branch is pruned, then bears new fruit. In the other gospels, the special relationship Jesus has with Abba makes him outgoing, loving, and giving: the Son of Man comes to be a ransom for many and to give his life away. He stands between God and humankind not as a wall, but as a bridge.

This understanding of incarnation is expressed in a hymn based on John 1:14 ("Good Is the Flesh" in the Gallery that follows this chapter). The Word becomes flesh, and one of the implications of this is that God loves the human body and calls it good:

> *Good is the flesh that the Word has become,*
> *good is the birthing, the milk in the breast,*
> *good is the feeding, caressing and rest,*
> *good is the body for knowing the world,*
> *Good is the flesh that the Word has become.*

Through our bodies we know the world, "sensing the sunlight, the tug of the ground," feeling and perceiving our environment through all five senses. The human body is loved by God, and lovely to God, "from cradle to grave, growing and aging, arousing, impaired." Finally, the hymn praises the open-endedness of incarnation:

Good is the pleasure of God in our flesh,
longing in all, as in Jesus, to dwell,
glad of embracing, and tasting, and smell,
good is the body, for good and for God,
Good is the flesh that the Word has become.

To see the incarnation as open-ended does not mean losing touch with Jesus of Nazareth. It means that in thinking about how "God was in Christ," we follow the guideline of the gospel records, where Jesus, aware of his own unique destiny, never uses that awareness to draw attention and honor to himself, but points us away from himself, to praise Abba-God and love our neighbor. The risen Christ does not strut the schoolyard of history, chanting, "True God, True Man, you can't be like me, nobody can." He says, "I must go, that the Spirit may come." The male for others bids us look for the freeing of women and men by the indwelling Spirit of God.

Gallery: Songs of Incarnation

Birthsong*

Her baby, newly breathing,
with wailing needful cry,
by Mary kissed and cradled,
is lulled in lullaby.
Long months of hope and waiting,
the thrill and fear of birth,
are crowned with exultation,
and God is on the earth.

The eyes that gaze at Mary
have yet to name or trace
the world of shape and color,
or recognize a face;
yet Holiness Eternal
is perfectly expressed
in hands that clutch unthinking,
and lips that tug the breast.

The milk of life is flowing
as Mary guides and feeds
her wordless Word, embodied
in infant joys and needs.
Enormous, formless strivings,
and yearnings deep and wide,
becradled in communion,
are fed and satisfied.

How mother-like the wisdom
   that carried and gave birth
to all things, seen and unseen,
   and nurtured infant earth:
unstinting, unprotected,
   prepared for nail and thorn,
constricted into maleness,
   and of a woman born.

Good Is the Flesh*
(Genesis 1:30, John 1:14, John 14:23)

Good is the flesh that the Word has become,
   good is the birthing, the milk in the breast,
   good is the feeding, caressing and rest,
   good is the body for knowing the world,
Good is the flesh that the Word has become.

Good is the body for knowing the world,
   sensing the sunlight, the tug of the ground,
   feeling, perceiving, within and around,
   good is the body, from cradle to grave,
Good is the flesh that the Word has become.

Good is the body, from cradle to grave,
   growing and ageing, arousing, impaired,
   happy in clothing, or lovingly bared,
   good is the pleasure of God in our flesh,
Good is the flesh that the Word has become.

Good is the pleasure of God in our flesh,
   longing in all, as in Jesus, to dwell,
   glad of embracing, and tasting, and smell,
   good is the body, for good and for God,
Good is the flesh that the Word has become.

New Disciples*

1

Woman in the night,
spent from giving birth,
guard our precious light,
peace is on earth!

Refrain after each stanza:
Come and join the song,
women, children, men.
Jesus makes us free
to live again.

2

Woman in the crowd,
creeping up behind,
touching is allowed:
seek and you will find!

3

Woman at the well,
question the Messiah,
find your friends and tell,
drink your hearts desire!

4

Woman at the feast,
let the righteous stare,
come and go in peace,
love him with your hair!

5

Woman in the house,
nurtured to be meek,
leave your second place:
listen, think, and speak!

6

Women on the road,
welcomed and restored,
travel far and wide,
witness to the Lord!

7

Women on the hill,
stand when men have fled,
Christ needs loving still,
though your hope is dead!

8

Women in the dawn,
care and spices bring:
earliest to mourn;
earliest to sing!

Magnificat*

(Luke 1:26–55, Mark 3:20–35, John 19:25–27)

Daughter Mary, saying yes
to the angel's visitation,
   no disgrace
   shall cloud your face.
Thrill us with your expectation:
     As in heaven, so on earth,
       God will work salvation
     as the child you bring to birth
     checks the wealthy, feeds the poor,
     ends all domination.

Mother Mary, crying no
at your son's disruptive vision,
   he must roam
   away from home,
breaking family cohesion:
     Planting heaven here on earth,
       God's new invitation
     brings the outcasts to rebirth,
     lifts the humble, shifts the proud,
     ending domination.

Sister Mary, pierced and torn
as the child your arms protected
   chokes and dies
   before your eyes,
trust again the unexpected:
     Love has broken free on earth!
       Tiers of domination
     tumble as the Spirit's mirth,
     weaving friendship, sparking hope,
     sings of new creation.

8

The Dance in God Begun

A woman in the crowd
quietly hides her defiling blood.
    Who can tell
twelve years of tiredness, longing to be well?
Yet trusting her Spirit, refusing to be cowed,
she touches a coat-sleeve, and feels God is good.

A beggar always blind
washes his face, and is dazzled by light.
    How can he,
punished by blindness, claim that he can see?
Yet trusting his Spirit, while many close their mind,
he greets God in Jesus, and sharpens his sight.

An immigrant from Tyre
argues for crumbs from the table of grace.
    Should her child
get special treatment, foreign and defiled?
Yet led by the Spirit, she senses the Messiah,
and knows that he comes to the whole human race.[1]

I said earlier that something set Jesus free from the drives of patriarchal malehood, and that the gospels speak of that "something" in terms of his anointing by the Holy Spirit and special relationship with God. The above hymn expresses that threeness. There is the free male, *Jesus,* in whom others feel and greet *God,* and in whom they recognize the *Spirit.*

At first, that threesome experience was simply praised, proclaimed, and lived with. But Jewish faith is founded on the knowledge that there is only one God. Sooner or later, the threesome experience had to be thought about and related to the founding conviction of God's oneness. At that time it could only be thought about within the KINGAFAP metaphor system. Tertullian (b. A.D. 160) laid the first foundations. In his treatise *Against Praxeas*, his primary data were the oneness or unity of God, and the Father-Son relationship, as recorded in Christian Scripture. From this he concluded that the Son was equally to be worshipped, and in some sense of the same identity as the Father. Like the Son, the Spirit had also been recognized as divine from early times.

In a polytheistic environment, it was essential to avoid any suspicion that Christians were talking about three distinct gods, and Tertullian's illustrations reflect this concern. Father, Son, and Spirit are compared to a root, its shoot, and its fruit; to a spring, leading to a river, leading to an irrigation canal; and to the sun, its sunbeam, and the patch of ground it lights up. Later reflection showed the inadequacy of such metaphors. The root, shoot, and fruit are merely stages of one plant, just as the other two metaphors only suggest stages or aspects of running water and sunlight. Such illustrations safeguard oneness but lose any real sense of threeness in God.

In Cappadocia (Asia Minor), two centuries later, Basil (b. 330), his brother Gregory of Nyssa (b. about 334), and another Gregory, of Nazianzum (b about 330), worked with the same data and metaphors, but considerably refined them. Like Tertullian, they accepted the sequence given in the KINGAFAP system, where the King sends the Crown Prince to do his work, and then sends the Spirit, either through the Son or jointly with the Son. We know God from the one Spirit through the one Son to the one Father, says Basil, "and conversely the natural goodness and inherent holiness of the royal dignity extend from the Father through the Only-Begotten to the Spirit." In his *Treatise to Ablabius*, Gregory of Nyssa says that the Father, Son, and Spirit do not act on their own, but that every operation from God to creation has its origin in the Father, proceeds through the Son, and reaches completion in the Spirit.

Though this sequence was the story line of Christian worship, these theologians knew it was inadequate. If all three Persons are fully divine, they must be coequal: there cannot be grades and rankings of divinity. So though they accepted the sequence as basic data, revealed in Scripture, they broke through it into a new understanding. "Whoever receives the Father virtually receives *at the same time* both the Son and the Spirit," said Basil (Letter 38 to Gregory of Nyssa). Gregory of Nyssa agreed that the sequence did not mean a subordination of Spirit to Son to Father. Instead, the three Persons in the godhead "jointly, inseparably and mutually exercise their divine power and activity." Moreover, though any movement must ordinarily entail a time interval, however small, this is misleading when applied to God, since it would be incompatible with the idea that all three persons act together. Thus Gregory concluded that "no delay exists or is to be conceived in the movement of the divine will from the Father through the Son and to the Holy Spirit."

In their illustrations, the Cappadocians were less afraid of tritheism. Though Gregory of Nazianzus rejected all images as inadequate ("for it is not possible to trace out any image exactly to the full extent of the truth"), he used the image of three men acting together to illustrate the three Persons, and at one point suggested the biblical family of Adam, Eve, and their son Seth as a parallel.

A little later, Augustine showed the same awareness of the difficulty of expressing threeness and oneness. It takes time to say the words "Father, Son and Holy Spirit," he observed, but the oneness of the Trinity is not like that, for it can have no intervals of time or place (*De Trinitate*, 4:21–30). His metaphors follow Tertullian rather than the Cappadocians. For example, he compared the Trinity with contemporary understandings of memory, intellect, and will, which saw them as separate aspects of a person, acting together. All three are involved in the act of naming any one of them: I have to *will* or want to speak of my *intellect*, and *remember* what "intellect" means in order to speak of it, for example. Yet even in Augustine's time the three were aspects of *one human individual*, thus stressing oneness against threeness.

Augustine began a helpful train of thought by speaking of the three Persons in terms of love, which has the advantages of being biblical and potentially nonsexist. Thus he says that in a love relationship there are three things: the one who loves, the one who is loved, and the love between them. The Holy Spirit can be called "that absolute love which joins together Father and Son" (*De Trinitate*, 7:3–6, 8:10–14). Scripture proclaims that God is love, and the Holy Spirit is especially called love because "he" is the greatest gift of God and is the Spirit of love uniting the Father and the Son (*De Trinitate*, 5:19–37).

These examples illustrate important trends in trinitarian thinking. First, it is not free speculation, but an attempt to make sense of what has been revealed in Christian history. Second, illustrations of the trinity have either emphasized oneness at the cost of threeness, or less frequently overemphasized threeness, and this seems to be an inescapable problem, whatever images are used. Third, trinitarian thought has remained in close orbit around its original metaphors, attempting to redefine or qualify them to overcome their inadequacies. Basic to the original metaphors are an interpersonal relationship between two of the Persons (Father and Son); a different metaphor for the Third Person (Spirit); and a KINGAFAP-based sequence with the King-Father giving orders to his Son and the Spirit being sent by the Father alone or Father and Son together.

These trends continue into modern times. Jürgen Moltmann is a good example.[2] He starts from the biblical record and focuses first on the threesome experience: if we take it seriously, he argues, our problem is not how the one God can be three, but how the threesome experience can be one God. Our best attempts at explanation will fail, because the answer will only be clear to us when all God's purposes are accomplished. Moltmann's other starting point for trinitarian doctrine is the crucifixion, where Jesus dies forsaken by God. God can only appear in our history as God really is, not because God is limited, but because it is not in God's nature to deceive us. The experience of separation in Jesus' cry is therefore an experience within the life of God and poses the first trinitarian problem: how can oneness be so utterly rent asunder, and how can such separation be an unbreakable oneness?

It is interesting to watch Moltmann dealing with the Father-Son metaphor. In keeping with the biblical record, "Father" is Abba, and the "kingdom" of God is marked not by hierarchy, but by freedom. "In this kingdom there are no servants; there are only God's free children. In this kingdom what is required is not obedience and submission; it is love and free participation," demonstrated by the Son's brotherliness and friendship.[3]

When Moltmann speaks of relationships within the Trinity, however, he uses different language. The love of Father and Son is that of like for like, he says. "In eternity and out of the necessity of his being the Father loves the only begotten son . . . with a love that both engenders and brings forth. In eternity and out of the very necessity of his being the Son responds to the Father's love *through his obedience and his surrender.*"[4] If obedience and submission are not required in the kingdom of God announced by Jesus, what are they doing in the eternal relationship between First and Second Persons of the Trinity? What Moltmann's own exposition logically demands is an adult, coequal relationship between Father and Son, based on friendship, love, and care. Instead, the traditional associations of the metaphor lead him back into a patriarchal framework.

The maleness of the metaphor also hinders Moltmann's attempts to escape from its gender reference. If the Son proceeds from the Father alone, he argues, this is both a begetting and a birth, meaning that the relationship between First and Second Persons must be modeled from both male and female roles in the bringing forth of new human life. A "Father" who begets and bears is not a father in the male sense. "He is a motherly father too." This is not a new thought, but was expressed in an early Christian council, at Toledo in A.D. 675: "It must be held that the Son was created, neither out of nothingness nor yet out of any substance, but that He was begotten or born out of the Father's womb [Latin: *de utero Patris*], that is, out of his very essence." On the most favorable interpretation, this is an attempt to move beyond the limitations of the male metaphor of Father and Son. Yet the attempt founders on the maleness of that metaphor. Incorporating female functions into a divine life imaged in male terms is simply a repeat, on a cosmic scale, of the male-as-norm syndrome. The male stays in control and either admits some aspects of the feminine into himself or takes over female functions. This is not a breakthrough from patriarchy, but a reassertion of it.

Moltmann pinpoints some longstanding problems relating to the third center of personhood in the Trinity. Augustine saw the spirit as the bond of love between Father and Son, though only as an illustration. Moltmann criticizes Karl Barth for following that line of thought too far. "If the Spirit is only termed the unity of what is separated," he argues, "then he loses every center of activity. He is then an energy, but not a Person."[5] It has always been difficult for Christian faith to know and worship the Holy Spirit as fully coequal with the "Father" and "Son," because the doctrine of the Holy Spirit "really has no organic connection" with the doctrine of God the Father and the Son. In his own way, Moltmann sees that the Spirit belongs to a different metaphor system, whereby "the Father utters his eternal Word in the eternal breathing out of the Spirit," so that both Word and Spirit issue simultaneously from the Father. The problem is how to integrate these two metaphor systems (he calls them "patterns") in trinitarian discussion, namely, "the logic of the Father and the Son and the logic of the Word and the Spirit."[6]

This misstates the problem, for not only are the metaphor systems incompatible, but the Father-Word-Spirit triad reduces the Second and Third Persons to aspects of the First (since words and breath cannot be coequal with their speaker), while neither set of metaphors shows the Holy Spirit as on a par with the other two centers of personhood. If Moltmann's route is adopted, it will prove endlessly necessary to explain that "Word" and "Spirit" are *not really* as subordinate as the metaphor makes them.

Principles and Problems

If a God-metaphor has serious limitations, we can try to mitigate them by explaining that it doesn't mean exactly what it says. Yet if it is a basic metaphor, a metaphor we live by, it will continue to shape the way we think and will limit what can be said and known. In worship, the qualifications and explanations of theologians have little effect, since what counts is the metaphor's impact on the imagination. Our knowledge of the Trinity as love-in-relationship is limited by the male metaphor of Father and Son, its patriarchal formation, and by the difficulty of naming the Holy Spirit as a fully coequal center of divine personhood. In worship, the traditional doxology pictures God as an all-male one-parent family with a whoosh of vapor. Our images of God are male and monarchical, however often we sing "Holy, Holy, Holy" or talk about the Trinity—and few of us do that very often.

There are as yet no widely accepted alternative metaphors to stand alongside Father-Son, Spirit-Word, and their combinations.

Most recent attempts retain Spirit/Holy Spirit for the Third Person of the Trinity, and replace Father and Son with such words as *Creator, God, the One, Provider of all,* and *Word, Christ, Jesus Christ, the Christ.* Though less overtly male-imaged than the traditional formula, they break no new ground and are often inadequately trinitarian.[7] Alternative doxologies are most likely to emerge from experiment based on trinitarian experience: from habits of thinking, praying, and praising that delight in the complexity of the one God. Some have only limited use, for example:

> *Praise the God who changes places,*
>   *leaves the lofty seat,*
> *welcomes us with warm embraces,*
>   *stoops to wash our feet . . .*
> *Praise the Rabbi, speaking, doing*
>   *all that God intends . . .*
> *Praise the Breath of Love, whose freedom*
>   *spreads our waking wings.*[8]

Though this experiences God as Trinity, it does not condense into an adequate doxology. We need more experimentation, and more theological work, before new trinitarian formulas can emerge and gain acceptance.

One issue is whether our metaphors should veer toward oneness or threeness. Historically, trinitarian metaphors have inescapably veered one way or the other, suggesting either that there are three separate Gods (tritheism) or one God who only appears to be three. This latter distortion is known as Sabellianism, after an early proponent, Sabellius, who taught that the one God appears to us in three different forms: in the form of the Father as Creator; in the form of the Son as Redeemer; and in the form of the Spirit as the Giver of life. This implies that the three forms are a single center of divine personhood seen, as it were, from different angles. Talking of God as Creator, Redeemer, and Sustainer is a step back to that distortion, not a step forward in nonsexist language.

Tritheism has always been more feared than Sabellianism. Even today, theological fingers wag in disapproval against any whiff of tritheism. This is odd, since Western Christianity no longer lives in a polytheistic environment (the situation may be different for Christians living among a dominant Hinduism). In Britain or America, the risk of small-town congregations going tritheist is about as likely as their town electing a Communist mayor.

We should be more concerned about the recurring tendency to collapse back into a divine duo (God and Jesus) or a simple monotheism. Such tendencies accommodate perfectly to patriarchy, which always looks for a single leader. Fear of tritheism may be a patriarchal twitch, since patriarchal religion is mon-archic at heart. For Western Christians at the end of the twentieth century, tritheism is a dead issue. We should treat it as such and be willing to risk trinitarian metaphors of God as three partners in close cooperation, to do justice to the threesome experience, which is unique to Christianity. God should not be imagined as "a being" alone in solitary splendor. On the contrary, God longs to see communion, cooperation, sharing, and the flowering of free individuals in relationships of mutual love because such relationships and communion are rooted in how God is, deep within the godhead.

Trinitarian tradition has often glimpsed this, despite the limitations of its founding metaphors. In the seventh century John of Damascus used the Greek word *perichoresis* (literally "dance around") to describe how the three divine Persons relate to one another (the Latin translation replaced this with a word meaning sitting together, which lost the dynamism of the Greek). Perichoresis means that the three Persons continually exchange energy, being, and power, so that each partakes of the other. It suggests a beautiful intertwining, unending dance, whose movement flows to and fro between the dancers. Trinitarian metaphors should strive for that sense of dynamic, intertwining movement.

In speaking of the Trinity, problems arise with the word *person*. This has changed its meaning since early times, and though historical reflection helps us recapture earlier meanings, there is no way back to them in the devotional mode, where contemporary connotations are bound to be uppermost. Our problem, therefore, is what *modern* understanding we should work from and try to establish in the imagination. A person is, roughly, a human being in all her aspects, unique and aware of her individual existence, to whom all other human beings are "other," though some may also be very alike. In capitalist society we are strongly aware of each person as a self-contained individual and are encouraged in that

awareness by the approval our society gives to competition between individuals.

   To understand the "persons" of the Trinity in that way is a
nonstarter, for the three must be seen as in the closest communion: it would be ridiculous to picture games of Monopoly between them. Yet our experience of personhood has another strand
to it. No one is an island, though some of us try to be. We know
from child psychology that a human being only becomes a person
in a loving relationship with parent figures and others. To be a
person is to be in relationship with others, part of a social network, and we are most truly free to be ourselves when we know
that we are valued and loved by other persons.[9]

   We should therefore seek to name God in terms drawn from
the communal and relational meanings of human personal existence. Because of its individualistic connotations in our culture,
person may not be the best word to suggest this. What trinitarian
faith tries to express is the conviction that God is "a unity of three
centers of awareness and centeredness who are also perfectly
open and interdependent on each other . . . three centers of
divine identity, self-aware and self-giving in love, self-possessed
yet freely transcending the self in eternal trinitarian intercon-
nectedness."[10] The phrase "centers of personhood" seems to me
a useful way of suggesting this, because it includes the word *person*, but in a way that suggests we are not talking about "persons"
as we know them, and certainly not about individualists.

The Personhood of the Spirit

Personal and relational metaphors have always been available for
the first and second centers of divine personhood. The third has
been recognized as coequal, but without receiving names that do
justice to that recognition. Sallie McFague argues that "friend" or
"companion" is a better metaphor than "Spirit" and develops
models of God as mother, lover, and friend to depict God's creating, saving, and sustaining activities in relation to the world.[11]
Her reasons for rejecting "Spirit" are that the word is amorphous,
vague, and colorless; that the limitation of Spirit language to

divine activity in human beings disqualifies it from speaking of divine activity as the breath of life in all things; that it reinforces the entrenched separation between "spirit" and "matter" and tends toward an individualistic understanding of God's action.

It may be granted that by itself the word *Spirit* (or *Holy Spirit*) suggests something vague and amorphous, or minimally useful images of haunting and intoxication. In worship, however, it frequently appears with metaphors conveying more richness and power. To take one example, a recent British hymnal names the third center of personhood as comforter, redeemer, lord, breath of God, dove, guest, giver, guide, counselor, paraclete, well, advocate, fount of our being, love divine, God's voice, father of the poor, and Word of God.[12] The most common metaphors suggest powerful energy, wild and untamable: wind, fire, breath, and water, as in the following:

> *Holy Spirit, storm of love,*
>   *break our self-protective walls . . .*
>
> *Deep, cool well of peace,*
>   *wine of mercy at the feast,*
>   Holy Spirit, come!
> *Green, strong, living oak,*
>   *seed and root and flower of hope,*
>   Holy Spirit, come!
> *Fire, flame, blazing light,*
>   *judgement, justice, truth and light,*
>   Holy Spirit, come!
> *Great, wild eagle-dove,*
>   *storm and breath and song of love,*
>   Holy Spirit, come!
>
> *Come, singing fire, of truth, compassion, right,*
>   *and scorch our hardened apathy*
>   *till love is new and bright . . .*
> *Come, singing breeze, from world's already new.*
>   *Blow in and out of weary minds*
>   *till faith is singing too . . .*
> *Come, singing light, from new creation's dawn,*
>   *where trees of healing deck the streets*
>   *and joy is newly born.*[13]

What we should be considering is not the word *Spirit* alone, but *Spirit* together with its most commonly associated images.

On McFague's second point, I am not convinced that the historical emphasis on the Third Person's activity in individuals prevents us from widening our vision. When I began hymn writing in the early 1960s, our hymnbook had plenty to say about the Holy Spirit's gifts to the individual, somewhat less about the Spirit in the church, hardly anything about the Spirit in human life and history, and nothing at all about the Spirit in creation. My reading of the situation now is that though powerful movements still overemphasize the Spirit's gifts to the individual, there are more hymns on the Spirit in the church and the world, and that it is certainly *possible* to widen the understanding and associations of "Spirit" still further in preaching, prayer, and praise. Images like the following are a beginning, and McFague's critique is a stimulus to take this line of thought further.

> *Great soaring Spirit,*
> *sweeping in uncharted flight*
> *across the bounds of time and space,*
> *God's breath of love,*
> *you fill the outflung galaxies*
> *and move through earth's long centuries*
> *with aching, mending, dancing grace.*[14]

I therefore prefer to regard the question as open, as Sallie McFague also does in relation to her preferred God-metaphors of "friend" and "lover," whose past individualistic associations don't apparently disqualify them from communal and creational developments.

The word *Spirit* has undeniably been used to emphasize God's actions in individuals, and it is difficult to resist our culture's divisions of spirit and matter, as in the common misuse of the word *spiritual* to mean things inward, nonmaterial, uplifting, but without political consequences, in contrast to the material, political, and fleshly aspects of existence. Though such dichotomies are not derived from biblical experience,[15] they are difficult to dislodge. Yet though her reservations are well founded, Sallie McFague's suggestion that we replace "Spirit" with "friend/companion" is unhelpful. To begin with, it isn't practical politics: however well founded the reservations, there is unlikely to be much support for such a move. The problem is better dealt with by highlighting the many other metaphors available in tradition for the third center of divine personhood, and using the word *Spirit* more sparingly. Another way forward is to ensure that the words *Spirit/ Holy Spirit* are used in combination with other strong metaphors, including metaphors of community and relationship. With those provisos, a modified form of "friend" may be illuminating, as we shall see.

Many Third Person metaphors are nonpersonal: for example, fire, wind, breath, water, dove, and hovering wings. Sallie McFague does not distinguish between "spirit" and these other metaphors, but her preference for "friend/companion" suggests she would reject them as well. She certainly shows the importance of *personal* God-metaphors. Since they draw on experiences we know from the inside, they have more credibility and immediacy for us than any others. They are also the richest model: it is not human-centered pride to say that we are the most complex creatures we know, with depths we ourselves cannot fathom, and thus the best model by which God can be revealed to us.[16]

Yet nonpersonal God-metaphors are frequent in the Bible,[17] and are vouched for by McFague's own discussion. For if God indwells creation, so that we can think of all nature as God's child or even God's "body,"[18] there must be aspects of the divine that only metaphors drawn from nature can point to. Nonpersonal metaphors are needed to protect us from cozy God-images tailored to our own perceptions, and to encounter God's strangeness and otherness. Without nonpersonal metaphors, our image of God becomes domesticated; without personal metaphors, God is unknowable and alien. Both are needed, in harmony and dissonance.

Many of the nonpersonal metaphors uplift the value of "wildness"—nonrational, untamable, unpredictable energy. If we are trying to escape from hierarchical separations of reason from the emotional and intuitive aspects of human experience, these metaphors will become more valued, not less. The rushing, mighty wind, the storm and breath of love, the fire of empowering and inspiration, and the hovering wings of the eagle-dove suggest that the third center of divine personhood can't be pinned down or controlled—and what applies to one center of personhood applies, of course, to all three.

The second center of personhood, constricted into maleness and revealed to us in Jesus, is by no means an epitome of cool reason. Jesus is anointed and possessed by the Spirit, who drives him into the wilderness. He withdraws unexpectedly from crowds and speaks and acts unexpectedly in his encounters with individuals. "The wind blows where it wills; you hear the sound of it, but you do not know where it comes from, or where it is going. So with everyone who is born from spirit," says Jesus (John 3:8). In saying this he speaks not only of his disciples, but of himself.[19]

Whether or not we use the word *Spirit*, the third center of divine personhood was known from the beginning of Christian experience as the one who creates unity, in whom we communicate with each other, and whose highest gift is interpersonal love. John V. Taylor gives a helpful model of the Holy Spirit as an anonymous go-between not only between one person and another, but between human beings and the world of nature. What makes a person, a landscape, an idea, come to life for me and become a presence toward which I surrender myself, he asks? I recognize, respond, fall in love, yet it was not I that took the first step, but the third center of divine personhood, who activates awareness and makes human beings aware—of the nonhuman as presence, and of each other as persons.[20] Making us aware is itself a work of love, for "one cannot choose to be open in one direction and closed in another. Vision and vulnerability go together."[21] To human beings there is a certain anonymity about the third center of personhood: "You cannot commune with the Holy Spirit, for he [sic] is communion itself." We cannot know the otherness of the Holy Spirit, only the aliveness brought by the Spirit's presence, and the inertness felt in the Spirit's absence.[22] The fullness of the Spirit is marked by a communal awareness of the reality of God and Jesus, and a new communal awareness toward other people (and, one may add, toward other life forms and nature itself). Christian Scripture speaks of the communion of the Holy Spirit (2 Cor. 13:14).[23]

To summarize, Christian experience of the third center of divine personhood is of Someone known through both nonpersonal and personal metaphors, the anonymous Go-Between who creates love relationships in community and opens us to the impact of the divine in other life forms and inanimate things. This Someone has an element of wildness and unpredictability, and reminds us that God is not under our control. To know the Trinity more adequately, we need fully personal names for the Third Someone. What we can say of this Someone will also be applicable to the other two centers of divine personhood, as they each exchange their gifts, experience, and energies. To speak of the Third Someone in personal names is the unfinished business of trinitarian theology, because without such names the Trinity is reduced to a duality linked by a less than personal love bond. Yet when the work is done, we shall do well to be suspicious of neat and tidy formulas, for our experience is that this Someone, like the other two centers of personhood and the Trinity as a whole, eludes our grasp and cannot be pinned down.

The Keynote Is Love: Trinitarian Possibilities

We need a trinitarian naming of God that escapes from the patriarchal formation of our founding metaphors. Such a theology will take seriously the Hebrew-Jewish-Christian story that gave us the threesome experience of God and will try to express the full personhood of that Third Someone, traditionally known as Holy Spirit.

In previous chapters, God has been imaged as creating in several ways, as birth-giver, spinner and weaver, the gambler who spins the wheel of randomness and chance, and especially as the Lover whose act of creation involves a letting go of control. God has the capacity to be delighted and surprised by us, and by the workings of creation. God is the Questioning Lover, who passionately cares for us and planet earth, and calls us critically to account; and the Mother who gives birth to all creation, longs for a fair ordering of our planetary home, and rises in impassioned anger when her human children mistreat one another and their companion species on earth. The fullness of God can be named as Womb and Birth of time, Nudging Discomforter, Weaver of Stories, Strong Mother, Warm Father, Listening Sister, and Loyal Brother, as Life-giving Loser, as Companion and Friend. Jesus as friend reveals the impassioned friendship of the whole Trinity, who calls us to be friends of God as we befriend our planet and its varied life.

Though diverse, these metaphors are connected, since their keynote is love-in-relationship. As a connected group of metaphors they are the seed bed of alternatives to KINGAFAP. The key word is *love*, and the focusing metaphor is of *God the Lover*: of creation, history, all life forms, and every human person.

Love is the key word for trinitarian namings, since love is by definition about personal relationships and is not prespecified in terms of gender. Yet three is an odd number in human love relationships. Most close relationships are paired, and group relationships are usually larger than threesomes. The test will be whether we can find metaphors through which we encounter all three centers of divine personhood as fully personal, and which are acceptable in worship as well as in theological reflection. The three centers of personhood are coequal and coeternal. Each is revealed to us as having a unique character (and presumably unique experiences), different from the other two. Yet such is the interchange of energies and experience in the divine dance that the "otherness" of the centers of personhood to each other never causes the separateness we experience from each other, in our broken mirroring of that divine otherness and likeness.

In a trinitarian theology, as opposed to a divine duo in a love bond, each center of personhood will be named by particular metaphors, some of which will be nonpersonal. Yet each must also be nameable by a personal metaphor we can make sense of by connecting it with the other two. It is not enough to speak of the Lover, the Beloved, and the bond or communion of love between them, for though we know people who are lovers and beloveds, their "bonding" is not another person, but merely an aspect of their relationship. A test of the validity of personal metaphors is whether they can be interchanged and attributed to the other two centers of personhood, thus mirroring the exchange of energies and experience between them.

Using these principles, we can already speak of the first two centers of divine personhood. One is the Lover, the other the Beloved. Yet the Lover is also beloved, so can be called the beloved Lover, while the Beloved, who loves in return, can be called the loving Beloved.

How, then, do we name the Third Someone in the Trinity with a name that is fully personal and attributable to the other two centers of personhood? Breath, wind, storm, communion of love, fire, and water are impersonal and will not suffice. The biblical names of Counselor and Advocate are useful pointers and suggest an "agency" function, as does Taylor's picture of the anonymous go-between. In human relationships we know of the go-between, the matchmaker, or the mutual friend, who introduces two people to each other; values, protects, and delights in their mutual love; and does not seek to claim one or the other in an exclusive relationship. Though infrequent, this is an apt model, for the Trinity is the one "eternal triangle" where there is neither possessiveness nor jealousy. Because it rarely happens in human relationships, this function is not easy to name, but it would be getting close to say that the third center of divine personhood is the Love-Mediator, the Meeting-Maker, Matchmaker, Love's Companion, and Mutual Friend. I shall work with the last named, since it has more semantic resonance and may sound more acceptable in worship.

We now have three personal gender-free names: the Lover, the Beloved, and the Mutual Friend. I shall try and speak of their relationships, to test the coherence of the metaphors. As a move away from patriarchy, I'll use feminine pronouns, recognizing that both *she* and *he* are inadequate.

The Mutual Friend creates communion in the Trinity, community between human beings, and common feeling between humans and their environment (including other life forms). The Mutual Friend is also beloved, by the Lover and the Beloved, who know their Mutual Friend more intimately than we, who are often unaware of her presence. To us, the Mutual Friend is often anonymous, but to the Lover and the Beloved she is fully present, recognized, and loved. The Mutual Friend is also loving, the lover par excellence. It is through her outgoing, inclusive, nurturing, freeing love that the Trinity loves humankind through all history. The Mutual Friend, storm and breath and song of love, is God's growing and learning point, since history has real developments of love and community, as well as terrible setbacks and evils.

The Beloved loves the Lover, so can be called the loving Beloved. She is also our mutual friend, who in the free male, Jesus, calls disciples into community and seeks to create friendship and trust (reconciliation) between humankind and the Lover, through incarnation and dying in forsakenness on the cross. The relationship between Lover and Beloved is one of equality, not subordination: by definition the Lover is beloved, and the Beloved is lover. The Mutual Friend is their equal partner, delighting in their mutual love, knowing each and by each fully known, the whole effortlessly enclosing all creation and inviting all things to join the great ongoing dance.

The Lover of Creation is also beloved. She is both beloved Lover and mutual friend, for with the Beloved and the Mutual Friend, she creates every conceivable possibility of loving relationship, between people and people (relationships of peace and justice), people and other life forms (relationships of care), and people and nonliving nature (relationships of respect and delight).

Since the cross is for us the supreme point of trinitarian disclosure, it should be possible to speak of it coherently with these metaphors. In human terms, a lover and beloved are equals if both are adult. So in this metaphor system, the equality of the three centers of personhood is safeguarded. The Lover sends the Beloved, but this sending is not by command from authoritarian Father to submissive Son; rather it is by agreement and communion with the Mutual Friend, who watches over their unity. One is not active and the other passive, nor one acting and the other responding, nor one commanding and the other obeying, but all in love act together in this sending forth, and in complete communion with one another. The built-in inequality of King and Prince is overcome, and the third center of personhood is seen as a coequal partner in divine action.

Our metaphors suggest three dimensions of God's suffering in the cross. The Beloved and the Lover endure separation, one letting go of the other and feeling the pain of that lost communion, the other experiencing abandonment and desolation. The grief of the Mutual Friend cannot be known to us, but can be inferred: it is like the torn grief of a mutual friend when the couple she loves separate and she feels each one's pain as well as the loss of their common bond. In the cross, the Mutual Friend feels the agony of the Lover and the Beloved, and grief at their separation, yet so strong is her love that the Lover and Beloved are held in unshakable unity.

Speaking of this, Moltmann says that the Trinity is the love of like for like. But how do we know this? Our distinctions between Like and Other fail when we speak of the Trinity, for the Trinity surely knows both likeness and otherness more fully than we do. Even in human experience, anyone like us is always, in the end, Other, and even those who are most Other are, in the end, like us (though it may be difficult to realize this). Translating Moltmann's discussion into my own metaphors, there is acute separation between the Lover and the Beloved. The Lover withdraws from the Beloved, so that the Beloved will know the human experience of suffering and death to the full, and feels the pain of that withdrawal. The Beloved knows that withdrawal as the experience of being forsaken. Their Mutual Friend is grief-stricken at the suffering each endures and unbearably hurt by the fact of their separation. Though exchanged in the divine dance (perichoresis), these experiences are different and constitute Otherness.

Praising the Trinity

The personal metaphors above can be cast in hymnic form (see the Gallery that follows this chapter). In speaking of the whole Trinity, the most powerful metaphor for me is that of the great dance:

> *God is One, unique and holy,*
> *endless dance of love and light . . .*
>
> *When minds and bodies meet as one*
> *and find their true affinity,*
> *we join the dance in God begun*
> *and move within the Trinity,*
> *for all the good that's seen and done*
> *in every kind of unity,*
> *begins with God, forever One,*
> *whose nature is Community. . . .*
>
> *Praise, until we join the singing*
> *far beyond our sight,*
> *with the Ending and Beginning,*
> *dancing in the light.*[24]

This dance is not a solo performance, but a communal enterprise, like an eightsome reel, square dance, or barn dance. The metaphor suggests cooperation in movement, where each dancer becomes the center of the whole and then contributes to the honoring of another, as in this visionary passage from C. S. Lewis's novel *Perelandra (Voyage to Venus)*, where the hero, Ransom, sees the great dance of God:

> It seemed to be woven out of the intertwining undulations of many cords or bands of light, leaping over and under one another and mutually embraced in arabesques and flower-like subtleties. Each figure as he looked at it became the master-figure or focus of the whole spectacle, by means of which his eye disentangled all else and brought it into unity—only to be itself entangled when he looked to what he had taken for mere marginal decorations and found that there also the same hegemony was claimed, and the claim made good, yet the former pattern not thereby dispossessed but finding in its new subordination a significance greater than that which it had abdicated.[25]

Lewis's vision is close to contemporary concerns for ecological wholeness, for in the Great Dance all things are included: peoples, institutions, civilizations, arts, sciences, individual entities, flowers and insects, a fruit or a storm of rain, crystals, rivers, mountains, and stars. The ancient metaphor of divine perichoresis is an apt metaphor for trinitarian life and the life of all things in God, as in this portrait by Patricia Wilson-Kastner:

> Such is the depth and commitment of the shared life of the Trinity that this eternal dance makes the three one: unfettered love creates a living stability stronger than an enforced bond through coercion or assertion of a preexisting divine substance of an ill-defined nature. As in a dance the diversity and unity co-exist; the unity of the dance is an active common life created by the dancers, whose very being as dancers is established through their full participation in the unity of the dance. In the universe the divine perichoresis summons everyone to join it in trinitarian eternal harmony.[26]

Peace and Justice from the Trinity

The preceding section has important implications for Christian social ethics. I will state them briefly, for others to elaborate. If the

Trinity is a dynamic unity of Mutual Friend, Beloved, and Lover in an inclusive, open, unfinished, and coequal dance, it follows that the Trinity is the fullness of peace and justice, and longs to see that fullness reflected and developed in human society. In the Father-Son-Spirit metaphors, there is no built-in need for human justice and peace, except by identifying them as the will of the divine Father. But in the unity of the Beloved, Lover, and Mutual Friend are a mutuality, wholeness, *shalom* (peace), and coequality that express what we know as peace and justice and model them for us. For this is a divine oneness whose nature is community, a love dance in which each divine partner and human or nonhuman participant is fully honored and valued, in which the divine dancers and their human and nonhuman partners abolish domination, manipulation, oppression, subordination, self-centeredness, enmity, and morality and know the excitement of the peace that the world cannot give.

Gallery: How Wonderful the Three-in-One*

How wonderful the Three-in-One,
whose energies of dancing light
are undivided, pure and good,
communing love in shared delight.

Before the flow of dawn and dark,
Creation's Lover dreamed of earth,
and with a caring deep and wise,
all things conceived and brought to birth.

The Lover's own Beloved,** in time,
between a cradle and a cross,
at home in flesh, gave love and life
to heal our brokenness and loss.

Their Mutual Friend all life sustains
with greening power and loving care,
and calls us, born again by grace,
in Love's communing life to share.

How wonderful the Living God:
Divine Beloved, Empow'ring Friend,
Eternal Lover, Three-in-One,
our hope's beginning, way and end.

9

Consequences

It is said that Christ occasionally walks the earth incognito, to see if the time has come to end all things. The elders of a large American congregation got wind of this and were given audience.

"Sir," they began, "we have a problem and need your advice."

"Speak on," came the reply.

"Some years ago our church took an important step. After much prayer and thought, we knew that the time had come to include a woman minister on our staff. We searched diligently and called a young woman, just out of seminary, as our associate pastor. She worked very well with our senior pastor, but had only been with us for six months when he had a heart attack and died. We were deeply distressed, but after a time we appointed a search committee and eventually called another man, younger, with a good record of ministry. We asked our associate to stay during the transition, and she worked so well with the new minister that it was obvious she would continue with us. After five years he moved on to another congregation, and again we cast about, and eventually called a returned missionary, who stayed for nearly eight years. And again, our associate was asked to stay on, and again she worked so well with him that we knew we had done well in calling her. She has become indispensable to us, and when she retires next year, she will have worked successfully with no less than seven senior pastors. So you will understand that we have never regretted our decision."

"Well and good," said the Lord, "but what then is your problem?"

"Our problem is this," said the elders. "In the resurrection, whose associate will she be, since she worked with all seven?"

Pending the establishment of a sane, humane, and ecological planetary society, where women and men shed patterns of domination and subordination and respect the integrity of creation, what immediate changes are suggested by the preceding chapters, and what issues most need action and exploration? I shall touch on a few, moving from the simplest to the most far-reaching.

We shall be on the lookout for patriarchal patterns and assumptions in worship. In a reasonably literate society, liturgies do not have to be written on the assumption that the shepherd says lots of interesting things and the sheep say "baaa." Congregations can say more to and see more of one another, and worship can be enacted so as to highlight its communal intention. Even in churches built on the general-addresses-the-troops pattern, that pattern can be subverted, to some extent, by inviting people to stand and face one another across a center aisle. Better still is an educational process leading to an informed decision to install flexible seating. We do not have to begin worship with the unimportant people expectantly waiting and the important people processing in. Worship leaders can begin worship seated in the congregation and be called out from among the congregation, to symbolize both the importance of leadership and its accountable derivation from the whole community. Where vestments are worn, worship leaders can be called out and vested *among the congregation* at the beginning of worship. Details of language are important: we don't have to go along with our culture's customary listings from most to least important: "men, women, and children," "priests and people," "clergy and laity," "bishops, priests, and deacons," "Father, Son, and Holy Spirit," or even "Lover, Beloved, and Mutual Friend." Conscious attempts to vary such sequences are like dusting and polishing the furniture. If you don't intend to move the furniture and rebuild the house, they will seem unimportant; if you do, they are a reminder of larger intentions.

To elaborate on the trinitarian examples, it is difficult to think about the Trinity without using the traditional monarchical sequence, from first to second to third centers of personhood, as I have done in preceding chapters. But it is not satisfactory, nor should it be the unquestioned pattern in worship. Taking the co-equality of the centers of divine personhood seriously means varying the order of our doxologies, starting sometimes with the second, sometimes with the third, and sometimes with the first: we might gain new insights that way, in both worship and theology.[1]

We shall recognize the importance of the nonverbal and intuitive in worship. Dance, music, and the visual arts will be valued: not used only to illustrate the Word, but allowed to communicate on their own terms. We shall not feel the need to control what they communicate by always finding words to interpret it. Though congregational involvement is important, there will be an equal and honored place for music, dance, painting, photography, and fabric work as skilled, professional offerings, on a par with those of priests and ministers, and in partnership with them. As a weaver of words, I am excited by the emerging theology of nonverbal forms;[2] I have seen worship come alive with a power beyond the accomplishment of individual contributors when musicians, dancers, artists, poets, and preachers work together.

We need to think carefully about how we describe the relationship between different metaphors for God. Postpatriarchal Christianity will not think in terms of a *controlling image*. Sallie McFague speaks of *root metaphors*, which suggests growth from an origin, but doesn't allow for variety. We could speak of a *drama* in which some metaphors play leading roles, but supporting roles are equally vital and even the crowd has an essential part to play. God-metaphors can be seen as partners in a *dance*, in which some become briefly central and then give place to others; or as an *orchestra*, its instruments giving different texture and rhythm, in harmony, dissonance, or clashing time signatures.

Theologians and preachers need to work on these and other models, since our choice of model will shape thinking and action. When we speak in terms of *creeds*, the statement "We believe" (or "I believe") carries the assumption that "we" or "I" believe something, and that there are others who don't believe it: naming such statements as creeds makes polarized assumptions of truth and untruth, right and wrong. I'm not saying that truth is unimportant, only that the true-untrue, right-wrong polarization of credal statements is inadequate, because of its exclusiveness. But what if we say, "This is my *story*, this is my *song*"? If belief is a song we sing, it's something we want others to hear, enjoy, and join in; if it is a story, it's the story that moves and inspires us, and we want to tell it and hope it will speak as powerfully to others. Such metaphors are as evangelical as "I believe," but less exclusive: my song leaves room for the beauty of your song, and my story allows you to have your story also.

We shall move forward with programs and processes based on respectful dialogue, not monologues or edicts from leaders to led. There are many educational materials on language and gender issues, but they will only be useful if their users have a grasp of dialogical and participatory methods.[3] An example may be helpful. At a conference in Dunblane, Scotland, I asked the participants, working in fours and fives, to list reasons and feelings against, and then for, speaking to God as "Mother." Scotland was an appropriate country in which to raise the question, since the General Assembly of the largest church was so antagonistic to female God-talk that it had refused even to debate its own report, "The Motherhood of God."[4]

Eight minutes of work produced an impressive list. The main reasons in favor were that some biblical images are female;[5] "Mother" brings out the gentler aspects of God; it reminds us of a sacrificial, unconditional love; and it conveys images of carrying, bearing, nurturing, strengthening, and enduring. To call God Mother is appropriate, because fathers often leave home and abandon their wives and children, giving a negative image of fatherhood. To call God both Mother and Father reminds us of the limitations of human language, prevents us from thinking we have God neatly categorized, and helps us to get beyond seeing God as having gender.

Reasons against included the fear of worshipping a different God; a sense of discomfort, insecurity, nameless fear; the fear of change, or being changed; the weight of tradition and church authority over two thousand years; the fact that men have largely determined the structure of church and society, implying that a God not depicted in male terms would be incredible; the belief that Jesus had only male disciples; a feeling that men could not relate to, and would be alienated by, a motherly God; the power of Mother and a feeling that recalling that earliest experience of utter dependence would keep us in an immature relationship; a loss of old certainties, and feeling that to speak of God in this way would be like making God in our image; the fact that Jesus taught his disciples to pray "our Father"; and a feeling that female terms devalue God because they suggest weakness, and we need a strong God to have any impact on the world.

This wide range of response came after brief work on the nature of God-talk, without any analysis of patriarchal society. Yet several responses show an implicit awareness of patriarchy, and that the group knows more about this than it thinks. This is of great importance for counterpatriarchal education, since it shows how people's own awareness can be a gateway to insight. The group feels the weight of tradition, and justifiably so, since patriarchy has been with us for even longer than two thousand years: this leads to questions of how and why patriarchal society arose, and how it might be changed.

The group also recognizes that men hold the dominant place in society and sees this either as a reason for speaking of God in male terms (so that faith is not at odds with our culture) or for using a mixture of images, so that God is *not* imaged as male: here also the group's own findings suggest areas for further exploration. The worry that men might not be able to relate a "motherly" God to male experience makes it possible to suggest that an all-male God has a similar effect on women. Recognizing that attributes stereotyped as "feminine" are downgraded and seen as "weak" is an opening into issues raised in earlier chapters and can prompt the realization that a decision to use female God-metaphors must go hand in hand with a revaluation of "the feminine," since it would not be a step forward to incorporate a devalued femaleness into God-talk.

The group recognizes that "Mother" is a powerful image, and that we may need to be reminded of our dependence on God. But the image has both value and limitations: it can suggest unconditional love or a continued babylike dependence. Yet "Father" is equally problematic, in a society where many marriages break down and fathers don't give enough companionship to their children. In discussing "Mother" and "Father," the group has itself clarified the nature of God-metaphors, and raised profound issues about women and men in society. If the educator holds up such insights and invites the group to reflect on them, she is assured of committed participation, since the issues have come from the group, not been handed down from outside or above.

All church traditions will have to move away from overt and covert structures of hierarchy and domination. Few priests and ministers know how to work cooperatively and nonhierarchically. Many don't want to, and few are trained how to, though some churches have a theology that ought to contradict patriarchal practice (for example, "the priesthood of all believers"), or terminology that sounds cooperative but isn't (as in "associates," who are in fact assistants). In part, this is because churches take their models of ministry uncritically from their culture, so that paid staff are seen as members of the professions or managers with authority to hire, fire, and produce religious goods (sermons, prayers, sacraments, music, counseling, and forgiveness) for the people to consume.

A counterpatriarchal church will stop ordaining ministers or priests into a caste that gives them power to do and say things that others are excluded from, as when presiding at the Lord's Supper/Eucharist. At present, "the symbols of clerical power duplicate on the level of ecclesiastical hierarchy the symbols of patriarchal domination of men over women, father over children. It is impossible to liberate the Church from patriarchy and retain a clerical definition of the ministry."[6]

The comment is from a Catholic, but Reformed theology and practice are equally questionable. Catholic theology is at least explicit. Ordination to the priesthood confers "holy orders," a rank or status conferring power to perform certain acts that only a priest can perform. For Roman Catholics, the Second Vatican Council softened but restated the traditional view. The Decree on the Ministry and Life of Priests (*Presbyterorum Ordinis*) says that priests are to be servants who do not use their authority in an authoritarian way, but willingly listen to the laity. Yet they are still able, "by the sacred power of their office," to offer sacrifice (preside at the Eucharist) and remit sins, and are "marked with a special character" in ordination. This is an understanding of the church that starts from the power and status of bishops and priests and fits the laity into it.

In Reformed theology, ordination is not supposed to be an act of power, but a matter of "order." People appointed to preach, lead worship, administer sacraments, and exercise pastoral care are not said to be elevated to superior status, merely given particular functions. Reformed ordering of the church's ministries was originally thought to derive from Scripture, but this is now untenable, because Christian Scripture (the New Testament) lacks the clear distinctions between ministries that the Reformers found there. When one looks at what Reformed ministers and Catholic priests actually do, the allegedly fundamental differences about ordination vanish like morning dew, and what we see are groups of paid professionals, with lifelong tenure of their religious status, in the garb of servanthood, but with the power to do and say certain things denied to the majority of their fellow church members. Both Reformed and Catholic traditions operate within thoroughly patriarchal structures. Admitting women to positions of ordained power, though a step long overdue, is not a step forward unless we question the nature of ordination and its patriarchal framework.

For both author and readers, the preceding chapters disturb and undermine the social predominance and personal identity of men. Some of us want to become more caring fathers to our children, or wish we had been, but we all have a long road to travel. Though patriarchal society is now being questioned in Western society, reported sightings of the New Man are premature. Though many younger men have significantly different attitudes from their parents, this has not yet led to widespread changes in practice. A recent survey in the European Economic Community tested the "margin of male exaggeration" (the difference between what men claimed to do in their household and what their wives were willing to vouch for). For British men it was 10 percent, halfway between the self-confident Italians (21 percent) and the more self-critical Danes (5 percent). Overall, many European men were willing to do some of the shopping (73 percent), washing up (53 percent), and organizing a meal (43 percent)—but most would wait to be asked. Though most men would smile at a fellow male who believed in Father Christmas, we keep a childlike faith in the Home Hearth Fairy, who picks up the litter, changes the toilet roll, magically transports the clothes from dirty basket to folded cleanliness, and does all the other things we don't quite notice. According to one recent book, the average man in Michigan contributed 81.39 minutes a day to house tasks and child care in 1965 and 82.4 minutes daily in 1975, an increase of 25 seconds in ten years, despite having gained an extra *40 minutes* per day of leisure time.[7] Men will have to accept new patterns of child care for themselves, and promote them through legislation, until our economy encourages men in paid work to be equal partners in child care.

Men will need to support women's leadership in ministry and be willing to work with (and, in unreformed structures, for) women ministers, priests, and bishops. As one male minister observes, "We men have grown up assuming that if we have certain gifts and are good stewards of them, we will be recognized with positions of responsibility in the church. Some of these expectations will be disappointed if the church develops a true sense of justice and mutuality in women-men relationships. Men will need to learn to grieve about that loss. We may also then become aware of the feelings of our sisters who have been excluded for generations."[8]

So what's in it for men? Letting go of privilege and dominance may be harder than we think. A woman minister told me of her time as an "associate" pastor in a large American congregation. The male senior pastor constantly assured her of his support, but rarely allowed her to preach and lead worship (she is an able preacher). "I could fill a room with those assurances of support," she said, "and I would have traded an ounce of real power sharing for the whole roomful of them." I hear many similar stories.

We men will know what's in it for us as we begin to develop *men's theology.* It will be a sign of progress when theological journals are publishing articles on it by our best male biblical scholars, historians, and systematic theologians, both black and white, and by male liberation theologians from Asia, Africa, and Latin America.

As a *theology of repentance,* men's theology will look at the traditional subject matter, subject divisions, and primary questions of theology from a penitent awareness of male dominance and patriarchal formation. It will be a theology of listening and self-critique and will lead to substantial changes in the way theology is done, and the way ministers and priests are trained. It will reflect on Jesus as the male who repudiated control over others, and ask how men in our culture can embody this as the supreme male value and live the consequences.

As a *theology of redefinition,* men's theology will search deeply and widely for redefinitions of what it is to be "a real man." It will draw on empirical psychology and the powerful myth stories of Jungian and Freudian approaches, together with the rituals and stories of other cultures and religions.

As a *theology of caring maleness*, men's theology will uplift the importance of caring as a male activity, and grieve over, reflect, and act on the painful contradiction between the image of God as the reliable, caring, companionable father and the loss of fatherly companionship in our culture. It will redefine ministry as an all-around caring servanthood and dream of the day when congregations look askance at married male pastors who want to work full-time.

Men's theology will be a *theology of male particularity*, speaking from the limited but important perspectives of male experience. The creation of the first professorships in men's theology at Princeton, Yale, Oxford, Cambridge, Edinburgh, McGill, Uppsala, Tübingen, Sydney, and Auckland will mark seismic shifts in male self-awareness, achieved at considerable cost and against deep opposition, because *naming* the activity as "men's theology" undercuts the assumption that traditional male approaches are unbiased and impartial. Male theologians will no longer think they speak for the whole human race from nowhere in particular, but begin to discover the beauty and worth of specifically male experience.

One gain from such shifts will be the recovery of *primal male energy*. The American poet Robert Bly has done important work on this, as he retells and comments on the ancient story of Iron Hans (or Iron John), collected by the Brothers Grimm but actually much older.[9]

Bly suggests that when men take feminist critiques seriously, we start looking for the feminine in ourselves and become more gentle, caring, and peaceable. Though this is an important step forward, we also need something else (women may need it too, but we can only speak of our own needs and experience).

The story of Iron Hans has some intriguing suggestions about that "something." A man goes hunting in a forest where previous hunters have mysteriously disappeared. In the middle of the forest he finds a large pond. As he stands by the edge, a hand reaches from the pond and grabs his dog. The hunter doesn't want to lose his dog, so he gets some other men with buckets and they empty out the pond. The story suggests, then, that getting in touch with whatever is at the bottom of the pond requires painstaking work—bucket by bucket.

At the bottom of the pond they find a large man covered with hair down to his feet; it is reddish, like rusty iron. Hair is a symbol of primal male energy, of intensity, living on the edge, delighting in challenge and risk taking. Such energy is not macho brute strength, but energetic, exuberant action undertaken with compassion yet resolve. Another writer suggests that the cult of male toughness may be what happens when that primal maleness is repressed and denied: it doesn't go away but manifests itself demonically.

The Wild Man is brought back to the castle from which the hunter had set out on his quest and is put in an iron cage in the courtyard. His long hair suggests the instinctive, sexual, and primeval elements in maleness. He is a disturbing presence, which order and civilization want to contain—hence the cage, an archetypal symbol of male order, right in the middle of the castle.

One day the king's eight-year-old son is playing in the courtyard and his golden ball rolls into the cage. He asks the Wild Man to give it back, and the Wild Man refuses unless the boy opens the cage. The boy is afraid to, but keeps coming back to ask the Wild Man for the golden ball. The golden ball suggests light, wholeness, and a sense of unity and probably symbolizes the wholeness of childhood innocence, which boys and girls alike lose at about that age.

Three times the boy asks for the ball and gets the same answer. The third time he finally unlocks the cage (the Wild Man has to tell him where to find the key, which is under his mother's pillow, suggesting that the boy can only grow up by moving away from his mother's encompassing energy). Then the boy decides to go with the Wild Man back to the forest; they go off together, the boy sitting on the Wild Man's shoulder, and have adventures.

The great hairy man represents a primal energy: ancient and rusty, deep and dark, wet, moist, and male. It can't be defined and conceptualized, only pictured and put in stories. Getting in touch with the Wild Man is not something we do lightly: the Wild Man is either way down in the deep dark pond or safely locked up in the cage, contained by civilized order. Letting the Wild Man out of the cage is risky: he looks too dangerous, a huge hairy figure with a big laugh and exuberant strength. Yet the story assures us that, once released, he is not a rampaging macho brute but a gentle giant who can safely become part of our psyche. The man in touch with his Wild Man has compassionate strength. He loves challenge and risk, but no longer links them with conquest and gaining control over others. He knows who he is, and what he wants or needs, and can respond from his own centeredness to the new energy in women, facing and valuing it because he knows his own maleness better. Greater emphasis on caring maleness will help to release this primal energy, because father-son companionship will be able to express it and pass it on in a wholesome way.

Challenge and risk are what Jesus appealed to in his male disciples when he called them to leave their nets and customs posts. To his women followers, on the other hand, he offered healing and wholeness, because they needed a different route to self-discovery. When we men meet the Wild Man within ourselves, and embrace him, we shall find our own wholesome, compassionate strength and be ready for new adventures. We shall be able to meet the energy and self-confidence flowering in women and partner it without domination or subservience, exchanging our gifts and experiences in a human perichoresis. We shall be able to say, in this time of women coming into their own, "She must increase, and I must decrease." We shall say it and not feel diminished, knowing that we are quoting a Wild Man par excellence, who gained his honored place in history because he knew how to give place to another.[10]

Epilogue: KINGAFAP Revisited

What is to be done with KINGAFAP? Even when we have alternatives, it will meet us when we read the Bible, sing hymns, or recite creeds.

Analyzing and Reimaging

One way forward is to analyze KINGAFAP metaphors and reimage from their root intentions. For example, the Ascension story shows the resurrected Crown Prince going up to the heavenly throne and sitting at the right hand of his Father-King-God. The imagery expresses the following convictions:

1. Jesus is alive forever.
2. Jesus is as close to God as it is possible to get, and on the same level, not secondary or subordinate.
3. Everything he taught and showed about God is vindicated, and his whole human life is taken into the divine life and experience.
4. Jesus, with God, has access to all human life: past, present, and future (in the KINGAFAP system this is expressed as "oversight," control, sovereignty).
5. The active presence of the Holy Spirit stems from the closeness of Son and Father.

Imaging from the first three convictions led me to the following:

> *Jesus is with God,*
> *endlessly alive.*
> *All he did and said and suffered,*
> *all he hoped and all he offered*
> *beats with shimmering wings*
> *in the heart of things.*[1]

The last two lines try to express Ascensiontide convictions without using up-down language, adding a reference to the Holy Spirit's presence in the godhead.

The first line, "Jesus is with God," then led me to ask a different question: Where is God? One answer is that God in Christ comes to us through our oppressed and suffering neighbors (Matt. 25:31–46) and issues through them a renewed call to discipleship:

> *Jesus is with God*
> *where the victims cry*
> *from the crosses of oppression,*
> *praying for our intercession:*
> *"Leave your nets, and see!*
> *Christians, follow me!"*

All three centers of divine personhood meet us in our neighbor, especially our suffering neighbor. In each such neighbor we meet the Lover who gives birth to all creation and creates each human being in her image. Jesus the Anointed One, the Beloved incarnate, meets us personally in our neighbor's suffering. Their Mutual Friend, outgoing energy of love, is the go-between who opens our eyes so that we may see and respond.

In its third and final stanza, the hymn returns to convictions (4) and (5) above, and focuses on the future opened up by the resurrection:

> *Jesus stands with God*
> *by an open door,*
> *calling us to pray and follow*
> *through the struggles of tomorrow,*

sowing hopeful seeds
where the Spirit leads.

The hymn illustrates a method by which the traditional metaphor system can be respected and used as a basis for exploration. It replaces KINGAFAP, but is derived from important meanings in the original. It is gentler in tone, and its openness to the future is an improvement on KINGAFAP, which suggests a static sovereignty over all things until the end.

Yet changing a metaphor changes its meaning. It is worth asking what is *lost* when we depart from KINGAFAP. Three important elements of the traditional system are causation, oversight, and victory over opposition. The experience of seeing a command obeyed made it possible to conceive of God causing the universe to come into being. Yet the command metaphor suggests a lack of empathetic involvement, and metaphors of God as Mother and birth giver seem to me an improvement.[2]

Oversight is another connotation of sovereignty: the king on his throne commands his realm and surveys everything in it. In modern times this image has lost its original meaning and tends to suggest remoteness. The king over all is easily seen as "above it all," separating God from creation and the humiliated from the exalted Christ. One way of dealing with this is to use the traditional imagery, but deny its false meanings:

> *Not throned afar, remotely high,*
> *untouched, unmoved by human pains,*
> *but daily, in the midst of life,*
> *our Savior in the Godhead reigns.*
> *In every insult, rift and war,*
> *where color, scorn or wealth divide,*
> *Christ suffers still, yet loves the more,*
> *and lives, where even hope has died.*[3]

The oversight element in KINGAFAP cannot do justice to God as the Lover who surrenders control by allowing freedom and randomness. Yet we need metaphors to express one important implication of oversight, namely, that the God-King is able to realize his purposes. The greatness of God's vision for humanity is that everything is *not* cut and dried. We are co-responsible with God for our planet. Millions of human lives, from whom God could weave history's tapestry into unimaginable beauty, may or may not be lived, and whether they are lived depends in large measure on human action. Letting go of control, abjuring covert operations, and being present only in strictly human possibilities for good are hallmarks of God's risk-taking love. Here is a fruitful field for hymn writers, since such thoughts cannot be expressed within the KINGAFAP system.

Victory over opposition is another hallmark of KINGAFAP, but war and battle metaphors cannot express God's love for the enemy, because they have the built-in notion of hating, conquering, wounding, and killing the person who stands against us.

How then can we love yet resolutely oppose: oppose yet steadfastly love? In writing hymns on this theme, I have turned to the witness of women in the peace movement, committed to non-violent direct action, at a nuclear missile base thirty miles from my home. Their commitment to nonviolence means that they put their bodies in the way of the missile launchers, refuse to use physical force or verbal abuse, and speak personally to the police and soldiers who confront them.

One of them explains their action by pointing to a double meaning in the word *oppose* ("stand against," but also "do the opposite"). Nonviolent direct action "is about stating opposition clearly, standing face to face," she says. "If we make use of the threat of violence in direct action, *then we do not truly oppose, we are not opposite,* because we are using aggression to oppose aggression."[4]

Hearing that witness, I turn to 1 Corinthians 13 and write:

> *Love is the only hope*
>   *for peace on earth.*
> *Love isn't quick to take offense*
>   *at other nations,*
> *but listens and decides*
>   *with careful patience:*
> Love is realistic. Love isn't blind.
> Love is determined, caring and kind.
> Spirit of Jesus, friend and forgiver,
>   near us for ever,
>   fill us with love.[5]

This is a paraphrase of the New English Bible translation, restating the meaning of the text at an international level. The following stanzas do likewise for the local community and the individual ("Love is the only hope for peace at home . . . for peace of mind"). "Love is realistic / love isn't blind" interprets 1 Corinthians 13:7. If there is nothing love cannot face, this means that love is not self-deluding, but sees clearly (realistically) how things are.

Romans 12:9–17 is another helpful source. The stanzas of this hymn paraphrase the New English Bible, and the refrains seek the help of the Holy Spirit:

> *We want to care*
> *for blind or evil enemies,*
> *giving blessings,*
> *meaning what we say . . .*
>> Deep, cool well of peace,
>> wine of mercy at the feast,
>> Holy Spirit, come!
>
> *We want to grow*
> *in joyful, clear humility,*
> *facing trouble,*
> *never losing heart:*
>> Green, strong, living oak,
>> seed and root and flower of hope,
>> Holy Spirit, come!
>
> *We want to work*
> *with never-flagging energy,*
> *doing justice,*
> *freeing the oppressed:*
>> Fire, flame, blazing light,
>> judgment, justice, truth and right,
>> Holy Spirit, come!
>
> *We want to love*
> *with generous sincerity,*
> *shedding evil,*
> *clinging to the good:*
>> Great, wild eagle-dove,

storm, and breath, and song of love,
Holy Spirit, come![6]

Using KINGAFAP Creatively

I said earlier that, at its best, KINGAFAP arouses wonder. When the
shock of the original intersection ("powerful king" with "suffering servant") is retained, the news that the divine, all-powerful
King could humble himself and die for us has continuing imaginative power.

Triumphalistic versions in which the King's Son suffers as a
temporary measure are unacceptable. We should only draw on the
story if we rekindle its original shock, singing of the King whose
throne is a cross, whose bidding no one obeys, and whose crown is
made of thorns. We should tell how the suffering Prince rises from
death and takes his human experience forever into the dance of
divine love.

It would also be good to see hymns and prayers in which
KINGAFAP is one metaphor among many, thus highlighting its incompleteness. Another theme worth highlighting is of Abba the
caring Father and republican King, who is grieved if we rebuild
the pyramids of patriarchy. Here is a king who stands against the
demonic and authoritarian tendencies of human governments and
institutions, including the church. My plea to liturgists and hymn
writers is: if you must use KINGAFAP, use it in this creative and
liberating way; don't just repeat the story with its patriarchal flaws.

The Empty Throne

There's another way of dealing with the story, which G. A.
Studdert-Kennedy arrived at in the trenches of World War I. As he
tells the Christian story, "men" saw God's Crown Prince revealed
in suffering servanthood, but grew ashamed of the cross and could
not see it as God's *real* throne. So they invented the glorified
Christ: "White-robed angels stand about Him bowing to his least
command, shouts of triumph greet His entrance, the mighty gates

lift up their heads and the King of glory enters in. All the pageantry of earthly power, all the pomp of courts and kings which He on earth refused, are used to make him beautiful. . . . This glorified Christ in regal robes is a degraded Christ bereft of real majesty; these baubles are not worthy of the King."[7] The regal Christ sitting with God Almighty is an idol. The KINGAFAP story takes an unexpected turn, as the Heavenly King is pulled down from his throne, and Almighty God deposed by Mary's Magnificat:

> We may still worship idols, but in our hearts we despise them, and despise ourselves for worshipping them. The only thing we can respect and remain self-respecting, is loving service. . . . So, at last, the great suffering, striving God of service and of love is coming into His own, and as He comes into His own, so the High and Mighty Potentate, King of kings and Lord of lords, Almighty God, powerful, passionless, and serene, is being deposed from His throne in the hearts of men, and in His place there standeth one amongst us Whom we knew not, with bloody brow and pierced hands, majestic in his nakedness, superb in his simplicity, the King Whose crown is a crown of thorns. He is God.[8]

In other words, the true story of KINGAFAP does not end with the Prince returning to the throne and everyone worshipping the highest symbol of patriarchal power. It ends with God quitting the throne for good and being revealed as impassioned, suffering love. Thus love "triumphs," not because it wins battles with demonic powers, but because it is enduring, exuberant, and unquenchable. In speaking of this ending of the story, Studdert-Kennedy shifts prophetically to a different, female metaphor, saying that God "endures an agony unutterable *in the labor of creation,* but endures on still for love's sake to the end."[9]

A Fable

Once upon a time a king, a prince, and a royal ambassador lived in a castle with three great thrones high above all things. The king and the prince sat in state, while the ambassador came and went like the wind, going about through all creation. Choirs of angels sang their praises, throngs of elders kept on casting crowns at their feet, and the prayers of their devoted subjects rose like incense all around them.

One day the king could stand it no longer. He stopped the angel choirs in mid-chord and bade the elders put their crowns down quietly and leave them there. Heaven was filled with blissful silence, though the prayers kept on rising.

Just then the ambassador returned, and the prince, the king, and the ambassador pulled their thrones into a circle and made plans. "We're both tired of sitting here," said the prince to his father, "so what shall we do?"

"If you will," said the king, "I would like you to live among our people, know them from the inside, and show them who we are and how passionately we love and care for them."

"That's exactly what I had in mind," said the prince. "But tell me, dear Dad, and tell me, dearest friend, what will you be doing?"

"I'm going to go around and about," said the king, "until I find a more worthy occupation."

"And I," said the ambassador, "have places to visit, people to see, and meetings to arrange."

So the prince left his high throne and glorious robes and went to live among the people, who knew him as one of themselves and loved and hated and killed him. His body was laid in a rocky tomb in the middle of a garden and sealed with a great stone.

On the first day the sun rose and set, the tomb stayed shut, and those who loved the prince mourned his passing.

On the second day the sun rose and set, the tomb stayed shut, and some mourned while others said that life must go on and went about their business.

On the morning of the third day, before dawn, a gardener came to the garden. He rolled back the stone, and the prince came out full of life. In the same moment a traveler stood with them, and all three embraced, and wept, and laughed together.

"Well, Dad," said the prince, "I see you've changed your occupation."

"Yes," said the king, "I've always wanted to take up gardening. Can't stay long: there's the whole earth to look after. What will you do with yourself, now you're alive again? Your old room's up there if you want it."

"I don't see him sitting up there in solitary," said the traveler. "He's got all history before him."

"My thoughts exactly," said the prince. "I promised to stay with my friends, and I've still got my trade. Carpenters are always in demand. There are hopes to make and people to mend. And we'll all three meet again, here and there and as and when. But what will you be doing, dear friend of friends?"

"Ah, you know me," said the traveler. "Places to visit, people to see, meetings to arrange . . . "

Then the gardener, the carpenter and the traveler went their ways in time and space. Their thrones sat empty in heaven, while the elders dug and planted trees on earth, the people's prayers were fragrant with justice and peace, and the angels sang songs of new creation.

Notes

Introduction to Part I

1. Gerder Lerner, *The Creation of Patriarchy* (New York: Oxford University Press, 1986), p. 239.

Chapter 1. A Flawed Maleness

1. *Economist*, 3 May 1986.
2. *Guardian*, 7 January 1987.
3. Mary Ingham, *Men: The Male Myth Exposed* (London: Century, 1984), pp. 69, 70, 3.
4. Joseph Pleck, *The Myth of Masculinity* (Cambridge, Mass.: MIT Press, 1981). Pleck's discussion is technical, but his findings appear in a questionnaire (pp. 133–34) from which my summary is taken.
5. Antony Easthope, *What a Man's Gotta Do* (London: Collins/Paladin, 1986), p. 168.
6. Lily Macfarlane, "Would You Give a War Game for Christmas?" *Guardian*, 9 December 1986.
7. For a helpful discussion of the toughness-tenderness conflict, see Easthope, *What a Man's Gotta Do*, pp. 28–32, 35–54.
8. Pleck, *Myth*, pp. 140–41.
9. Barbara Ehrenreich, *The Hearts of Men: American Dreams and the Flight from Commitment* (New York: Anchor/Doubleday, 1983), pp. 135–39.

10. Andy Metcalf and Martin Humphries, *The Sexuality of Men* (London: Pluto Press, 1985), p. 3.

11. Ingham, *Men*, p. 213.

12. John Nicholson, *Men and Women: How Different Are They?* (Oxford: Oxford University Press, 1984), p. 109.

13. Philip Smith, *Language, the Sexes and Society* (Oxford: Blackwell, 1985), pp. 31–33.

14. Richard Dyer, "Male Sexuality in the Media," in Metcalf and Humphries, *The Sexuality of Men*, p. 38.

15. Ibid.

16. Ibid., p. 39.

17. Ibid., p. 41.

18. Nicholson, *Men and Women*, p. 176.

19. Smith, *Language, the Sexes and Society*, p. 55.

20. Many recent works suggest that the "flight from the feminine" stems from a boy's early experience of bondedness to his mother, which he is obliged to forego and has mixed feelings about. Though such theories are suggestive, they have insufficient empirical backing, and available research casts doubt on them. See Pleck, *Myth*, pp. 108–12.

21. Lerner, *Patriarchy*, p. 239.

22.. Marilyn French, *Beyond Power: On Women, Men and Morals* (London: Jonathan Cape, 1985). This is a detailed, well-researched, overlong, often epigrammatic, moving, and compelling book.

23. Lerner, *Patriarchy*, pp. 231–43.

24. Nicholson, *Men and Women*, p. 158.

25. This and preceding paragraphs draw on Lerner, *Patriarchy*, esp. chaps. 2 and 11. Traditional history is not simply an account about men. If it were, it would focus on all classes and kinds of men, including the poor and powerless. Nor is it only a history of power: if it were, it would give full attention to powerful women. Its focus is narrower: *power* wielded by *men*, where "greatness" usually means the degree of change imposed on a culture by a man or movement. Such history telling focuses on the MAWKI theme of control. It concentrates on "strategies, political maneuvers, or on the huge figure of the strong man striding across a landscape he barely regards, intent upon his destiny." Moral judgment may figure in the account, but frequently "melts away before the fascination, obsession, with the raw fact of power in a

man" (French, *Beyond Power*, pp. 264–65).

26. French, *Beyond Power*; Lerner, *Patriarchy*; and Rosemary Radford Ruether, *Sexism and God-Talk* (London: SCM Press, 1983), are useful introductions.

27. See *The Illuminations of Hildegard of Bingen*, with commentary by Matthew Fox (Santa Fe: Bear and Co., 1985).

28. Examples from French, *Beyond Power*, pp. 165–67, 189–94.

29. Ruether, *Sexism and God-Talk*, p. 172. The preceding paragraphs draw on pp. 165–73.

30. Nicholson, *Men and Women*, pp. 7–8, 19.

31. See Patricia Wilson-Kastner, *Faith, Feminism and the Christ* (Philadelphia: Fortress Press, 1983), chaps. 1–3.

32. Nicholson, *Men and Women*, p. 3.

33. Ibid., pp. 36–38.

34. Ibid., pp. 52–73; the quotation is from p. 69.

35. Ibid., pp. 122–23.

36. Ibid., pp. 130–32.

37. Ibid., pp. 15–19. Smith, in *Language, the Sexes and Society*, cites similar studies.

38. Nicholson, *Men and Women*, p. 90.

39. Ibid., p. 107.

40. Ibid., pp. 107–9.

41. Ibid., pp. 160–61. Nicholson summarizes many psychological studies, distinguishes between methodologically sound and unsound research, and makes a convincing case against sociobiological justifications of male dominance.

42. Vic Seidler, quoted by Tony Eardley, "Violence and Sexuality," in Metcalf and Humphries, *The Sexuality of Men*, p. 98.

43. Ingham, *Men*, pp. 135–36.

44. Ibid., p. 135.

45. See, e.g., Alice Cook and Gwyn Kirk, *Greenham Women Everywhere: Dreams, Ideas and Actions from the Women's Peace Movement* (London: Pluto Press, 1983).

Chapter 2. The Cost of Control

1. See Brian Wren, *Education for Justice* (Maryknoll, N.Y.: Orbis Books, 1977), chap. 1.

2. Genevieve Lloyd, *The Man of Reason: "Male" and "Female" in Western Philosophy* (Minneapolis: University of Minnesota Press, 1984).

3. Ibid., p. 24.

4. Carol C. Gould, "The Woman Question: Philosophy of Liberation and the Liberation of Philosophy," in Carol C. Gould and Marx W. Wartofsky, eds., *Women and Philosophy: Toward a Theory of Liberation* (New York: Putnam, 1976), pp. 5–44, quoting from p. 19.

5. Lloyd, *The Man of Reason*, p. 14.

6. Ibid., pp. 14–16; emphasis mine in the last quotation.

7. Ibid., p. 105.

8. Gould, "The Woman Question."

9. Robert Paul, "There's Nobody Here but Us Persons," in Gould and Wartofsky, *Women and Philosophy*, pp. 128–44.

10. Ibid.

11. L. Jordanova, "Natural Facts: A Historical Perspective on Science and Sexuality," in *Nature, Culture and Gender*, ed. Carol MacCormack and Marilyn Strathern (Cambridge: Cambridge University Press, 1981), pp. 42–96, quoting from p. 45.

12. Ibid., p. 54.

13. Examples from Brian Easlea, *Fathering the Unthinkable: Masculinity, Scientists and the Nuclear Arms Race* (London: Pluto Press, 1983), pp. 19–21. Emphasis mine.

14. Ibid., pp. 23–29, 38–39.

15. Quoted in Penny Strange, *It'll Make a Man of You: A Feminist View of the Arms Race* (Nottingham: Peace News Pamphlet, 1983), p. 15.

16. Jeff Hearn, "Men's Sexuality at Work," in Andy Metcalf and Martin Humphries, eds., *The Sexuality of Men* (London: Pluto Press, 1985), pp. 110–28. Hearn cites surveys by the Alfred Marks Employment Bureau, Trades Union surveys in London and Leeds, findings of a book by women managers, and a reader response in *Cosmopolitan* magazine. This last showed only 11 percent of readers experiencing harassment, which seems oddly low compared with the others (51, 59, 70, and 52 percent, respectively), so I have taken the higher range as more plausible.

17. Chief executive of Korn/Ferry, quoted by Andrew Phillips, "New Cult of the Golden Calf," *Observer*, 12 April 1987.

18. Raymond Williams, *Towards 2000* (London: Chatto and

Windus/Hogarth Press, 1983), pp. 88–101.

19. See Paul Ekins, ed., *The Living Economy: A New Economics in the Making* (London: Routledge & Kegan Paul, 1986); other publications from the New Economics Foundation; and "The Other Economic Summit" (annual conferences paralleling meetings of Western finance and trade ministers).

20. Alan Sugar, head of Amstrad Electronics, quoted in Phillips, "New Cult of the Golden Calf."

21. Mary Ingham, *Men: The Male Myth Exposed* (London: Century Publishing, 1984), chap. 4.

22. Barbara Ehrenreich, *The Hearts of Men: American Dreams and the Flight from Commitment* (New York: Anchor/Doubleday, 1983), pp. 104–5.

23. Davidson Loehr, "Individuals in Vietnam: Some War Stories and Reflections," *Criterion* 23, no. 3 (1984): 13–17.

24. Marc Feigan Fasteau, *The Male Machine* (New York: Dell, 1975), p. 163. I draw on chapter 12, "Vietnam and the Cult of Toughness in Foreign Policy," pp. 158–89.

25. Ibid., p. 174 (Fasteau's judgment).

26. Ibid., p. 181.

27. Ibid., pp. 170–72.

28. As early as 1904 Ernest Rutherford wrote: "If it were ever found possible to control at will the disintegration of the radio-elements, an enormous amount of energy could be obtained from a small quantity of matter." His colleague Frederick Soddy gave similar warnings. Both were horrified by the carnage of World War I and warned of what might have happened had nuclear explosives been available. Both continued their research. In the 1930s Rutherford, and later his German counterparts, alerted their governments to the war potential of nuclear energy. Though they rejoiced in its peaceful possibilities, they knew they were playing with fire; and moreover the play both fascinated and alarmed them (Easlea, *Fathering the Unthinkable*, pp. 49–58).

29. Ibid., p. 59.

30. Ibid., p. 63 (this and preceding quotation).

31. Ibid., p. 64.

32. Ibid., p. 62.

33. Ibid., p. 129.

34. Ibid., p. 85.

35. Ibid., p. 84.

36. Ibid., p. 211.

37. Ibid., p. 206.

38. Ibid., p. 137; previous quotations from pp. 107, 127, 130–31. Emphasis mine.

39. Rosemary Radford Ruether, *Sexism and God-Talk* (London: SCM Press, 1983), pp. 173–74.

40. Exodus 3:13. The Hebrew expresses an incomplete action without time reference, which my translation partly renders.

41. See hymn after Chapter 8, below.

42. Though some women also walk them, those paths are patriarchal nonetheless: women are not immune from the sins of dominance, just as men are not immune from being submissively manipulative.

Introduction to Part II

1. I owe the concept of "linguistic visibility/invisibility" to Susan Thistlethwaite, professor at Chicago Theological Seminary. She argues, I believe correctly, that it is a more accurate and acceptable indicator of what is at stake than the common terminology of "inclusive" and "exclusive" language.

Chapter 3. Language, Thought, and Action

1. S. I. Hayakawa, *Language in Thought and Action* (New York: Harcourt Brace Jovanovich, 1972), 3rd ed., is a helpful guide to clear thinking and the expression of thought in language, but covers different ground.

2. The "babytalk" quotations are taken from Brian Easlea, *Fathering the Unthinkable: Masculinity, Scientists and the Nuclear Arms Race* (London: Pluto Press, 1983), pp. 94–97, 103, 107, 113, 126–31.

3. Personal communication from Martin Miller-Hessel, a former student of Teller's, July 1986.

4. The relationship between preconceptual or prelinguistic awareness and linguistic expression and communication is an unresolved debate with shifting terms. Some writers stress the reality

of inner sensations, perceptions, and feelings and their importance as in some sense prior to their expression and communication in language; others are impressed by language as a public medium preexisting and pervading the individual and itself shaping our experiences. See, e.g., Thomas A. Russman, *A Prospectus for the Triumph of Realism* (Macon: Mercer University Press, 1987), chap. 2, contrasted with George A. Lindbeck, *The Nature of Doctrine* (Philadelphia: Westminster Press, 1984), chap. 2.

5. Stephen A. Tyler, *The Said and the Unsaid* (New York; London: Academic Press, 1978), pp. 14–15. Mistakes or slips of the tongue "may index our reluctance to say what we think or our intention to reveal only partially what we are reluctant to say, and may thus signify conscious deceit or unconscious intent." Similarly, "silence may communicate what is beneath words or beyond them."

6. Quotations from George Orwell are from "Politics and the English Language," reprinted in *Inside the Whale and Other Essays* (London: Penguin, 1962) and in C. Muscatine and M. Griffith, eds., *The Borzoi Reader*, 2nd ed. (New York: Knopf, 1971); his emphasis on the word *pacification*. The "nukespeak" example is developed from Haig Bosmajian, "Dehumanizing People and Euphemizing War," *Christian Century*, 5 December 1984, pp. 1147–50.

7. This is Stephen Tyler's conclusion, though he expresses it less concretely, in *The Said and the Unsaid*, p. 60. Tyler cites several other works on human thought processes.

8. This passage is widely quoted, as for example in Deborah Cameron, *Feminism and Linguistic Theory* (London: Macmillan, 1985), p. 97, and Haig Bosmajian, *The Language of Oppression* (1974; reprint, Lanham, Md.: University Press of America, 1983), p. 8.

9. Hebrew verbs are aspective, marking the completeness or incompleteness of an action, so do not themselves indicate whether the action is past, present, or future. Their calendars and other indicators, however, show that the Hebrews had a well-developed chronology. The timing of an event was indicated by context and other aspects of the language structure. See James Barr, *Biblical Words for Time* (London: SCM Press, 1962), and *The Semantics of Biblical Language* (Oxford: Oxford University Press, 1961).

10. Cameron, *Feminism and Linguistic Theory*, p. 99.

11. Ibid., p. 98.

12. German and French speakers tell me that similar considerations apply. "Argument is war" may be a metaphorical system widely shared in languages influenced by Western culture.

13. George Lakoff and Mark Johnson, *Metaphors We Live By* (Chicago: University of Chicago Press, 1980), pp. 3–6. They return to this metaphor several times in the book.

14. Ibid., p. 5. Proceedings in a Maori meeting house are close to my portrait of reasoning as dance. Each person speaks in turn, each contribution is valued, and the contributors find ways of evaluating and qualifying contributions without being "for" or "against" them, until consensus is achieved.

15. Tim Searson, "Time, the New Scarce Resource," *Southwest Spirit* (Magazine of Southwest Airlines), July 1986.

16. Lakoff and Johnson describe the three interlocking metaphors as "a single system based on subcategorization" (*Metaphors We Live By*, pp. 7–9).

17. Ibid., pp. 10–13.

18. Roy Harris, *The Language Myth* (London: Duckworth, 1981), quoted by Cameron, *Feminism and Linguistic Theory*, p. 138.

19. Tyler, *The Said and the Unsaid*, p. 15.

20. Cameron, *Feminism and Linguistic Theory*, p. 142.

21. Quotation and other points in the preceding paragraph from Lakoff and Johnson, *Metaphors We Live By*, pp. 231–32; emphasis mine.

22. Cameron, *Feminism and Linguistic Theory*, p. 143.

23. Tyler, *The Said and the Unsaid*, p. 459.

24. S. I. Hayakawa, *Language and Thought in Action*, p. vii.

25. Eugen Hadamovsky, *Propaganda und nationale Macht* (Oldenburg: G. Stalling, 1933), p. 16, quoted in Bosmajian, *Oppression*, p. 18. For this section see pp. 11–31 of Bosmajian's book.

26. Leo Lowenthal and Norbert Guterman, *Prophets of Deceit* (Palo Alto: Pacific Books, 1970), p. 6, quoted in Bosmajian, *Oppression*, p. 25.

27. Richard Grunberger, *A Social History of the Third Reich* (London: Weidenfeld and Nicholson, 1971), p. 330, quoted in Bosmajian, *Oppression*, p. 31.

28. Bosmajian, *Oppression*, p. 36.

29. Basil Davidson, *Black Mother: Africa and the Atlantic Slave*

Trade (London: Penguin, 1980), pp. 53–55, 284. Emphasis mine.

30. Peter Fryer, *Staying Power: The History of Black People in Britain* (London: Pluto Press, 1984), p. 133.

31. Ibid., p. 134.

32. Ibid., (chap. 7, pp. 133–90, is the source of the material in this paragraph).

33. The records of the conquest of the Incas suggest that the Spaniards were at first welcomed because they fit into a positive preexisting image of white gods from across the sea, whose arrival was signaled by a number of portents. The black/negative—white/positive contrast is probably not peculiar to Indo-European languages. In at least one African language, terms for blackness can also be negative and whiteness positive, though the connotations are more varied. In Swazi, black symbolizes the "impenetrability of the future," but also "the sins and evils of the past year." Black beads can symbolize marriage and wealth in cattle, but also evil, disappointment, and misfortune. The word *mnyama* means black, dark, but also deep, profound, unfathomable, confused, dizzy, and angry. The word *mhlope* (white) means "pale, pure, innocent, perfect," but can also mean "destitute and empty." The whiteness of the full moon relates to fullness, but another term for whiteness means "useless" (T. O. Beidelman, quoted in Bosmajian, *The Language of Oppression*, p. 49).

34. Fryer, *Staying Power*, p. 190.

35. Bosmajian, *The Language of Oppression*, pp. 71–75.

36. Lakoff and Johnson, *Metaphors We Live By*, pp. 245–46.

37. Rhodes quotation from Alex Callinicos and John Rogers, *Southern Africa after Soweto* (London: Pluto Press, 1977), pp. 21–26. See also the measured conclusion of *Towards Social Change: Report of the Social Commission of the Study Project on Christianity in Apartheid Society* (Johannesburg: SPROCAS, 1971), p. 23: "Deprived of land, many tribesmen had no option but to work as serfs on white-owned land or as laborers in white-owned industry. The need to work for whites was given impetus by the requirement of having to pay poll taxes in cash."

38. Mostly from the Indian subcontinent.

39. Cameron, *Feminism and Linguistic Theory*, p. 150.

40. Bosmajian, "Dehumanizing People and Euphemizing War."

41. On dominance and cultural oppression, see Brian Wren,

Education for Justice (Maryknoll, N.Y.: Orbis Books, 1977). I am not convinced that men control language itself (see Cameron, *Feminism and Linguistic Theory*, pp. 54–55, 90, 143, 147, 154, 171).

Chapter 4. The Nature of God-Talk

1. The suggestion that there is one subject, not two, and the use of the term "active together" are vindicated by Janet Martin Soskice, *Metaphor and Religious Language* (Oxford: Clarendon Press, 1985). Among the most important discussions are Max Black, "Metaphor," in his *Models and Metaphors: Studies in Language and Philosophy* (Ithaca: Cornell University Press 1962); I. T. Ramsey, *Models and Mystery* (Oxford: Oxford University Press 1964); and Paul Henle, *Language, Thought and Culture* (Ann Arbor: University of Michigan Press, 1958), chap. 7. All argue convincingly against "substitution" and "comparison" views.

2. Arthur Koestler, *The Act of Creation* (London: Hutchinson, 1964). Koestler gives many examples of creativity in aesthetic insight and scientific discovery.

3. On this, see Soskice, *Metaphor and Religious Language*, pp. 64–66, from which my definition of *analogy* is also taken.

4. Examples from "Deck Thyself, My Soul, with Gladness," Catherine Winkworth's translation of Johann Franck's hymn (see standard hymnals) and "Soundless Were the Tossing Trees," Thomas Troeger's superb evocation of Jesus healing the deaf-mute, in *New Hymns for the Ecumenical Lectionary: To Glorify the Maker's Name*, Carol Doran [music] and Thomas H. Troeger [words] (New York: Oxford University Press, 1986).

5. I concur with Soskice, *Metaphor and Religious Language*, in using *metaphor* to mean a precise type of *language*, among other rhetorical tropes. Allegory and parable are similar, but elaborated in different ways.

6. Soskice, *Metaphor and Religious Language*, chap. 3, pp. 24–53.

7. Ibid., p. 25.

8. G. B. Caird, *The Language and Imagery of the Bible* (London: Duckworth, 1980), p. 176.

9. Donald G. Bloesch, *Battle for the Trinity: The Debate over Inclusive God-Language* (Ann Arbor, Mich.: Servant Publications, 1985), p. 21.

10. Soskice, *Metaphor and Religious Language*, p. 15. The material in this section is drawn from pp. 15–23. Sallie McFague develops "metaphorical theology," meaning a way of speaking of God that neither literalizes and idolizes key metaphors nor dispenses with them, but gives license for speech about God as well as indicating the limits of such speech (*Metaphorical Theology* [Philadelphia: Fortress Press, 1982], p. 19). Despite her many insights, I prefer, for clarity's sake, to use *metaphor* for the particular type of *language use* analyzed in this chapter. Theological discussion would be clearer if other terms were found for the issues McFague is discussing.

11. Soskice, *Metaphor and Religious Language*, p. 18.

12. Ibid., p. 45.

13. Ibid., p. 46. Soskice uses the terms *tenor* and *vehicle* where I use *subject* and *intersecting image*. Though her terminology has a respectable pedigree, it was opaque to several readers of my manuscript, so I have tried to find something clearer.

14. The Amos and Hosea examples in this chapter are drawn from earlier work. They are chosen for convenience and come from near contemporaries who use language in ways similar to their successors, such as Isaiah of Jerusalem, Jeremiah, Ezekiel, Second Isaiah, and Micah. The Amos example has a translation that keeps the rhythms of the Hebrew. To see the text as a sequence, rather than two parallel similes (as in the New English Bible) is linguistically feasible and dramatically more convincing, since it first heightens the danger of the flight situation by confronting us with a bear, then lets us apparently reach safety before administering the coup de grace of a fatal snakebite. The preceding examples (Flaubert, *sun* and *biscuits*) are from Soskice, *Metaphor and Religious Language*, pp. 58–61.

15. Ibid., p. 59.

16. Terminology adopted by G. B. Caird, *Language and Imagery*, p. 153–59, drawing on my unpublished doctoral thesis, "The Language of Prophetic Eschatology in the Old Testament" (Oxford University, 1968), pp. 114–21.

17. See Caird, *Language and Imagery*, p. 153, and Leonardo Boff, *Church: Charism and Power* (New York: Crossroad, 1985), chaps. 12, 13.

18. Black, "Metaphor."

19. Soskice, *Metaphor and Religious Language*, p. 62.
20. Ibid., pp. 50–51.
21. Ibid., p. 51.
22. Ibid., pp. 47–48. I have extended and paraphrased Soskice's analysis.
23. Caird, *Language and Imagery*, pp. 18–19, 173, 177.
24. Bloesch, *Battle*, pp. 13, 21, 35, 36. "The Enigma of God-Language" is one of his chapter titles.
25. Hosea 2–3 and 11:1–9. I say "more definitive" because internal evidence suggests that Hosea sees forgiveness beyond judgment and destruction.
26. The examples in this section are drawn from George Lakoff and Mark Johnson, *Metaphors We Live By* (Chicago: University of Chicago Press, 1980), pp. 14–17, 29–31, 56ff. Their "orientational metaphors" are probably "analogies" on Soskice's definition (see n. 3, above), but the difference in terminology does not affect the point at issue.
27. John Nicholson, *Men and Women: How Different Are They?* (Oxford: Oxford University Press, 1984), p. 44.
28. A 1976 study by E. Goffman cited in Philip Smith, *Language, the Sexes and Society* (Oxford: Blackwell, 1985), p. 33. Goffman says the resulting configuration can be read as an acceptance of subordination, an expression of ingratiation, submissiveness, and appeasement.
29. We can also speak of the *following* weeks and *preceding* months, because we use two metaphorical systems for time (see Lakoff and Johnson, *Metaphors We Live By*, pp. 14–17, 29–31, 56ff.).
30. Caird, *Language and Imagery*, pp. 174–76. Useful references include Deut. 32:10–11, 18; Ps. 22:9–10 NEB, 23:1–4, 80:1–2, 82, 97:1–2, 99:1–4, 144:1–2; Isa. 42:13–14; Jer. 18:1–6; Hos. 1–3, 7:11–12 NEB, 11:1–4, 8–11, 13:4–8 NEB; Matt. 5:43–48, 6:31–33; the paired parables in Luke 15:4–10 (God's action seen in terms of shepherd and peasant woman); and Matt. 23:37. NEB is cited where it gives clearer translation than other versions.
31. Isa. 40:11–18, 21–26; 41:2–5; 42:5, 13–16; 44:2, 6; 45:1, 6–7; 46:3–4, 8–10; 54:4–10.
32. Clyde A. Holbrook, *The Iconoclastic Deity: Biblical Images of God* (Lewisburg: Bucknell University Press, 1984), p. 76.

33. On this, see Caird, *Language and Imagery*, chap. 11, "Linguistic Awareness," esp. p. 196. My biblical kingship discussion also draws on Caird, pp. 178–82.

34. Ibid., p. 179.

35. Quoted in Haig Bosmajian, "Dehumanizing People and Euphemizing War," *Christian Century*, 5 December 1984, pp. 1147–50.

36. Sallie McFague, *Metaphorical Theology* (Philadelphia: Fortress Press, 1982), p. 26, developing a sentence in Immanuel Kant's *Critique of Pure Reason*, trans. Norman Kemp Smith (New York: St. Martin's Press, 1929), p. 93: "Thoughts without content are empty, intuitions without concepts are blind. . . . The understanding can intuit nothing, the senses can think nothing. Only through their union can knowledge arise." My discussion of God-metaphors as expressing qualities of relationship is also indebted to McFague.

37. Soskice, *Metaphor and Religious Language*, p. 62.

Introduction to Part III

1. I am indebted to Gordon Kaufman for the suggestion that the dominant image of God in worship is divine kingship (*Theology for a Nuclear Age* [Philadelphia: Westminster Press, 1985]). It prompted my hymnological research ("The Roq:un Fragment") and some of my criticisms of divine kingship language.

Gallery: The Roq:un Fragment

1. Capitalized words are counted as titles, following the judgment of the hymnal editors as to which God-designations are titles or names. To make judgments about the variety of uncapitalized God-speech would be difficult and unlikely to alter the results.

2. The occurrences are: God, of whole godhead or First Person—320, of the Second Person—30, of the Third Person of the Trinity—7; Jesus—300; Christ—208; Holy Spirit/Ghost—190; godhead—9; Trinity, Three-in-One, etc.—20.

3. The full table is:

Lord	87	Shepherd	7
Father	91	Maker	6
King	34	Ancient of Days	4
Al(mighty)	13	Love	4

3 each—Alpha and Omega and First and Last; Holy/Holiest; Judge; Sun; Wisdom.

2 each—Defender, Friend, Giver/Donor, I Am, Light, Redeemer, Shield, Unsearchable.

1 each—Captain of Salvation, Creator, Eternal, Formless, Great, Great Reward, Guide, High, Immortal, Infinite, Parent of Good, the Presence, Star.

4. Out of 290 names, 3 titles of male authority predominate: "Lord," "Father," and "King," with 30, 31, and 12 percent of the total (73 percent in all). Further analysis confirms this pattern: *Names with clearly male reference:* Lord, Father, King, Shepherd, Judge (though some societies now have some female judges, the image is almost certainly seen as male when applied to God)—222 (76.5 percent).

Names with female reference—none.

Names associated with power as rule: Lord, Father, King, Al(mighty), Shepherd, Judge—235 (81 percent).

5. The full table of the 816 names and titles for the Second Person of the Trinity is:

Lord	262	Life	11
King	140	Word	11
Savior	105	Name (all in one text)	10
Son	61	Redeemer	16
Lamb	21	Shepherd	9
Love	16	Son of Man	8
Immanuel	15	Master	7
Light	12	Messiah	7

6 each: Truth, Prince of Glory, Man, Child.

5 each: Prince of Peace, Friend.

4 each: Priest, Captain.

3 each: Conqueror, Crucified, Incarnate, Joy, One, Son of David.

2 each: Advocate, Counselor, Feast, Heart, Maker, Prince of Life, Prophet, Rock, Servant, Son of Mary, Spring, Strength,

Sun, Victim.

1 each: Almighty, Beloved, Bridegroom, Brother, Crown, Day-Spring, Desire of Nations, End, High(est), Judge, Key of David, Stem of Jesse's Rod, Way, Zion's Friend, Rod of Jesse, Wonderful.

Titles associated with power as rule: Lord, King, Shepherd, Master, Prince, Captain, Conqueror, Victor, Almighty, Crown, Highest, Judge—507 (62 percent).

Clear titles of servanthood, humility, and suffering: Savior, Lamb, Redeemer, Love, Prince of Peace, Friend, Crucified, Servant, Zion's Friend—174 (21.3 percent).

6. In this short section, the names and titles are more varied:

Comforter	9	Guest	3
Redeemer	8	Giver	3
Lord	7	Guide	2
Breath of God	6	Counselor	2
Dove	6	Paraclete	2
		Well	2

1 each: Advocate, Fount of our Being, Love divine, G-d's Voice, Father of the Poor, Word of G-d.

7. *Well-developed* metaphors speak of the king, his reign, homage, commands; *less developed metaphors* mention the heavenly throne, rule, majesty, but as a background for other thoughts; and king metaphors are *presupposed* in texts with *mercy* and *pardon*, which imply a kingly authority figure.

8. "Father" and "King" are intertwined: not two separate systems but one. In hymns 1–218 (excluding the Spirit section), fifty-five texts speak of God as Father. Of these, thirty-five (63 percent) link Father with King or other language of kingly rule.

9. In twenty-nine of the texts the Prince leaves the throne; lives a human life; suffers, dies, and is raised from death; then returns to his royal state. Examples include "At the Name of Jesus" (no. 74), "Ride On, Ride On in Majesty" (159), "Thou Didst Leave Thy Throne" (154), and "The Strife Is O'er, the Battle Done" (214). In a further twenty-one texts the kingship language is held in tension with suffering and humility. Examples include "Jesu, Jesu" (145), "Trotting, Trotting" (162), "Son of the Lord Most High" (142), "O Sacred Head Sore Wounded" (176), and "Hail to the Lord Who Comes" (126). Phrases include: "Master who acts as a slave . . . kneels at the feet of his friends"

(145), "Many thought he should have come on a mighty horse leading all the Jews to battle [and] . . . were amazed to see such a quiet man trotting on a donkey" (162), "Not with the high and great his home the Highest made . . . O lowly majesty, lofty in lowliness" (152), and "How scornfully surrounded with thorns, thine only crown" (176). Yet more than half the texts are based on the KINGAFAP system. The self-emptying theme is submerged, and the dominant impression is of a Second Person who leaves behind the suffering, serving, humble mode on returning to the heavenly throne. This is expressed in sequences such as: "Hail, thou *once-despised* Jesus . . . enthroned in glory, there for ever to abide" (222), "Christ, above all glory seated, King triumphant, strong to save . . . on the eternal throne of heaven in thy Father's power to reign" (189), "See the Man of Sorrows now from the fight returned victorious. . . . In the seat of power enthrone him. . . . Crown him King of Kings and Lord of Lords" (201), and "The Father on his sapphire throne expects his own anointed Son. . . . Bow thy meek head to mortal pain, *then take, O God, thy power, and reign!*" (159).

10. Source: letter from the series editor, Stephen Whittle. Fifty-seven of these hymns appear in the first section of *Hymns and Psalms,* and a further sixty appear elsewhere in that collection. Analysis, therefore, supplements and helps to confirm my overview of *Hymns and Psalms.* Two texts could not be found, so my analysis covers 135 of the 137 mentioned.

11. Space forbids me from listing the hymns analyzed; bona fide researchers may write for it, via the publisher.

12. Examples taken from the *Consultation on Revision of the ICET Texts* (English Language Liturgical Consultation, 1986).

Chapter 5. Dethroning Patriarchal Idols

1. Though the divine King does not appear in the hymn "Amazing Grace," he is there behind the scenes. God's grace is a central Christian theme, and it was KINGAFAP that made it possible to articulate it, since its basis in human experience is the favor bestowed by a monarch with absolute authority to punish or forgive. "Grace" is the experience of meeting that absolute power and authority and finding ourselves pardoned, loved, and welcomed. Nowadays, this is often transmuted into the language of

personal relationships and understood as the unconditional *acceptance* of one person by another. Yet grace was first thought about, and only became thinkable, within the metaphor system of the great King-Father, and I suspect that modern metaphors of interpersonal acceptance still refer back to it.

2. One of the few is W. H. Vanstone's superb "Morning Glory, Starlit Sky," in *Hymns Ancient and Modern New Standard Edition* (Norwich: Hymns Ancient and Modern Ltd., 1983), no. 496, which praises God's love that "spares not, keeps not, all outpours," and therefore must hang helpless on the cross:

> *Here is God: no monarch he,*
> *throned in easy state to reign;*
> *here is God, whose arms of love*
> *aching, spent, the world sustain.*

If "he" could be changed to "high," the kingship metaphor would be strengthened and the language made inclusive.

3. "Come Let Us Love the Unborn Generations," no. 45 in *Faith Looking Forward: The Hymns and Songs of Brian Wren* (Carol Stream, Ill.: Hope Publishing Co., 1983).

4. "Great Lover, Calling Us to Share," in *Bring Many Names: New Hymns by Brian Wren* (Carol Stream, Ill.: Hope Publishing Co., forthcoming).

5. The fundamental change represented by human ability to end life on earth, and the inadmissibility of expecting biblical end-of-the-world imagery to sanction divine intervention preventing or hastening it, are well argued by Gordon Kaufman, *Theology for a Nuclear Age* (Philadelphia: Westminster Press, 1985); Jonathan Schell, *The Fate of the Earth* (New York: Knopf, 1982); and Robert Jewett, *Jesus Against the Rapture: Seven Unexpected Prophecies* (Philadelphia: Westminster Press, 1979).

6. Quotations and examples taken from David Nicholls, "Deity and Domination," *New Blackfriars* 66, nos. 775–76 (Jan.–Feb. 1985).

7. Theodore Klauser, quoted in Don Cupitt, "The Christ of Christendom," in John Hick, ed., *The Myth of God Incarnate* (London: SCM Press, 1977), p. 139, and Cupitt himself, p. 141.

8. Rosemary Radford Ruether, *Sexism and God-Talk* (London: SCM Press, 1983), p. 29.

9. G. A. Studdert-Kennedy, *The Hardest Part* (London: Wm. Heinemann, 1918), pp. 37, 39.

10. Ibid., pp. 40, 44.

11. Protestants who refer to the Heidelburg Catechism of 1563 know that "God may not and cannot be imaged in any way." Seventeenth-century Puritan William Perkins saw this and gave an early critique of KINGAFAP, saying, "So soon as the mind frames unto itself any form of God, as when he is popishly conceived to be like an old man sitting in heaven in a throne with a scepter in his hand, an idol is set up in the mind . . . a thing faigned in the mind by imagination is an idol." Taken literally, this means we can only speak of God in negatives, since metaphors and similes are created "in the mind by imagination." The biblical practice of using a variety of linguistic images tells against such a rigorous view. Against Perkins's sideswipe at "popery," it is doubtful whether the Old Man in the Sky image has ever been restricted to the mental apparatus of Roman Catholics.

12. The hymn "Immortal, Invisible, God Only Wise," by Walter Chalmers Smith (1824–1908).

13. Hebrew poets and prophets habitually put opposing thoughts alongside each other, without trying to resolve their apparent contradiction. George Caird gives many examples in *The Language and Imagery of the Bible* (London: Duckworth, 1980), pp. 110–21.

14. As *definitions* of God, names like father, mother, mountain, and sun are mutually exclusive; as *models* (metaphors with staying power), they are mutually enriching. See Sallie McFague, *Models of God* (Philadelphia: Fortress Press, 1987), p. 39.

15. See, e.g., Julio de Santa Anna, *Good News to the Poor: The Challenge of the Poor in the History of the Church* (Geneva: Commission on the Churches' Participation in Development, World Council of Churches, 1977), chaps. 4–6.

16. See Deborah Cameron, *Feminism and Linguistic Theory* (London: Macmillan, 1986), chap. 5, esp. pp. 84–90.

17. Here, as elsewhere, I must mention McFague, *Models of God*, which systematically explores the interconnected metaphors of God as Mother, Lover, and Friend.

18. Pamela Payne Allen, "Taking the Next Step in Inclusive Language," *Christian Century*, 23 April 1986. Other resources include *Words That Hurt, Words That Heal: Language about God and*

People (Nashville: Task Force on Language Guidelines, United Methodist Publishing House); Barbara Withers, ed., *Language and the Church: Articles and Designs for Workshops* (New York: Division of Education and Ministry, National Council of the Churches of Christ in the USA, 1984); and *In the Image of God: An Inclusive Language Educational Program* (Task Force on Inclusive Language, Diocese of Connecticut, 1986).

Chapter 6. Bring Many Names

1. Sallie McFague, *Models of God: Theology for an Ecological, Nuclear Age* (Philadelphia: Fortress Press, 1986). The love of God as Mother is *agape*, the Creator's love, love of all that is, the affirmation of all creatures by their parent. This love suggests an ethic of justice, whereby God is intimately and impartially concerned with the fulfillment of all forms of life, not just the human species. The love of God as Lover is saving love, *eros*. It is the passionate manifestation and incarnation of divine love for humanity, going to the limit, so that there can be no doubt that the last and the least are accepted and reunited. It suggests an ethic of healing, making whole, and reuniting all creation. This love values the universe, the earth, and us, finding all three attractive and precious, as lovers value their beloved. The love of God as Friend is *philia*, a companionable love that continues alongside us and suggests an ethic in which right living means working with our indwelling Friend toward the wholeness of creation (précis of McFague's systematic elaboration of the three metaphors, drawn from pp. 91–92 of *Models of God*).

2. Verbal creativity is released when people are given step-by-step tasks, each clearly explained, working singly or in very small groups (three to six people). In the brainstorming exercise mentioned here, groups of five to six people appoint one member scribe and record every name of God put forward, without discussion. Discussion and comment must be held back to allow our intuitive, associative processes to have free rein. Though the resultant list may be long and repetitious, it sparks new ideas as it is heard or read.

3. *Praising a Mystery: 30 New Hymns by Brian Wren* (Carol Stream, Ill.: Hope Publishing Co., 1986), no. 8.

4. Useful Scripture references are: 1 Cor. 13:12, Exod.

20:18–21, 1 Kings 8:10–12, Ps. 18:2–12 (esp. vv. 8–12), Deut. 4:15–24, 2 Cor. 4:5–7, Acts 9:1–9, Exod. 24:9–18 and 33:18–23, and 1 Cor. 2:7–11.

5. See Chapter 3, the "Language of Darkness and Light" section.

6. "Joyful Is the Dark," in *Bring Many Names: New Hymns by Brian Wren* (Carol Stream, Ill.: Hope Publishing Co., forthcoming).

7. Patricia Wilson-Kastner, *Faith, Feminism and the Christ* (Philadelphia: Fortress Press, 1983), p. 96.

8. McFague, *Models of God*, p. 8, quoting Harold K. Schilling, "The Whole Earth Is the Lord's: Towards a Wholistic Ethic," in Ian Barbour, ed., *Earth Might Be Fair: Reflections on Ethics, Religion and Ecology* (Englewood Cliffs, N.J.: Prentice-Hall, 1972), p. 102.

9. "We have only two real options: either to learn to use our intelligence to become servants of the survival and cultivation of nature or to lose one's own life-support system in an increasingly poisoned earth" (Rosemary Radford Ruether, *Sexism and God-Talk* [London: SCM Press, 1983], p. 89).

10. "Thank You, God, for Water, Soil and Air," in Brian Wren, *Faith Looking Forward: The Hymns and Songs of Brian Wren* (Carol Stream, Ill.: Hope Publishing Co., 1983), no. 7.

11. For this section I am indebted to John Hull, *What Prevents Christian Adults from Learning* (London: SCM Press, 1986), pp. 223ff.

12. I say "relatively" to indicate that our freedom is incomplete, being limited by (for example) our historical context, social conditioning, and unconscious drives.

13. When one possibility becomes actual, it creates a host of new possibilities. God's omniscience is not a controlling knowledge, but an enjoyment of all the possibilities flowing from one moment, and all the possibilities that will flow from the next moment, when another possibility has become actualized. God's all-knowingness is awesome to us, not because God determines and "fixes" every event, but because God's perfect knowledge of all the possible possibilities is instantaneous and effortless, one small, simple sequence in the communal dance of trinitarian life.

14. "The Horrors of Our Century," in Wren, *Faith Looking Forward*, no. 46.

15. Hull, *Christian Adults*, p. 223. Hull discusses issues aris-

ing from this line of thought.

16. Based on McFague, *Models of God*, p. 93.

17. "The Horrors of Our Century," in Wren, *Faith Looking Forward*, no. 46.

18. Gordon Kaufman, *Theology for a Nuclear Age* (Philadelphia: Westminster Press, 1985). Kaufman's discussion faces the radical newness of the situation in which human beings can end all human life. By calling "God" and "Christ" the "central symbols of Christian faith," he comes close to suggesting that words don't point to transcendent reality (several seminar participants got this impression). Yet Kaufman's careful conceptual work is essential if theology is to move forward; it proved helpful in sparking new images of God.

19. Ibid., pp. 33–34.

20. I gladly leave the "choice versus necessity" conundrum to others and suspect it is inappropriate to oppose them when talking about love.

21. McFague, *Models of God*, p. 134.

22. "Great Lover, Calling Us to Share," in Wren, *Bring Many Names* (forthcoming).

23. McFague, *Models of God*, p. 86.

24. Ibid., chap. 5, pp. 125–55.

25. "All-perceiving Lover," in Wren, *Bring Many Names* (forthcoming). To see God as Lover changes our understanding of evil and sin (see McFague, *Models of God*, pp. 133, 137ff., 145).

26. Reactions from groups in a workshop at Dunblane, Scotland, in 1986; for more details, see Chapter 9.

27. Naomi Janowitz and Maggie Wenig, "Sabbath Prayers for Women," in *Womanspirit Rising: A Feminist Reader in Religion*, ed. Carol P. Christ and Judith Plaskow (San Francisco: Harper and Row, 1979), pp. 174–78.

28. Donald Bloesch, *The Battle for the Trinity* (Ann Arbor, Mich.: Servant Publications, 1985), p. 100.

29. Ancient hymns to the goddess Ishtar are valuable if used as an image quarry rather than a theology factory. One such hymn reads:

> *Gracious Ishtar, who rules over the universe,*
> *Heroic Ishtar, who creates humankind,*
> *who walks before the cattle, who loves the shepherd . . .*

You give justice to the distressed, the suffering you give
justice.
Without you the river will not open,
the river which brings life will not be closed.

Unlike the Virgin Mary, who intercedes with God but remains a creature, Ishtar and other goddesses had divine power in their own right. The female and feminine were valued and appreciated, even at a time when men were consolidating their power over women in the political realm (Gerda Lerner, *The Creation of Patri-archy* [Oxford: Oxford University Press, 1986], pp. 142f.).

30. "Dear Sister God," in Wren, *Faith Looking Forward*, no. 3.

31. "Go Forth in Faith," in Wren, *Bring Many Names* (forth-coming).

32. "The Horrors of Our Century," in Wren, *Faith Looking Forward*, no. 46.

33. One of a group of prayers I wrote for Christian Aid, Brit-ish Council of Churches, 1982.

34. McFague, *Models of God*, pp. 109–13.

Chapter 7. A Male for Others

1. The central Christian experience is that the self-giving love of God, encountered in Jesus, overcomes all estrangement between human beings and God. In the New Testament, this ex-perience is expressed in a variety of metaphors. In one passage, God "cancels the bond" (debt) that pledged us to the decrees of Mosaic law, while Christ "discards cosmic powers and authorities like a garment," then "leads them captive" in his triumphal pro-cession (Col. 1–2). Elsewhere, the experience is expressed in metaphors drawn from animal sacrifice, as when Christ's death is described as a sacrifice for sins (Heb. 10:12) or sacrifice to God (Eph. 5:2). It can be seen as a ransom (Mark 10:45), as redemp-tion (i.e., of slaves), and as propitiation or expiation. As regards the last named, there is no division in God, but rather the recog-nition that God is active in Jesus, doing what needs to be done. Neither metaphor is used in a strong enough sense to suggest God's anger had to be placated. To feel ourselves ransomed is a

vivid way of describing the experience of meeting God in Christ
(especially in an era of renewed hostage taking), but theology runs
into the sand if we start asking who the ransom is paid to, and
whether whoever-it-is (usually the Devil) has the right to be paid
off. All these metaphors (and others that may become appropriate
to us) describe something, for someone, about the unnameable
experience of salvation. It is a fundamental error to try and elaborate
them into logically coherent systems. To do so is to read the New
Testament as if it were a mixture of rule book and philosophical
treatise by a consortium of judges and logicians. It isn't, thank
God.

2. Diane Tennis, *Is God the Only Reliable Father?* (Philadelphia: Westminster Press, 1985), p. 95.

3. Ibid., p. 94.

4. Ibid., pp. 95–96.

5. "LORD, Thank You for the Jews," in *Praising a Mystery:
30 New Hymns by Brian Wren* (Carol Stream, Ill.: Hope Publishing
Co., 1986), no. 28.

6. "Who Comes?" in Wren, *Praising a Mystery,* no. 30.

7. For this section I am indebted to Elisabeth Moltmann-
Wendel, *The Women around Jesus* (London: SCM Press, 1982), esp.
pp. 61ff., 31ff.

8. As Gordon Kaufman points out, Jesus showed and shared
a Way, characterized by love, joy, peace, patience, kindness, and
reconciliation. As described by early Christians such as John and
Paul, it showed virtues recognized in the Hellenistic world, for
which the Greek language had common names. See *Theology for a
Nuclear Age* (Philadelphia: Westminster Press, 1985), p. 58. "How
These Christians Love One Another!" shows a recognition of a
human quality common to women and men and seen by non-
Christians. If Christian virtues were not recognized as such by
their pagan neighbors, they could not have heard the Christian
message as good news.

9. For the above I am indebted to Rosemary Radford Ruether, *Sexism and God-Talk* (London: SCM Press, 1983), pp. 29,
121–22, among others. Important Scripture references are Mark
9:30–37, 10:41–45; Matt. 23:1–12; and Luke 22:24–30. By juxta-
posing the reference to the disciples sitting on thrones (Luke
22:28–30) with verses 24–27, Luke characterizes the "en-

thronement" promised them as the abandonment of hierarchical authority.

10. Tennis, *Father*, p. 105.

11. The temptations are among those that particularly beset men in patriarchal society, though women are not exempt from them.

12. "Dear Sister God," in *Faith Looking Forward: The Hymns and Songs of Brian Wren* (Carol Stream, Ill.: Hope Publishing Co., 1983), no. 3.

13. "The Human-Not-Quite-Human," in Dorothy L. Sayers, *Unpopular Opinions* (London: Gollancz, 1946).

14. No. 6 in Wren, *Faith Looking Forward*. The original reads "Lord God," and so appears in several hymnals. I would now change it to the version quoted, to move away from the maleness of "Lord."

15. "Praise the God Who Changes Places," in Wren, *Praising a Mystery*, no. 21.

16. For example, Sallie McFague, *Metaphorical Theology* (Philadelphia: Fortress Press, 1982), pp. 178ff., and *Models of God: Theology for an Ecological, Nuclear Age* (Philadelphia: Fortress Press, 1986). McFague focuses on God as the Friend who invites us to join Godself in a common vision of salvation as the earth's well-being. Although this is a valuable metaphor, the friendship of Jesus, or the Christ, has stronger traditional associations.

17. "True Friends," in Wren, *Praising a Mystery*, no. 26.

18. See Joachim Jeremias, *The Prayers of Jesus* (Philadelphia: Fortress Press, 1978), chap. 1; and James Barr, "Abba Isn't 'Daddy,'" *Journal of Theological Studies* 39 (1988): 28–47, and "Abba, Father," *Theology* (May 1988): 173–79.

19. Jürgen Moltmann, *The Trinity and the Kingdom of God* (London: SCM Press, 1981), p. 58.

20. For this section I am indebted to James B. Nelson, *Between Two Gardens: Reflections on Sexuality and Religious Experience* (New York: Pilgrim Press, 1983), chap. 2.

Chapter 8. The Dance in God Begun

1. "An Immigrant from Tyre," in *Praising a Mystery: 30 New*

Hymns by Brian Wren (Carol Stream, Ill.: Hope Publishing Co., 1986), no. 27.

2. Jürgen Moltmann, *The Trinity and the Kingdom of God* (London: SCM Press, 1981).

3. Ibid., p. 70.

4. Ibid., p. 58; emphasis mine.

5. Ibid., p. 142.

6. Ibid., pp. 169–70.

7. The United Church of Canada has two examples:

Praise God from whom all blessings flow;
praise God, all creatures high and low;
give thanks to God in love made known:
Creator, Word and Spirit One.

and:

Gloire soit au Saint-Esprit!
Gloire soit au Dieu de vie!
Gloire soit à Jesus Christ,
notre sauveur, notre ami!

("Glory be to the Holy Spirit! Glory be to the God of life! Glory be to Jesus Christ, our savior and friend!" *Songs for a Gospel People* [Winfield, British Columbia: Wood Lake Books, Alberta and Northwest Conference of the United Church of Canada, 1987], hymns 11 and 89.) The first is a singable nonsexist version of the popular doxology, but its Creator-Word-Spirit triad has the problems already indicated, and the third line loses the repeated "Praise God," which is part of the attractiveness of the original. "Praise God, great Three, in love made known" is one possible improvement. The second alters the traditional order, thus enhancing the coequality of the persons; but "God of life" for the First Person could suggest that the First Person is more truly God than the other two. The Episcopal Church in the United States has a number of experimental variants, including:

Honor and glory to God, and to God's eternal Word, and
to God's Holy Spirit: as it was in the beginning, is now,
and will be for ever. Amen.

Provider of all . . . guide us . . . through Christ, who is revealed and dwells with you and the Holy Spirit, one God, now and forever. Amen.

Blessed be God, the One in Three: The One who creates us, the Christ who redeems us, The Spirit who is poured into our hearts.

(Liturgical Texts for Evaluation [New York: Church Hymnal Corporation for the Standing Liturgical Commission of the Episcopal Church in the United States, for use in selected evaluation centers from 20 September through 14 October 1987].) The items quoted are the most frequent doxology (p. 13 and frequently); a collect (p. 99, similar formulas elsewhere); and an opening ascription of glory in an alternative rite for "The Holy Eucharist: The Nurturing God" (p. 113). These are preliminary texts, not officially authorized by the Episcopal church, or for general use.

The first of these uses the Word-Spirit metaphor, replacing "Father" with "God" for the First Person, which reduces the Trinity to one Person ("God") with two secondary emanations, "God's Eternal Word" and "God's Holy Spirit." The second suggests three distinctive centers of personhood who are together one God, but the metaphors are disparate, and provide no clues about trinitarian relationships. The third example makes an unfortunate choice of name, since "the One," following closely after "the One in Three," suggests that oneness is an attribute of the First Person alone. Two other attempts are: "Creator, Redeemer, Sustainer" (in common use) and "God unbegotten, God incarnate, God among us," in Janet Morley and Hannah Ward, eds., *Celebrating Women* (London: Movement for the Ordination of Women and Women in Theology, 1986), p. 39. The former shows three functions belonging to the whole Trinity and fails to safeguard the distinctiveness of each center of personhood. The latter is a useful variant, though too abstruse to convey trinitarian personhood.

8. Wren, *Praising a Mystery,* no. 21; see also no. 26, "Who Is She?" reprinted in the Gallery preceding Chapter 6.

9. On this, see Patricia Wilson-Kastner, *Faith, Feminism and the Christ* (Philadelphia: Fortress Press, 1983), pp. 125–26.

10. Ibid.

11. Sallie McFague, *Models of God: Theology for an Ecological,*

Nuclear Age (Philadelphia: Fortress Press, 1986), pp. 169ff., 91ff. McFague says that "the three metaphors of God as parent, lover, and friend form a 'trinity' expressing God's impartial, reuniting, and reciprocal love to the world" (p. 91). This falls short of a trinitarian understanding, since it speaks of one divine being engaging in different activities, and the word *trinity* is put in quotation marks, presumably to distance it from its full meaning.

12. See n. 6 to "The Roq:un Fragment" Gallery.

13. Wren, *Praising a Mystery*, nos. 11, 24, 40.

14. "Great Soaring Spirit," in *Bring Many Names: New Hymns by Brian Wren* (Carol Stream, Ill.: Hope Publishing Co., forthcoming).

15. In Hebrew culture, the spirit of a human being is not the most rarefied element beyond the mind, but the power of personhood which "is never uniquely mine as are my body, my life, my individuality [but] resides only in my relatedness to some other" (John V. Taylor, *The Go-Between God: The Holy Spirit and the Christian Mission* [London: SCM Press, 1972], pp. 50, 8).

16. McFague, *Models of God*, p. 82.

17. See above, Chapter 3, p. 103.

18. McFague, *Models of God*, pp. 69–78.

19. I am indebted for this insight to Taylor, *The Go-Between God*, pp. 110–11.

20. Ibid., p. 17.

21. Ibid., p. 19.

22. Ibid., p. 43.

23. Ibid., p. 201.

24. The quotations are from *Faith Looking Forward: The Hymns and Songs of Brian Wren* (Carol Stream, Ill.: Hope Publishing Co., 1983), nos. 1, 4, and *Praising a Mystery*, no. 21.

25. C. S. Lewis, *Voyage to Venus (Perelandra)* (London: Pan Books, 1953), p. 185.

26. Wilson-Kastner, *Faith, Feminism and the Christ*, p. 127.

Chapter 9. Consequences

1. Monarchic views of the Trinity pervade worship and theology. The teaching of "the doctrine of God" typically begins with God the Creator, moves on to God the Word Incarnate, and

then fits the Spirit in at the end. Hymnals typically start with God the Eternal Father, have a long section on God the Son, then see what few hymns they can find on the Holy Spirit. It would be interesting to read a theological investigation that started at the other end, with the third center of personhood, and moved to the second and first. Varying the order might yield new insights.

2. On the theology of music and dance, see Judith Rock and Norman Mealy, *Performer as Priest and Prophet: Restoring the Intuitive in Worship Through Music and Dance* (San Francisco: Harper and Row, 1988).

3. On education as dialogue, my earlier book, *Education for Justice* (Maryknoll, N.Y.: Orbis Books, 1977), is still useful.

4. In April 1982 Anne Hepburn, then president of the Church of Scotland Women's Guild, used a prayer of mine to "God Our Mother" at a guild meeting. This caused controversy and led that church's General Assembly to invite the guild to join its Panel on Doctrine in a working party on the theological implications of such usage. The working party produced a report for the 1984 General Assembly. This was correct procedure, since the assembly had commissioned it. The report's authors aired it at the Women's Guild meeting a month before the assembly, as a courtesy, since the guild had been partly responsible for its commissioning. The report is very moderate in tone and gets as far as saying that it is appropriate to speak of God as a "motherly father." Maybe its title, "The Motherhood of God," caused misunderstanding, in a setting where many identified such language antipathetically with the Marian devotion of Roman Catholicism. At all events there was a storm of protest, and by the time the assembly met, many ministers had been lobbied by members of the guild to speak against the report. Some of the comments in the assembly, and most of the press coverage, show a strongly patriarchal reaction marked by fear and anger. The assembly resolved to "depart from the matter," refusing even to debate the contents of its own report. The report sat in an Edinburgh basement until 1986, when the Presbyterian Church in the United States ordered a thousand copies for study groups in its own congregations.

5. God can be imaged as, for example, a mother bear (Hos. 13:7–8), a mother (Deut. 32:18), a woman in labor (Isa. 42:14–16), a mother eagle protecting its young (Deut. 32:8–12), and a mother who teaches a toddler to walk with guiding strings, bends

down to feed the child, and lifts it to her cheek (Hos. 11:1–4, 8–11). The last passage is often read as an image of God the caring Father. Some fathers act that way today, but the actions depicted would in their historical context have been mainly associated with a mother's role.

6. Rosemary Radford Ruether, *Sexism and God-Talk* (London: SCM Press, 1983), p. 207.

7. Polly Toynbee, "The Incredible, Shrinking New Man," *Guardian*, 6 April 1987.

8. Edgar Metzler, "Men Need Liberation, Too," *Gospel Herald* (Mennonite Church publication), 15 October 1985.

9. Keith Thompson, "The Meaning of Being Male: A Conversation with Robert Bly," *L.A. Weekly*, 5–11 August 1983.

10. John the Baptist, John 3:30.

Epilogue

1. "Jesus Is with God," in *Praising a Mystery: 30 New Hymns by Brian Wren* (Carol Stream, Ill.: Hope Publishing Co., 1986), no. 17.

2. See above, Chapter 6, pp. 161–69.

3. "Christ Is Alive," in *Faith Looking Forward: The Hymns and Songs of Brian Wren* (Carol Stream, Ill.: Hope Publishing Co., 1983), no. 20 rev.

4. Alice Cook and Gwyn Kirk, eds., *Greenham Women Everywhere: Ideas and Actions from the Women's Peace Movement* (London: Pluto Press, 1983), p. 67.

5. "Love Is the Only Hope," in Wren, *Praising a Mystery*, no. 20.

6. "We Want to Care," in ibid., no. 24.

7. G. A. Studdert-Kennedy, *The Hardest Part* (London: Wm. Heinemann, 1918), pp. 72–73.

8. Ibid., p. 97.

9. Ibid., p. 71.